A JUMP IN THE RIVER

A JUMP IN THE RIVER

A MEMOIR

Clayton C. Hoskins

The Wooster Book Company
Wooster • Ohio
2000

The Wooster Book Company
205 West Liberty Street
Wooster Ohio • 44691
www.woosterbook.com

© 2000 Clayton C. Hoskins

All rights reserved. No part of this book may be reproduced, utilized, or transmitted in any form or by any means, electronic or mechanical, including photocopying, internet access, and recording—or by any information storage and retrieval system—without permission in writing from the publisher.
Printed in the United States of America.

ISBN: 1-888683-24-4

Library of Congress Cataloging-in-Publication Data

Hoskins, Clayton C., 1924–
  A jump in the river : a memoir / Clayton C. Hoskins.
    p.   cm.
  ISBN 1-888683-24-4 (trade paper : alk. paper)
  1. Hoskins, Clayton C., 1924– 2. Lawyers—Ohio—Biography. I. Title.

KF373.H642 A34 2000
340'.092—dc21
[B]   00-032069

Carlisle Printing
WALNUT CREEK

CONTENTS

	Prologue	III
	Introduction	VII
1	About That Title	3
2	Uncle Sam Wanted Me	5
3	Romance Among the Hill People	19
4	Religion In the Hills	25
5	The War Ends and College Begins	31
6	Law School and Finding a Job	63
7	Leukemia for Beginners	85
8	The Practice of Law	93
9	The Domesticated Lawyer	111
10	But First ... Golf	125
11	Bricker & Eckler	145
12	Mother and Matt	159
13	Back to the Good Life	171
14	A New Career for Me	203
15	Flying for Fun	211
16	August 1, 1927	225
17	Life After Death	241
18	My World of Wonders	255

Life is no subtle, greening thing,
   it takes the world by storm.
Each tender shoot asserts itself,
   defying all the odds—
      of gnarled limbs by winter stripped,
      of timbered ridge with cold winds whipped,
   of barren ground in dead leaves gripped.
And there, yes there, a bud bursts through!
A blossom blazes in the wood.
   A flower rages at the sun,
     returning fire with fire,
   a jump in the river unaware
of mysteries so near.

—Pastor George R. Wilcox
Oak Hill Presbyterian Church
St. Louis, Missouri

"I was only five years old, and the only thing I remember about the drowning is Clayt jumping on the couch at Grandma and Grandpa Clarks', and yelling THIS IS THE WAY MY DADDY JUMPED IN THE RIVER. *That has always stayed with me."*

—*in a letter from Cousin Catherine Enright, 1999*

A JUMP IN THE RIVER

PROLOGUE

You do not have to believe, as I do, that we were star-crossed lovers in a former life. But as you peruse the pages of *A Jump In the River* I think you will conclude that the life of which you are about to become a silent partner has been, in fact—is, a blessed one.

I missed part of it. I was not there to participate in the tragic early years, which included the traumatic training of a Navy pilot. But I can look back over the past 51 years which I have been privileged to spend as a partner. I view the kaleidoscope of fast-paced events as often hard won; but, nevertheless, the result of a man demonstrating grace in action.

You will feel the huge love and respect which he held for his mother and step-father. It goes without saying that both of us wanted our marriage to succeed as well as had our parents' marriages, whose underlying faith and support will be understood as a given.

Now you will have an opportunity to be moved, as was I, by this man of passion. Early in our courtship at Ohio Wesleyan, he stole my heart with a Scott Joplin "rag" which he improvised on a piano in an empty practice room in Sanborn Hall. I recall the vision I had that here was a man who would not restrict my independence, even as he would demand of life a non-conformist role for himself. It was scary, but he was able to convince me that the risks would be worth all the uncertainties.

Of late, I have come to realize that this is also a person with a photographic memory. Thus he is able to take one into the worlds of law practice, flying, and golf writing in ways that make you feel right there beside him. A day or two ago I overheard him on the telephone telling our son-in-law about an auto trip we took in California some thirty years ago. "It is just after you cross the Pass from Oregon and are about half-way down that we stayed at a place with a breath-taking view of Mount Shasta," he reminded him. I thought to myself, give Clayt another minute or two and he will come up with the name of the inn.

What is the matter if the truth is sometimes dressed up with a touch of hyperbole, if it in turn unearths a deeper more essential level of truth? And truth, to this person, is often arrived at following a myriad of questions others had not even considered. This is but one example of a creative mind at work. Another, in an entirely different vein, is when he relaxes at our piano, listening intently as his fingers change from key to key. Still another example: when he creates plans for bookcases, pantry shelves, unusual ceiling decorations for our game room—and then goes into his shop and builds them into beautiful reality.

You will find in these pages a man not afraid of work. Indeed, you will sense the passion of a lawyer in defense of his clients. There was more than once that a family trip was delayed, or canceled, due to the more immediate needs of a client. It was then that I was convinced that this was a shared marriage with the law, and sometimes with golf and flying. At that time it was often hard to forgive: a birthday dinner growing cold on the range, comes to mind. But then you become aware of the single-minded focus on each moment's happening, forged out of a fierce energy, ingenuity, and always explained with winning good humor. By way of personal confession, this gave me extra time to enjoy to the max our kids' growing-up years. And perhaps I still take unconscious pleasure in that all three of them grew up to follow my favorite political party, and not his.

You will want to see how this gentle man handled leukemia, which mercifully struck later in life. Yet perhaps this was all the more upsetting to his habits that had become ingrained over such a long span of life. You will sense that facing this health challenge brought this man and wife closer together, increasingly aware of the enduring nature of our love.

I can do no better than to quote the poet, Rainer Maria Rilke: "For one human being to love another, that is perhaps the most difficult of all our tasks, the ultimate, the last test and proof, the work for which all other work is but a preparation."

—Margaret Eleanor Hanna Hoskins
July 2000

INTRODUCTION

Early in 1999 we discovered that I am suffering from either leukemia or lymphoma. The oncologists aren't sure which. These spooky diseases are similar, and come in many varieties. My brand seems to be a combination of the types two fellows, both named Paul, incurred in the mid-1990s. Paul Azinger, the famous golfer, was one of those, and he returned to playing PGA Tour golf in a little over a year. The other, the Honorable Paul Tsongas, a former United States Senator from Massachusetts, also overcame his cancer and was able to mount an aggressive race for the Presidency. His life was cut short, and he died from complications related to the cancer.

Based upon those two Pauls, you might think that I have a 50-50 chance of living much longer. Who knows? No doctor, including our oldest daughter, an up-and-coming physician in Seattle, has suggested that my life is even so much as threatened.

I want to make that clear so that you will not conclude that you are about to read some kind of a morbid Final Statement.

A lot of people my age write a memoir, and we always claim that we are doing so not for public consumption. We always insist that we are baring our souls for the benefit of our grand and great-grandchildren.

Not me. I am a professional writer. I wrote this tale from the back nine of my life, for the benefit of every single (and married) man, woman and child of reading age throughout the civilized world. That includes our grandchildren, and those to be.

I sent my manuscript to a couple of dozen of those frenetic editors, book publishers and agents who seem to cluster in and around New York City. It is possible that none of them had time to read it. If Matthew, Mark, Luke and John had sent the Gospels to those people we would still be waiting for the New Testament.

I hope I don't sound cynical. There is so much to be cynical about these days. I considered writing a chapter on how the Internal Revenue Service has been bleeding me dry for years. But I didn't. I was going to say something about the lack of moral leadership in high places, but I suppressed it. If I appear to be misanthropic, or even antisocial, forgive me. I could have been worse.

You need a huge ego to write a memoir. If I didn't have a huge ego, I wouldn't be an aviator, a lawyer or a writer. I believe that life has taught me some lessons worth re-telling, worth hearing. Anyway, when you have leukemia you have a lot of time on your hands between the chemotherapy orgies.

I am grateful to my family and friends, and to a few of my law partners and fellow flyers who helped me recall the facts. The late Jim Reider, a senior executive at Industrial Nucleonics Corporation when I worked there, read the chapter on the beta gauge, and reminded me how the thing works. He did this for me a few days before he died in March of 2000. My boyhood friend, Phil Matheny, permitted me to quote from his memoir. Richard C. Pickett, my partner, read the chapters on flying, and set me straight on when we bought our airplanes and how much we paid for them. Dr. Chris Rhoades, a distinguished oncologist on the staff of the Arthur G. James Cancer Hospital at The Ohio State University, approved my chapter on leukemia. Aaron Cunningham, an ordained pastor, and his wife, Donna, who live on Asbury Ridge, where I spent my youth, checked out what I have to say about my grandparents' religious ideas, and they think I have it mostly right. Ken Bowden, the best golf writer in the world, looked over my chapters on golf and golf writing, and encouraged me, as he has since I began to write nearly 17 years ago. He is too nice to say so, but he could have written them much better. I thought I better let my high school girl friend take a peek at what I remember about her. I did not hear from her lawyer, or her husband, so I think I have a green light there.

One of my closest and oldest friends is the Honorable John David Holschuh, a senior US District Judge for the Southern District of Ohio. We go way back to the days when he was one of the best trial lawyers in Ohio. Last year at the depths of my illness, he came to my home, a 60 mile trip each way, and comforted me. For years it seemed that we either opposed one another, or represented co-defendants, in so many significant cases. Judge Holschuh read, and complimented, my chapter on how a law firm organizes itself in complex litigation. His wry remark was that if he had known I was so well organized, he would have been terrified. Thanks for your friendship, John.

All the errors are my own responsibility. Those include typos and misspellings, of course, but also the errors I have made in the way I have lived my life. It will occur to you that I did a lot of things wrong. I know it. They are all my fault. I wish I could live life all over again.

DEDICATION

Margaret Eleanor Hanna Hoskins is my spirit, my life. During this illness she has kept me alive. For 51 years she has laughed along with me. We make a good team. Anyone will tell you that. So to you, my dear one, I dedicate this book, as I have dedicated my life. Mmmmmm ... Thanks.

—CCH
July 2000

ABOUT THAT TITLE

On the evening of August 1, 1927 my father became a hero the hard way. He jumped into the Muskingum River, fully clothed, to save the life of a young woman who was drowning. He saved her. He drowned. His body was found the next day a mile downstream.

The text at his funeral was, "Greater love hath no man than this that he lay down his life for his friends."

Doris Logston was not exactly a friend. My dad never met her. He kept his barber shop open until about six o'clock that evening. After a hearty dinner, he, my mother, and I went over to the river bank to relax. None of us had any intention of going swimming.

The tragedy happened in front of our eyes. My mother became a 24-year old widow. I was five days short of my third birthday. I have no memory of the occurrence, which can be relied upon. I do have a nebulous feeling, more a sense than a memory, of my mother calling out "Jim … Jim …" across the gloomy waters of the Muskingum.

For weeks and months after his drowning, I called attention to myself by jumping on to sofas, and jumping off wagons and walls and anything else I could find, and yelling: *This is the way my Daddy jumped in the river.*

I got over it. My daddy jumped in the river all right, and that was the end of him. And of us as a family. It wasn't the end of my mother or me. She remarried and had a happy life. I grew up with many fathers instead of one. I became a carrier-based Navy pilot, graduated from college and law school, practiced law in a tiny town, and then in a small city, and then as general counsel of a publicly owned corporation, and finally as a senior partner in a blue chip law firm in the capital of Ohio. I gave up that good life years ago, to pound out pieces for golf magazines.

I have wondered what my life would have been like if there had been no jump in the river. If I wrote that story now, it would be a novel.

Who wants to write a novel?

This story is true. There was *a jump in the river*.

UNCLE SAM WANTED ME

It may not be logical, and certainly it is not chronological, but telling you now of my Navy career makes sense. It was a short and non-heroic career. I won't dwell on it. There is not the slightest doubt in my mind that the 34 months I spent as an aviation cadet and a carrier-based pilot, shaped my next 50 years.

I enlisted in the Navy in December of 1942, a year and a day after the attack on Pearl Harbor. Because the training facilities were overloaded, the Navy did not order me to active duty until the following August. I reported to a cadet processing facility in Detroit, where I met about 50 young men who would start training with me. After walking around most of the day stark naked, in mid-afternoon we left on a train, fully clothed, for Delaware, a small city in central Ohio. Delaware is the home of Ohio Wesleyan University, a small liberal arts college which in many ways unrelated to the Navy, has played a large role in my life to this day.

When our train pulled into Delaware at twilight, it was met by an Ensign who mustered us, and somehow or other assembled us into a loose formation. We were wearing our civilian clothing, and had not yet had our memorable haircuts.

The Ensign marched us east on the south side of West William street, toward the Ohio Wesleyan campus, a distance of less than a quarter of a mile. When we arrived in the vicinity of the university, we did a column right and proceeded up a narrow walkway toward Styvesant Hall.

The City maintained a concrete barrier in the middle of the path, to discourage vehicular traffic. I didn't see it and ran right into it. I skinned my leg rather badly and began to bleed all over my socks and both trousers legs.

If there is a moment in time when the boy turns into the man, that was it for me. If the accident had occurred the day before, my mother would have fussed over me. I might have gone to the doctor for some stitches. It wasn't yesterday anymore. It was today, and the Navy didn't care a bit whether my leg was broken in three places. The Ensign ordered me to stay in line, and quit whining.

As we entered the area immediately behind Styvesant Hall, the entire cadet battalion, several hundred youngsters, gave us a welcome. They leaned out of the windows and doorways, and shouted at the tops of their voices, "Go Back ... Go Back ... Before it is Too Late!!" and "You'lllll be sorryyyyy!!" A month later I gave the same greeting to the new squadron which came in after us. By then I was an Old Salt.

When I started cadet training I was not an incorrigible brat who particularly needed discipline. I was an only child of a widowed mother, who watched me like a hawk. Among other no-nos, I was never permitted to go swimming, because my father jumped in a river and drowned when I was little. The Navy had a lot of fun with that one, and taught me to swim in about 15 miserable minutes. By the time I became an Ensign, I could tow a battleship with my feet strapped together.

That's the way the Navy works, at least in war time. We all had strange mind sets in 1943. In my case, there was never a moment while I was undergoing aviation training that I was not thinking about some young, healthy, Japanese youngster my age, who was undergoing the same training somewhere in Asia. I convinced myself that someday we would meet in the skies over the Pacific, and one of us would not survive. That was on my mind as I learned to call the floor the deck, and learned how to tie knots and put up with other silly things mandated by the Navy, which had little to do with dive-bombing or dog-fighting.

Later in my training, when primary and advanced flying came along, I became determined to find out, and remember, how far I could take my airplane without pulling off its wings. I would think of that other youngster—everyone called them "Japs" in those days—as I practiced aerobatics and high and low gunnery runs hour after hour. I believed that no one in the world, including US Air Force pilots, could take off in any kind of weather, find the enemy and destroy him any more effectively than I could. I think a mind set less vicious than that would never have survived the rigorous Navy training.

That viciousness has waned over the years but never left me entirely. I impaneled scores of juries as a trial lawyer, and I can not remember ever intending to accomplish less than a total dismantling of the other side. One of the rare times I ever broke 80 at Muirfield Village Golf Club, near Columbus, was in a member-member tournament. By the luck of the draw, I was paired with a very polite Japanese executive at a nearby Honda plant. He was about my age, and all day I tried to kill him. I kept thinking that maybe at one time in his military career he might have been the one who trained to kill me. There were other vicious acts: I didn't buy a Nikon camera for years, although the evidence was clear that it was the best one for me. The only Japanese cars we have owned were made here in Ohio.

During the early part of 1943, while I was waiting for the Navy to call me to duty, I helped manufacture bomb racks at Chrysler Airtemp in Dayton during the days. Six nights a week I played a trumpet in a dance band which frequently was booked into the Kitty Hawk Room of the Biltmore Hotel in downtown

Dayton. Because I owned a bugle and had a leather lip from playing in the dance band, the Navy appointed me battalion bugler. I had to get up a little earlier each morning to blow reveille, but that was offset by the fact that I missed some of the physical training in order to blow the call to colors and other tattoos during the day.

Each night at 2200 hours the cadet day came to a close when I stood on the front porch of Styvesant Hall, where we were bivouacked, and played taps as melodically as I could. I put my heart into it each time, and it is a beautiful piece of music. Only Harry James could have done any better.

One minute after I played taps on the porch, I went down into Styvesant Glen, which was then a semi-wilderness area in front of the Hall, where I carefully played the "echo" to taps.

A good solid 3-wood shot to the north of Styvesant was an OWU dormitory known as Austin Hall. I didn't know it then, but the beautiful young lady I would meet when my Navy days were over, and who would be my wife for more than 50 years, was then a lonesome and homesick freshman. Her oldest brother was at that moment involved in some of the most perilous duty the Navy had to offer. He was an officer on a vessel which was escorting American troopships across the North Atlantic in the midst of the U-boat threats. His family did not know from trip to trip, or from day to day, whether he was living. "Harry James" blowing taps down in Sty Glen each night at ten o'clock, was more than she could take. She cried herself to sleep every night. It was so much fun consoling her, three years later, and for that matter, until this day.

Although I was an honor student in high school, the Navy's academic training was very difficult for me. I had earned varsity letters in basketball and baseball, but the physical training also was taxing. The Navy had physical education specialists who, before they were called to Naval duty, had been coaching various sports at some of our best known universities. They were totally committed to beating us into shape. Many of our academic instructors were senior members of the Ohio Wesleyan faculty, who one day might be teaching music to civilian students, and Morse code to cadets the next day. History professors taught us the Naval Regulations. We sometimes had the feeling that they were only a day or two ahead of us in the curriculum.

The days were long and exhausting. Sometimes after taps, I nearly cried myself. I was often near physical collapse. I never had time to long for civilian life. My body became hard as a rock, and I ran a mile in five minutes. Every day I was required to climb hand-over-hand on a rope to the top of Selby Stadium, a distance of 30 to 40 feet. A muscle cramp could be disastrous. The Navy simply did not fool around.

My Navy days at Ohio Wesleyan lasted about two months. Shortly before I shipped out, I met a young and talented cadet whose first name was Kenneth. I think he may be the best pianist I ever heard up close. Prior to joining the Navy he played with several prominent bands, including one of the early "herds" of Stan Kenton. He confided to me one day that he liked the way I played my bugle, and I had the nerve to suggest that we might put on a little concert for our shipmates some evening. I had a nearly new King cornet with me, as well as my bugle. The Navy, with or without OWU's knowledge, commandeered a grand piano from Sanborn Hall, the music school which was nearby.

Ken could play any music he had ever heard, in any key and in any rhythm. Because he had a couple of years at Julliard, he could read any music ever written and transpose it on the spot into any other key. My talents and horizons were much more limited than that, but because of my own "big band" experience I knew all the standards. I had committed nearly everything Harry James was playing in those days: "It Seems to Me I've Heard That Song Before," "I'll Never Smile Again," "The Music Makers," etc., etc.

They were all second-nature to Ken, and together we made some soft and sweet entertainment for the cadets who liked to swing a little. I never heard of Ken after the short time we had together. Our paths never again crossed in life.

In this day and age of computer searches, I could look him up in a data base, if I knew his last name. I have wondered whether his young enemy counterpart, who was at that moment training somewhere in Asia, and who loved life as much as we did, might have got Ken lined up in his sights, high over the Pacific.

When I concluded my training at Ohio Wesleyan it was clear to me that I would have to dedicate all of my time to Naval matters, and I shipped my bugle and cornet back to my home. To this day I have never played either of them enough to redevelop any kind of a lip. Navy, college, law school, raising a family, practicing law, playing lots of golf and rekindling my interest in flying through the ownership of several small airplanes, all of which I intend to tell you about, crowded out music entirely.

I reported to Bowling Green State University, in northwest Ohio, in mid-October. The duty was totally different, as was our mood. We were about to fly, and we thought of nothing else from 0545 each morning until taps, played by someone else. The first two weeks we had extensive ground school, but it was not theoretical or general in nature. It was devoted entirely to the mighty machine we would soon fly: a 65-horsepower Piper Cub.

After we learned the location and purpose of every gadget on the J-3 Cub, we finally got to go out to Bricker Field, BGU's local airport, and fondle one. Our instructor, a civilian flyer from the hills of West Virginia, gathered several of us around that beautiful little yellow airplane, and said gravely: "Gentlemen, this here thing is a airplane."

From that moment, we were hooked on flying for life.

I was lucky to have Dick Gauthier (Go-Shay) as my roommate at Bowling Green. I was 19 and he was 23, a world of difference.

He was the son of a famous football coach and athletic director at Ohio Wesleyan, George Gauthier. Dick had a BS from Ohio Wesleyan and a masters from Ohio State, in chemical engineering. He was just what I needed. When I got a little discouraged because I couldn't seem to fly well, he knew how to bring back my confidence.

Flying did not come easy for me. My instructor sensed that I was trying hard, so he stuck with me. I was almost the last in our group to solo the little bird. According to my logbook, it happened early in November, 1943, after I had 12 hours of flight instruction. Some of the hot pilots soloed after only eight hours. Like many exciting things in life, it happened rather naturally. My instructor simply got out of the airplane, and told me I was ready. He went over my "mission" with me one more time, and said: "Take it away ... you are a flyer."

I taxied to the tip of the runway, and opened up the throttle as quickly as I could before the instructor changed his mind. The little cub had much more power without him in it, and the view out the windows was better. I was airborne in nothing flat and up to 300 feet in a few seconds. I made my left turn, and stayed right in the traffic pattern. My downwind leg was precisely at 500 feet above ground level, and I did a beautiful 180 degree turn to the left losing altitude gradually, so that I could put my tail down before the wheels, right in front of my instructor. He must have had his heart in his throat. I sure did.

He waved me around for another touch-and-go and another perfect landing at his feet. The third time around, he gave me the cut sign to come to a full stop. He got back in the airplane, and had the good sense to taxi himself back to the hanger. He knew I was "wrung out" from all that serious flying. When we parked at the flight line, the cadet corps was gathered, and they proceeded to tear my shirt off my back. All hands autographed it, including my instructor. I still have the tattered shirt packed away carefully—one of the great traditions of Naval aviation. In the following two years, I must have soloed a dozen other Navy trainers, dive bombers, torpedo bombers, and fighter planes. But nothing ever compared to the first time around Bricker Field in the little yellow Cubby.

Bricker Field was named after Governor and Senator John W. Bricker. In 1964, 20 years after I soloed, Mr. Bricker invited me to join his law firm in Columbus, and I practiced with him until his death in the 1980s. There will be more later about him, and those exciting days.

There were many more thrills at Bricker Field, 71 hours of flying in all. Most of it was anticlimactic. Shortly after the beginning of 1944, I was on my way to the University of Iowa, to commence the famous SeaHawk physical training and ground school. It was famous because so few cadets got though it successfully. In my squad of 33, only 17 of us completed the full syllabus. The others either quit or were washed out to the Great Lakes Training Center north of Chicago, where they became enlisted men in the Navy for the duration of the war.

The syllabus, which involved no flying, took three months. The day we checked in we were issued huge book bags which contained materials on theory of flight, engineering, and the tables and charts needed for the study of celestial navigation. A complicated plotting board was fitted into the bag, upon which we would learn to calculate wind vectors. There were technical books on how aircraft radios and other flight instruments were made, and how they worked, and extensive flash cards on friendly and enemy aircraft recognition.

Most of our courses were taught in the academic rooms of the University of Iowa, and were conducted throughout the afternoons and evenings. Our instructors were eager, young Naval officers, many of whom were fresh out of Annapolis. No more liberal arts professors.

Each day started at the traditional 0545. Our bunks had to be made up as if each day were inspection. Our clothing had to be rolled and stowed according to regs, and the slightest mistakes or oversights, however innocent, resulted in demerits and extra hours of duty after taps.

All of our days were about the same. We fell in for muster on the parade grounds at 0630, and had about a half-hour of calisthenics, followed by a five-mile run, often in bitter-cold, midwinter weather. The last mile of the run was over the SeaHawk obstacle course, which was famous enough to be featured in *Life* magazine. During the remainder of the day until ground school started, we studied hand-to-hand combat, wrestling, boxing, and worked endlessly on the gym equipment, such as the parallel bars, rings, and vaults. Most of the cadets could swim like fish, and found it easy to pass the various required tests, in the first Olympic size pool I had ever seen. It was 16-feet deep and had no shallow end.

Because of my swimming deficiencies, I had to take "sub swimming" at both Ohio Wesleyan and Bowling Green. By the time I got to Iowa, however, I was over the fear of the water and doing rather well. I was trying hard, and it seemed to me that the Navy was pulling for me. Of course there were exceptions.

There always seems to be an exception to every rule. There was a swimming specialist at Iowa who had it in for me. No matter how hard I tried, I could not satisfy him. I think that secretly he wanted to be an aviation cadet himself, but his eyesight was not so good. In civilian life he had trained US Olympic swimming teams. A less than average swimmer like myself, was annoying to him.

One of the swimming tests we all had to pass consisted of breaking the hold of a specialist, who would jump on us from the shore, and take us to the bottom of the pool with his arms and legs wrapped around us. We would be treading water faced away from the shore, and would not know for sure when we would be jumped. The specialist was not supposed to drown us, and most of them would let us up after a minute, if we were not making any progress breaking their holds. Unfortunately, I was jumped by my friend at a time when I had very little air in my lungs, and I think he had in mind holding me down for a little longer than normal.

I have always reacted reasonably well at times of emergency, and this was one. I did exactly what any other red-blooded American boy would do who had learned to survive on the streets and playing fields of a small town in southeastern Ohio. My friend was wearing a skin-tight, Spandex-like swim suit, and I simply reached around behind him, got a generous handful of his most precious anatomy, and gave the whole apparatus a meaningful twist.

His legs came loose first and then his arms and we shot to the surface like Roman candles. I was gasping, and he was swearing. A senior instructor told me later that the procedure I used was okey under the circumstances, but it was not taught in the movies and lectures we endured on how to break the holds, because it was thought to be an extreme measure.

I was assigned a friendly new athletic specialist who treated me carefully, always with respect. I noticed that all of the specialists kept their distances from me after that episode. I passed all my swimming requirements, easily.

I mentioned that 17 of us completed the training. Unfortunately, all 17 of us did not move on to primary flight training. We were packed and ready to go, but several days passed and we began to realize that something was wrong. One morning we were called to the parade grounds a final time, and asked to count off. Even numbers were ordered to take one step forward. I was one of those. The commander announced that the eight of us would leave immediately for primary flight training at a naval air station near Ottumwa, Iowa. The buses were ready to load. On the double.

We had no opportunity to say good-bye to the other nine of us, the uneven numbers, who were sent to Great Lakes Naval Training Center for "processing." It was explained to them that they were not washed out of the cadet program. They were going to stand by at Great Lakes, until room opened up later at a primary flight location, and then they would be right back into flying. It didn't work out that way for two of them, the two who had been my roommates and therefore had lined up on each side of me. After a "decent period," they were permitted to resign from the Navy, or ship over as enlisted men for the duration of the war. This elimination process, which was so unfair, became known throughout the aviation cadet program as the "Purge." I said it before: the Navy did not fool around. A war was on. Winning it was everything.

Right here is where we are going to end my tale of Navy Life. I served another couple of years, but not with any particular distinction. If you want to read about flying heroics, read something about Ensign George Gay, or Colonel Marion Karl, or Colonel John Glenn (later to become my client and friend), and hundreds of others including a future president of the United States who flew the same torpedo bomber in which I was fleet-ready. I was sorry I never met Lt. George Bush.

I believe that when I left the Naval Flight Preparatory School at the University of Iowa, the Navy had finished its attempts to prepare me for manhood. I had a 30-inch waist, I weighed 155, and there was no fat on me. I could do 100 pushups without breaking a sweat. I no longer had a killer desire to take on just one Japanese opponent in combat, assuming that the poor guy lived through his training. I now wanted to take on about six of them at a time, so the odds would be even.

The Navy now intended to forget my manhood, and to concentrate on making me a lean, mean, flying machine. We stayed in shape with daily exercises, but the athletic specialists were out of our lives. I left at least one of them hobbling around for a few days.

From that time on, it was flying, flying, flying. After primary flying, it was intermediate flying, then advanced flying, and then instrument flying. I can think of only three times that flying with the Navy ever became other than routine for me. At Bowling Green I became disoriented in the air, at a time when I had about 20 hours in my log book. With less than 30 minutes of fuel in my tank, I decided that the smart thing might be to shoot an emergency landing, telephone my instructor and get a bit of help. This seemed to be what my inner voice was calling out for me to do, even if the incident brought my Naval flying career to an early end. The thought of a fiery crash never had much appeal to me.

I knew the Navy procedure for an emergency landing: (l) find the biggest, flattest, smoothest-looking field you can find on the horizon; (2) drag it once at low altitude looking for stumps or ditches, or parked farm equipment; (3) land into the wind, and let the airplane slow to a stop without brakes; and (4) cut the power and get out of the airplane without taxiing; and (5) walk to the nearest farm house and ask to use the telephone.

I did everything in the right order, and my instructor asked me to stand by in the farmhouse, until he could get there. The farm family and I became friendly, but in the end I could have killed the farm owner. Just as my instructor was congratulating me for landing in such a nice, safe field, the farmer butted in and said: "Hell, he should have landed in the big field over across the road ... I got a field over there three times as big as this little patch he picked!" I was relieved that my instructor only smiled, without taking any notes.

The other two incidents were exciting at the time. They also involved getting lost, once in very bad weather while serving as a utility pilot in the general vicinity of Cuba. The other was in the dead of night while I was flying a square search in the waters west of Point Loma, which guards the North Island Naval Air Station at San Diego. I was looking for a carrier I was supposed to intercept, and all navigation equipment was off. I had with me that plotting board which had been issued to me at the University of Iowa. What I needed was one of those recently graduated Annapolis instructors, who made everything look so easy in the classroom.

Exciting? You bet. But no one ever shot at me. I never had to drop a live bomb. I never strafed a village. I never shot up a Chinese Embassy by mistake.

My Navy Wings of Gold were pinned on me by my mother at special graduation ceremonies in May of 1945, at the naval air station at Corpus Christi, Texas. Mother had the audacity to toss me my first salute. I was an officer and a gentleman by an act of Congress, and I was three months short of my 21st birthday.

And now ... something much less viscious

ROMANCE AMONG THE HILL PEOPLE

To call yourself a true "Ohio Hill Person" you have to prove you were born in a narrow region along a line which meanders uncertainly to the southeast from Columbus to the Ohio River. Across the river you might be a mountaineer. Outside that tract you might be a drylander, or a clodhopper.

"Hilligan" can be pejorative, even rude, if used by a non-hilligan. So it is better to say Hill Person. We are tightly knitted by family, and in a neighborly way. We stick together and look out for each other. Almost entirely we are Anglo-Saxon, often Scottish or Irish. Also, there are a lot of Jones' and Evans' around at all times who claim to be from Wales, and like to sing a lot.

One of my very best friends when I grew up in Hocking County, the heartland of hilliganism, was Paul Stivison. He was one of the smartest boys in our class, very quick and very bright. By far he was the most polite and gentle of us all.

I doubt if he knew it, but I tried to emulate him. Mother encouraged that, because she knew that Paul was a worthy role model. When we both hit 16, our glands began to rage at about the same time. Paul always was kind of neat, and overnight I began to groom myself meticulously. I had to have every hair in place, actually pressed some of my clothing, shined my shoes now and then, and found myself talking to the girls quite a bit.

It was innocent enough. Girls were nice, I found out. They smelled a little differently, and they were soft when you bumped into them. They must have had some glands, too, because they no longer snarled or retreated into the school books when Paul and I got braver and braver.

There was no way I could get into even an inexpensive relationship, because I was dead broke. Didn't have a dime, and there was no way to get any. My father's sudden drowning left us penniless. Even without a tragedy like ours, nearly everyone else was penniless too. This was the Great Depression.

About the only families that had any money to speak of were the folks who owned small businesses, and did not have to depend upon others for work. My friend Dick Brown's father owned his own insurance agency, and so Dick had a modest allowance which he sometimes shared with me. My friend Jack Lee's dad owned a retail store, and he shared a little too. Of course I never asked for loans or for money. Dick and Jack, and others, would just grab the tabs quickly when they could.

Mother was a deputy in the prosecuting attorney's office in Hocking County, a job which paid her about $600 a year. The hero's pension I will tell you about later, provided a little more. We were well fed and clothed. Many families were not.

Paul Stivison and I had to rely upon our boyish charms to entertain the ladies. Wining and dining were out of the question. Naturally, Paul had very high standards when it came to women, and that meant that I had to have them too.

One of the nicest families in town, and perhaps one of the more prosperous, was the family of Mr. and Mrs. Joe S. Case. Mr. Case and his father before him owned Case's Drug Store for as long as anyone could remember. Their oldest son, William, graduated with high honors from Ohio Wesleyan, and from a seminary in Chicago. He became a professor of religion, which meant that around our town he was an eminent theologian. The oldest

Case daughter was Sue, and it didn't take Paul long to cut her out of the pack for his very own. They married shortly after World War II, and they still are. It was a case of true love at first sight.

Following in Paul's steps, as I did a lot, that left the youngest Case daughter for me, and for nearly every other 16 year old boy in town who knew she was alive. We all tried to get her attention, in a nice way. Her name was Jody Case, and my glands were telling me that she was the cutest thing that ever lived and breathed.

There was not much reason for Jody to notice me. But she did, mostly because she was naturally friendly. When I smiled she smiled back, a reaction I am sure I misinterpreted. She played a saxophone in the marching band, and I was one of the louder trumpet players in that same band. When I asked her to sit with me on the band bus, she accepted. I definitely misinterpreted that one. Before long, in my mind, she was "my girl." In her mind, I would imagine, I was one of several young men she liked about equally well. I am sure we were all fantasizing about her in the same, harmless way.

I was two years older than Jody, and that may have made me a bit more intriguing to her. Her mother, Mrs. Bess Case, did not seem to be concerned about our difference in age, and even commented once that she felt that Jody was as safe with me as Sue was safe with Paul Stivison. Jody's father always had those same reservations which every father has when a young man begins to show an interest in his daughter. Later, I would live through those reservations with each of our daughters, only to be blessed with the two best sons-in-law in the world.

Jody and I became an item in the school paper. We were going steady. Using her money was unthinkable, and since I had none, we went to such free things as school functions and church picnics. I did not belong to her church, but she invited me anyway, and I was right at home because every kid in town knew every other kid. I even knew the Catholics. Heck, I was the shortstop on their baseball team in the church league.

Now and then I would cheat a little on my steady. I met and admired a young lady who just moved to town. She was my own age and had a wonderful singing voice, which landed her in the cast of our junior class play. I had a kissing part opposite her, which because it was well rehearsed nearly brought the house down the night of the performance, as all my buddies cheered and called for more. I thought it was kind of funny, until I learned that Jody Case was not amused.

There was nothing enduring about my relationship with Jody, although I found every minute of it exciting. She soon began drifting back to some of her many other suitors, including the fullback on our football team. He was an Adonis type who could have folded me like a paper airplane and tossed me out a window. His ex-girlfriend asked me if I could do something to break them up so she could get him back. What a laugh. I told her as guilelessly as I could that I had no desire to lose all my front teeth. After a brief period of disappointment I found myself not too worried about Jody's dumping me, as I became very busy with school work, American Legion baseball, piano lessons, golf, varsity basketball, and a brass sextet which I helped organize, and which began to win statewide and even national honors.

I found out an interesting thing about teenagers' raging glands: if no one takes them too seriously or tries to suppress them too abruptly they will usually stop raging about as fast as they began.

Romancing among the Hill People is not reserved for teenagers. When I was about ten, I began to notice that Matthew P. Chesser's automobile was pulling up in front of our house quite often, and he was inviting my mother to movies and parties. She was just 31, and had been a widow about 7 years. My existence did not seem to scare him away.

Mother would not have dated anyone but Matt. They were both Hill People. She was born on Asbury Ridge in Starr township in Hocking County, and the Chesser family lived on the adjacent farm to the north. He was five years younger than she, and that made him like a little brother after the death of my dad.

Mother and Matt were married when I graduated from high school, and nothing nicer could have happened to either of them. They had 44 years together before cancer took him in 1986.

There is nothing like hilligan romance, which is not to say that it is the only kind of loving there is. I am sure that if Jody Case and I had married, the theme song of our life, probably a blissful one, would have been something like, "Don't Sit Under the Apple Tree With Anyone Else But Me." When Margaret Hanna and I were married, the mature and endless theme which has reverberated for more than 50 years for us is Tchaikovsky's "Fantasy Overture to Romeo & Juliet."

One tune is not better than the other. There is no moral issue here. But there is a difference.

RELIGION IN THE HILLS

Of course there is a God. How could any thinking person believe otherwise? Glancing up at the stars and realizing that each of them is in a predictable place at a given moment should tell you there is some sort of order at work here. Listening to a seven year old Yahudi Menuhin play the violin, or watching a ten year old Jack Nicklaus hit a golf ball, should tell you that some of that talent had to be developed in an earlier life. The soul must survive death. It follows that someone or something must be in charge of that process.

Faith aside, I would be hard pressed to prove the existence of God. But even if I could assemble hard, irrefutable evidence that there is in fact no God and there never has been one, I wouldn't do it. What a dirty trick on mankind that would be. I am glad that no one took such evidence to Mozart before he created the Requiem, or to Martin Luther as he was about to start a commotion in Europe.

My introduction to spiritual matters took place during my preschool years on my Grandpa and Grandma Clark's farm on Asbury Ridge in southeastern Ohio. After my father's death, Mother parked me there while she finished business school in Columbus and found employment with a brokerage firm. A brokerage firm was not a great place for steady employment in 1928.

But in Mother's case she was not looking for security in the Columbus area, because she intended to collect me when I was ready for school, and establish a home with me in Nelsonville, a small city near Asbury Ridge.

Asbury Ridge is a special place. The Clarks, Chessers, Hefts, Mitchells, Campbells, Kennards, Weeds, Whites, Dabritzs, McDaniels, and Todds all sleep silently these days in the hilly cemetery next to the Methodist Church. In the 1920s and 30s, the hub of all spiritual, social and community life on the Ridge was the church.

Grandpa Clark was the hub of the hub. He was the lay preacher, which meant that he was in charge of the pulpit on the Sundays when the regular minister was serving other churches on his circuit. Rarely could one church in the Hill Country support one pastor. Grandpa, his name was Josh Clark, could not preside at funerals, weddings or at communion; but if you wanted my grandfather to say a few words as your mother's casket was being lowered into the warm, sweet earth, you only had to ask him once.

He was a kindly man, although outspoken on any subject. He was largely self-educated. As a young man he was a blacksmith. For many years he studied electricity with the help of a correspondence course. Eventually he was selected to be the Electrician at the coal mine where he had labored for part of his childhood and most of his adult life.

Without my grandfather's influence, we would never have had Old Bill, the dispirited mine pony who for years and years had pulled the loaded coal cars out of the mine. Grandpa felt sorry for him and brought him home. After we washed him several times, and curried him, he turned out to be a pinto. With proper food and rest he became a heckuva pony. My Grampa bought me a cowboy hat.

For Josh and Ida Clark, religion was the most natural thing in the world. It was all in the Bible. If it wasn't in the Bible, it wasn't. They were saints by any theologian's definition. She cleaned the church, taught a Sunday School class and cooked enormous dinners for anyone in the congregation who wanted to come home with Grandpa. Their faith sustained them. Their religion was just right for them. It brought them peace of mind. It gave them heart. It kept them alive.

Grandpa's sermons followed a familiar theme: if you were not born again, you were a goner. It's entirely up to you: you can come down to the altar and pray your way through to Heaven, or you can continue to put it off until God Himself loses all patience with you. Grandpa would talk endlessly on how good it felt to know that you are right with the Lord; that you will see your loved ones upon your death; and that you won't have to worry about spending eternity shoveling ashes in Hell. That point came across to the many men in his audience who were retired coal miners.

His father before him, along with his father's brother, arrived from Darbyshire, England around 1860. They left because there was no opportunity. The British mines were unsafe, the pay terrible—all the usual reasons. Those very same conditions existed in southeastern Ohio. As a young man it looked to me as if they had not bettered themselves. Late in his life I asked my Grandpa Clark about that, and I will never forget his reply: "They did not do it for themselves, my boy. They did it for *you!*"

Grandpa and Grandma Clark could quote the Bible by the hour. She was my first Sunday School teacher, and each week I was required to recite a verse from the Bible. I thought it was very funny to embarrass my own grandmother, week after week, by reciting the shortest verse in the Bible: "Jesus wept."

In retrospect, it seems to me that my grandparents were concerned almost entirely with personal salvation, and only rarely with man's interaction with man. The parishioners were frustrated by poverty and unemployment. They yearned for a better life. Week after week Grandpa would make them feel better by telling them what a problem it will be for the rich men to enter the Kingdom of Heaven. They shouted their Amens on that one. That will teach those rich people.

But you would seldom hear my grandfather remind the congregation that if you " ... do it unto the least of these thy brethren, you will do it unto me." Perhaps he was just being practical. His friends and neighbors were hanging on for dear life. They were trying to get through this life to a better one. He told them how, often at the top of his voice. Keep in mind that under the circuit system, my grandfather preached several Sundays for each time the regular minister appeared.

That was my first introduction to religion. I knew no other religious ideas. I was reminded constantly that it was up to me to avoid the rages of Hell. When I was around 14 or so, I succumbed to the relentless pressure which for years my grandparents had placed upon me to get my own life in order by giving myself to the Lord. I hardly knew what to do. I wanted to save my life, of course, and at the same time please my grandparents. But it was not clear to me that taking on the religious life was the proper thing to do. One evening at a prayer meeting, my grandfather seemed to be pointing his sermon directly at me. I was scared to death as I accepted his invitation to come to the altar. With the tears streaming down my face, my grandfather finally declared that indeed I was now born again. Exactly how he knew that I have often wondered.

By this time, which was around 1938 or so, mother and I had moved from Nelsonville, where she was the secretary to an attorney in private practice, to Logan, another ten miles or so further from Asbury Ridge. Now, she worked in the prosecutor's office. Because my religious conversion was embarrassing to me, I insisted that we not make so many weekend trips to the Clark farm, and that we find things to do on our own in the Logan area. I also did everything I could to keep my new "birth" a secret from my sophisticated high school friends.

The immediate significance of my being born again was that it cooled my relationship with my maternal grandparents, a relationship that had been special since my third year, when I was overcoming the trauma of watching my father drown, and those blessed souls took me in and kept me alive.

The long term effect of my conversion at such an early age, has been to make me a bit cautious of persons who seem to have an excess of religious fervor. I saw a debate on C-span recently on the question of which is more dangerous, religion or science. I voted for religion. I think in the wrong hands religion can ruin lives, start wars, and generally disrupt the community.

My religious education in the Hill Country was unfortunate for me; but I came out of it without permanent damage, perhaps only a few scars. When I entered Ohio Wesleyan after the War, I came under the care of Professor Goldie McCue, who had taught religion for 40 years. Her approach was the opposite of anything I had ever known. I was given no universal truths to memorize or take on faith. Professor McCue gave us vast reading lists, and urged us to engender our own thoughts on why any thinking person should run the risk of trying to be a Christian. She knew the Bible, including a couple of "new" translations which were coming out, but she never flaunted that knowledge.

After a year with her, I began to understand that personal salvation is only a part of the equation. To love the Lord and to love our neighbors as ourselves are equally important. In fact, it is written that upon these two loves, hang all the law and the prophets.

Professor McCue, "Goldie" to me after we graduated, retired in California. We visited her regularly until her death in 1974. By that time my spiritual health had recovered to the point where I was teaching an adult religious education class, and serving on the board of trustees of a Presbyterian college. After Goldie's death, I continued to "grow." I became a Ruling Elder in the Presbyterian Church.

My personal commitment became so ecumenical that I began to pre-order kosher food on the airlines, just so I could give my seat mates a merry "shalom."

I served as attorney for our presbytery, and later our synod. In that capacity I argued numerous matters of church law on the synod and general assembly levels. After a few years I was appointed to the permanent judicial commission of our synod, and later was named moderator of that court. For years we applied church law without fear or favor to the princes and the paupers, and to the washed and the unwashed.

In recent years I have been unattached to any congregation. This is by choice, and has not resulted from any fights or feuds. I do not necessarily recommend such an independent attitude to others, and especially not to persons who haven't enjoyed a rich congregational experience. There is no question that my family and I have benefited from our long years of participation in the life of several wonderful churches.

For me, at this time, the opportunity to distance myself from the organized church has been rewarding and refreshing. If the minister wants to—or refuses to—marry two men, or two women, I will never know about it. If he assists the choir director with her secret abortion, he need not worry about my jumping to the wrong conclusion. If the church treasurer wants to attend a conference on stewardship in Las Vegas, he should go right ahead. I am not paying for it.

I have decided that God not only exists, but He exists within me, in my heart. I also know that after more than 60 years of service, I need to get away from denominational discord for awhile. No more every-member canvasses, no turgid meetings, no trips to presbytery, no teaching of classes—just a plain old cooldown. I need to worship at my own speed, and in my own way.

Now and then I hear a fundamentalist preacher yell through my TV that I can't do that.

Watch me.

THE WAR ENDS AND COLLEGE BEGINS

Life as a civilian student at Ohio Wesleyan began for me in mid-December of 1945. The six to eight months preceding that date were very busy. Shortly before my mother pinned my Navy wings on me in Corpus Christi, in May, my relationship with Jody Case underwent a brief and intense resurgence. She was now grown up and was just finishing her first year at Ohio State. I was grown up too and very lonely. I received a letter from her congratulating me on my commission and wings, and wondering whether we might get together the next time I got leave.

It sounded like a fantastic idea to me. The day after I graduated, I left Mother and her husband, Matt Chesser, in Texas so they could do some sightseeing, and I caught a Braniff flight to Dayton. I took a cab to our home, got the family car, and headed for the bus station to meet Jody, who was coming in from Columbus.

We had a wonderful reunion. She had lost much of her teen-age cuteness, and was a gorgeous young adult. In those days, college students were the pacesetters in fashion, and Jody was wearing a brown, tailored suit which was totally becoming. I had never seen her in heels, and her hair was styled quite differently. We had an amiable conversation on the way to her folks' house in Logan, and they were kind enough to make one of their guest rooms available for me for the next couple of nights. I slipped down to Asbury Ridge to visit my grandparents, and Jody went along.

I think I need to clarify something. Here I am, a Navy pilot home on his first leave in months. I pick up an old girl friend at a bus station and describe my reunion with her as "wonderful." I also mention an "amiable conversation." I can hear you calling out, "Come on … why don't you tell us what really happened."

I just did. That's what happened. Laugh if you want to, but that is the way we used to behave ourselves in this country. I have a high school friend, Phil Matheny, who also wrote his memoir of growing up in our home town. This is the way he put it:

"In our little town if you wanted sex you got married. I know that will be hard to believe in the late 20th Century, but it was true. If you were going steady you might get away with a little groping in the dark, but there was a line you didn't cross. The reason was that the girls didn't permit it. The girls I knew in high school were very arbitrary about this. There may have been some who didn't feel that strongly about it, but I didn't know them. It was the morality and ethic of the times. It was a matter of pride and self-respect, and I don't think any of us suffered any psychological damage."

Jody had to get back to Ohio State after a few days, and I took her to Columbus and met her roommates at Mack Hall. We agreed that we had a fine time, and that we would write to one another. I left her in Columbus, and returned my folks' car to our home in Dayton after filling the tank, using gas ration coupons issued to me by the Navy. The next day I flew back to Texas. Much to my pleasure, I started getting a daily letter from Jody.

I found out about that time that my next duty station would be Opa-Locka Naval Air Station, just north of Miami. My mission was to learn to fly the latest model torpedo bomber. This one was known as the TBM, because it was made by Martin rather than by Grumman. It had a heavier Pratt & Whitney engine and its hydraulic system was technically different. This meant back to ground school for me, and long hours of poring over details of an engineering nature.

After a couple of weeks, a brand new TBM was parked in front of Operations and my name was stenciled on the side of it. I was free to solo it, which I did that very day with enormous enthusiasm. My permanent crew, a gunner who sat behind me in his own turret, and a radio-radar man who sat in the belly of the airplane, were assigned to me, and we had to go through a period of getting to know each other.

It was comforting to see how trusting and loyal those two crewmen were. We had half a dozen orientation flights the next few days, during which they became convinced that I was the best pilot ever trained by the Navy. The radar man had an initial fear of flying, because from his position in the plane's belly he had only two, small windows. I took him up a couple of times by himself, with him sitting in the gun turret behind me. I demonstrated a number of maneuvers we would be doing, and shot several touch-and-go landings so he could gain confidence. It helped him to get out of his tiny compartment with the two little windows.

I continued to be very lonesome. I had a roommate, Ensign Jack Stuart. Every night when I returned to the Bachelor Officers Quarters, Jack would be lying on his bunk fanning himself with another of Jody's letters to me, all of which were elegantly perfumed. Jack ran a much-publicized poll up and down the corridors of the BOQ, and the consensus was that the perfume was Evening in Paris.

My commanding officer asked if I would like to get in some extra flying time which would not involve my own airplane or my crew. At nearby Ft. Lauderdale, the Navy was operating an advanced radar school for non-pilots. Most of the students were lieutenant commanders and higher, and the radar work they were doing was very sophisticated. They needed a few pilots to take them out over the Caribbean each evening so they could practice intercepting various pre-arranged targets. I talked it over with my crew, and they had no objection to my participating in the program, as long as the night flights did not interfere with our main mission of getting fleet-ready as soon as possible.

The Navy ferried us over to Ft. Lauderdale at 2000 hours each evening and we tried to get airborne by twilight. The older model TBF's in use at the school had more radar gear than I knew existed, which made the planes hard to fly. I merely flew the headings and the times radioed to me by the students, who operated out of the small compartment with two little windows. There were usually two students on each flight. Shortly after midnight when they had enough practice, they would give me radar vectors back to Ft. Lauderdale.

The radar was sophisticated but not foolproof. I took along a plotting board, the one from Iowa City, and did my own dead-reckoning navigation. The only exciting time was the event I mentioned earlier when we were lost one evening before darkness set in, near Havana. It all worked out by the end of that evening when the radar came back on line just as quickly as it had shut itself off without any warning. I did this utility flying for about 30 straight nights.

I couldn't get Jody's tailored brown suit out of my mind. Her letters indicated that she thought my dress blues were kind of impressive too.

Jack Stuart insisted that I "take the bull by the horns," as he put it, a metaphor which seemed to me not in the least appropriate. He went with me to a jewelry store in Miami, and helped me pick out a modest diamond ring. His bright idea was that I should send it to Jody with a letter asking her to wear it, but with the thought that we would not consider marriage at this time. As Jack said, " … the worst that could happen is that she will send it back to you."

She didn't. She wrote that she had discussed it with her parents and they agreed that she would consider herself engaged, but with the understanding that there should be no immediate plans for marriage. She mentioned that by coincidence, Paul Stivison and Sue Case had a similar understanding. Jody also sent me a black onyx ring as a gift.

By the end of July, my crew and I had completed all of our flying requirements. My gunner turned in the highest score in our squadron, shooting his turret gun at a target towed by another airplane. My radar man was required to vector me around the Caribbean for an hour or so, and then give me headings back to Opa-Locka. He pulled it off successfully.

The only thing between us and joining the fleet was my completing the program at the Carrier Qualification Training Unit (CQTU) at Glenview Naval Air Station northwest of Chicago. Getting over this hurdle was my responsibility alone, and did not involve my crew. They got liberty with orders to report to San Diego. A ferry pilot took my airplane to North Island Naval Air Station. I was off for Glenview on a train. I was about to get my first experience landing on a carrier, the thing most Navy pilots dream about from the time cadet training starts.

At this time, the middle of the summer 1945, none of us could foresee any end to the war. There was talk of invading Japan, and I was sure that I would be right in the middle of that. I was convinced that, God willing, I was going to be on active duty for a long, long time. This all changed in a big hurry.

On August 6, coincidentally my 21st birthday, the United States dropped the atom bomb on Hiroshima. Along with several million other people, a busload of pilots from CQTU, including myself, went to the Chicago Loop to mob-watch. I have never seen such a gathering of happy humanity, before or since. I completed the carrier landings at the CQTU by mid-August, but did not get new orders right away. It was obvious that the Navy was re-evaluating its entire mission in the light of Hiroshima, Nagasaki, and the unanticipated surrender of the Japanese government.

When my orders came in late August, they were to North Island, San Diego, with enough report time for me to spend a few days with my family in Dayton. During the leave, I went to her home to visit Jody, whose letters had become shorter and less frequent. I learned that she was no longer wearing my ring. She was kind and honest with me, as she explained that the quick end to the war in the Pacific, and my probable discharge within a few months changed things. I tried my best to understand why that was true. I was very disappointed. This rejection was much harder for me to take than her first one, when we were kids.

I flew to San Diego after a few days, and time and distance helped a lot. For months the lyrics of the ballads seemed to be aimed at me: I see your face in a crowd ... I'll never smile again ... sometimes I wonder why I spend these lonely nights. It is clear to me now, 55 years later, that Jody made the right decision for both of us. I never again received a perfumed letter.

I just re-read that last sentence. Actually, I did get one more perfumed letter, but I am not sure why. In very late 1945, after I had been a civilian for less than a month, I received a telephone call from Margaret Mackey, a family friend, who told me that Mrs. Bess Case, the mother of Sue and Jo, had died suddenly of a heart attack. I sent a letter to Jody and told her how sorry I was, and how much I enjoyed knowing her dear mother. Jody's tender and poignant reply was heartfelt, because she obviously was under stress. What was hard for me to understand, because at that time I was still on the rebound, was that the letter was perfumed, and she tucked in her new photograph. Within a very short time, she married a young fellow from Ohio State.

I asked my Phi Gamma Delta fraternity brother, Bill Scott, whose survival skills were honed on the streets of Cleveland, why

Jody's final letter to me was perfumed. He came up with a solution which was simplistic, but it made me feel better: "She had just one sheet of that Evening in Paris stationery left, and it was either send it to you or wrap the garbage."

I was separated from active duty with the Navy in late November, 1945, but it was very important to me that I kept busy the final three months. I reunited in San Diego with my crew, very briefly, until both of them were discharged and sent to Great Lakes for their own separations. It was a solemn but not a tearful good-bye for us, because they were tickled to death that their active duty days were over. They were kind enough to say that they would have been proud to fight the war with me. I felt the same way about them.

I applied for duty as a ferry pilot and for six weeks flew two Navy airplanes each day from San Diego to Oklahoma, where they were parked wing-tip to wing-tip in a huge field waiting to be scrapped. I was glad that I was not assigned to the last trip for the new TBM with my name on it. I never saw it again. Presumably some other ferry pilot flew it to its final resting place in Oklahoma, wondering all the way who Ens. C.C. Hoskins might be.

I was attached to a research project which sought new and better ways to park and handle aircraft on carrier decks. This meant some extra training in Florida, a few day landings on a small carrier, plus a few night landings on an Essex-class carrier. I took some joyrides to places like Alimeta, directly across the Bay from South San Francisco. On one of my departures from that area, I flew low over Alcatraz and scooted underneath the Golden Gate Bridge. There are many Navy pilots who will admit to that adventure, now that the Statute of Limitations has expired. I took some extra instrument flying training at Brown Field, near San Diego. On my final flight in California, I performed some exciting flat-hatting at Salton Sea, at a time when my altimeter was indicating that we were below sea level.

My Navy flying days were then over. I bought two civilian suits in San Diego and caught a troop train for a very slow trip to Great Lakes. Within a week I was in Dayton wearing my civilian clothing, but still feeling like an expensively-trained, carrier-based Navy pilot—the best in the world.

My family and I decided, shortly after the atom bombs were dropped, that upon separation from active duty I should attend college. We turned rather naturally to Ohio State. With the help of the Chaplain in San Diego, I sent in application forms along with my high school transcripts. My instructions were to report to the veterans office at Ohio State upon my discharge. Early in December I borrowed the family car (gas rationing was now over) and headed for Ohio State.

I parked on North High Street and walked to the campus. There seemed to be thousands of persons looking for the veterans office. A class let out just as I was entering a building and I was nearly trampled. A few days earlier I had received a letter from Pan American Airways inviting me to apply for pilot training in Miami. All of a sudden it seemed like the smart thing to do.

I decided to drive around for awhile and let the crowds die down. I headed north through Worthington and soon was on the outskirts of Delaware, the home of Ohio Wesleyan, my first duty station in the Navy. I wondered where all my old friends were now, and walked down to the very spot in Styvesant Glen where in 1943 I blew the echo to taps. It was while I was standing there alone that it dawned upon me that the War was over, and I had lived through it.

A student who saw the tears in my eyes, asked me if I needed help. After I explained my prior life in the Styvesant Glen, he invited me to his fraternity house for lunch. He then escorted me to the Admissions Office, and within the hour I was enrolled in a special class for returning veterans. OWU's normal fall program began in September, but because many of us could not get out of the military in time, they set up a special class beginning in December. I had less than a week to get ready. My folks were astonished that I had left that morning for Ohio State and returned as a student at Ohio Wesleyan. But I could see that they were pleased.

I had a lot to do in a short time. My step-father had a colleague at work who throughout the war preserved a 1941 Plymouth convertible for the return of his son. The youngster didn't make it, and the father wanted to dispose of the auto as quickly as possible. It was still on blocks when we saw it, with all of its juices drained. It was cream color. Who could turn it down at $640 cash?

With respect to my need for clothing, I had my two San Diego suits, and I could wear many of my Navy shirts, flight jackets, socks, skivvies, etc. I came out of the Navy with a little money, largely because I did not spend much of my $240 monthly income. The GI Bill of Rights would pay all of my Ohio Wesleyan costs and $90 a month in cash.

I made it just in time for the first classes, and they were eye-openers. Never before had I studied anything, anywhere, where no one seemed to be in a hurry. My academic advisor was one of OWU's all-time distinguished professors, an icon of the institution, Dr. Ben Arneson. Among other good advice he suggested that I not take any science courses right away. He said that my Navy transcripts were on the way, and upon their arrival an Ohio Wesleyan committee would decide how much credit I would receive. He thought that most of it would be in the science area.

We put together a group of courses in the liberal arts which totaled about 18 academic hours, a normal load. I asked Dr. Arneson if I could take a few more because I considered myself the world's oldest college freshman. He understood perfectly, and said that if it turned out to be too much, we could always scale back. My program finally totaled 25 hours. Throughout my time at OWU I always took at least 23 hours each semester. As a result I graduated in two years and five months, after receiving 16 hours for my Navy studies.

I had to learn new ways of studying. During the first few weeks I would visit the library stacks with a mission in mind, and then become mesmerized by the endless rows of books and contemporary periodicals. I would spend hours reading something of interest to me which did not happen to be tomorrow's assignment. Because class sizes were small, it was unthinkable to be unprepared. Freshman classes were nearly all taught by lecture, but there were constant references to the reading lists.

I couldn't resist some extracurricular activities. I joined the debate team and participated in a few interscholastic events before finishing the first course in speech and debate. I also went out for varsity baseball, and played mostly when we were so far ahead we couldn't lose, or when we had no chance of winning. I became a pledge at Phi Gamma Delta which was more time-consuming than I thought it would be. My Plymouth convertible was a big hit around the Phi Gamma Delta house, but a nuisance to me because persons I hardly knew, constantly were borrowing it. A used car buyer from Tennessee came through Delaware one afternoon, and I sold the car on the spot for $1100. The prices of prewar cars were escalating because postwar production was stalled until late in 1946.

After about six weeks, as January was ending, I began to hear from several friends that it would be a good thing if I met Margaret Hanna of Geneseo, Illinois. Of course I knew who she was. It would not have been possible to be a student at OWU in 1946 and 1947 without being aware of her presence. It was not just a case of her being popular, although she was indeed well liked and friendly. It was more of a widespread admiration for her because she was deeply involved in programs at Ohio Wesleyan which were worthwhile. Long before I met her she had a reputation for really caring about things in life that are important. That intensity has burned through the years and is as bright as it ever was.

A fellow student, Gertrude Beattie, was most responsible for bringing Margaret and me together. Although Gert was a junior, I was in one of her classes, and we became friends. Several times she told me that her roommate, Marg, was the girl for me. She approached me in Slocum library one evening, and asked me to go with her to the Kappa Kappa Gamma study table which was nearby. She introduced me to this beautiful young lady, Margaret Hanna, and I began to hear soft music playing in the background. Marg and I remember that it was February 5. We always have a date on that date.

The feelings I had and have for her are profound. My life has never been the same since that wonderful evening. There has never been a moment when I have not wanted to be with Marg, to talk with her, to entertain her and make her laugh, to protect her and to tell her of my love. She set a very high standard for me on the Ohio Wesleyan campus. Because she was a prominent student, it seemed to me that her boyfriend should be a person with some dependability. Within days and weeks, we were together as much as possible.

We both had intimidating schedules. Marg had fewer academic hours but her extracurricular activities were endless. She was a member of Mortar Board before we met, and soon after she was elected to Phi Beta Kappa. She was president of the YWCA, and president of a group called CAP, which published a newsletter which shed light on most of the social ills of the day.

As we walked to her dormitory one evening, shortly after we met, she told me of an experience she had as an entering freshman in September of 1943. She "reminded" me that at that time there was a large group of Naval aviation cadets on campus, and every night shortly after 10 p.m. the bugler played taps, which could be heard all over the campus. She explained that she was so homesick and worried about her oldest brother, John, that she simply couldn't take it. She cried herself to sleep every night. With that she collapsed in my arms in tears.

Rarely does a young wooer have an opportunity like this to impress his maiden, but this bugle business had to be handled very carefully so that it wouldn't sound like a sales pitch. I started out by telling Margaret that she should always feel free to cry in my arms anytime she wanted to—and in *this* case, especially *my* arms. I then assured her that I could prove everything I was about to tell her. She then got the taps story straight from the battalion bugler himself. She was skeptical at first, but as she got to know me better she realized I wouldn't kid about anything that romantic.

From the moment we met we were inseparable. Neither of us planned any event without including the other. As part of her YWCA responsibilities Marg had to go on a "retreat" now and then, and those weekends seemed endless to me. I went on some trips with the baseball and debate teams, and of course our respective academic lives sometimes kept us apart. If she had a term paper due she had to concentrate entirely on it. If I had a test I had to prepare for it. We both understood those ground rules. Our reunions were so sweet when life returned to normal.

I was determined that I would not cause Marg's academic excellence to suffer. Looking back I can see that I could not have done that if I tried. She simply was a good student and it was natural for her to do well. She had been the valedictorian of her high school class. She expected to excel

On the other hand I was limping along as a slightly better than average student. Because of my extra load, I had to fit courses into my schedule where I could. This meant that sometimes I took a junior or senior course before I took the underlying, freshman course. There were some areas in which I began to do well. Anything dealing with government and political science interested me. I found debating to be my passion, putting Marg aside for the moment.

It was May and then June before we knew it, which meant that Marg was off to her home in Illinois for the summer. I was stuck in Delaware taking a load and a half at summer school. Very few of the senior faculty taught during the summer term, which was relatively short.

At one point, the Registrar, a dedicated gentleman, called me to his office to review my transcript. He was having difficulty determining whether I was to be enrolled in the September, 1946 term as a freshman or a sophomore. For the life of me I could not understand why it made the slightest bit of difference, but to him it was right up there with the other mysteries of the universe. He didn't like my schedule a bit. He kept mumbling, "I see the fine hand of Ben Arneson here …" He determined, but not joyfully, that I was approximately half way through my sophomore year. By the end of the September term, according to his analysis, I would be very close to being a junior. I could see no reason to disagree with him.

When the summer term ended I headed for my home in Dayton. Marg was kind enough to invite me to "Seldom Rest," her farm home in western Illinois, for the Labor Day weekend. I went out on a train, and our reunion was exhilarating. I think I met every member of the Hanna family, and saw every inch of the big cattle farm. That is not easy on a four-day weekend.

Before we were ready, it was time to restart the grind: Marg's last year, and my next-to-last one. It was becoming more difficult for me to find enough courses meeting at acceptable times to total 25 hours. I found myself taking a course such as "Comparative Government," which did not interest me much, simply because it met at a time available on my schedule. More and more I turned to courses in the History department, because there were so many offerings. I was called to the Registrar's office a second time and this time it was much more serious. The Registrar had continued to find my transcript intriguing. Now he was troubled because I had not declared a "major," which every sophomore must do.

I didn't really know how to handle that one, and sought permission to discuss it with my advisor. I hadn't seen much of Dr. Arneson in recent weeks, because he had made it clear that we needed to confer only when I had a problem. In our last meeting or two we talked mostly about what it's like to land a military aircraft on an aircraft carrier deck, at night.

Before I had a chance to state my problem, Dr. Arneson said he had some good news for me, and was glad that I had made the appointment. He said that the Norwegian government had been in contact with him because he served as a trustee of the Norwegian-American Society. They wanted him to recommend a few students to travel to Norway during the summer of 1947, and study at the University of Oslo. He said he had taken the liberty of submitting my name, " ... knowing that you would not want to pass up an opportunity like that!" Dr. Arneson always had a twinkle in his eye when he knew he had pulled off a coup. Now he was sparkling like a Christmas tree.

As I sat there gulping, Dr. Arneson became serious and asked me what my problem might be which caused me to call for an appointment. I explained that the Registrar was after me because I had not declared a "major."

"I will get in touch with him yet today," he stated calmly, "and explain to him that you are an Inter-departmental Pre-law Major." I was reasonably familiar with the catalogue of academic offerings and I hadn't noticed that one. "Are you sure there is such a thing?" I asked.

"There is now," he chuckled. When I left his office he was looking like a Christmas tree again.

As if my plate were not full enough, two additional opportunities came along in the summer and fall of 1946. I received a letter from the Navy concerning a new reserve unit at Port Columbus International Airport. If I wanted to get some time in a variety of single engine Navy planes, I should join up. I did. I wanted no more Navy life, but I liked the thought of closing the canopy and opening the throttle one more time on an F-6-F Hellcat fighter. Even today I would like that.

The second opportunity had to do with campus politics. For as long as anyone could remember, prior to 1947 the president of the student body was a man selected and elected by the fraternity system. The more powerful fraternities passed the job around. This year the new president was destined to be John Sagan, a selection that pleased me very much. He was my fraternity brother and a close friend. That friendship has blossomed over the years. John earned his masters and doctorate in economics before joining The Ford Motor Company. Within a short time he became vice president and treasurer of Ford, and found time to chair the Federal Reserve Board in Chicago. For more than 20 years we served together as Ohio Wesleyan trustees. He died two days before Christmas in 1999. Earlier in 1999 John and his wife Margaret, the daughter of a former Methodist Bishop, gave a million dollars to Ohio Wesleyan. I think that John was the second smartest person in our class. (The smartest person is Dr. Sherwood Rowland, who won the Nobel prize in Chemistry in 1995.)

John Sagan asked me to be his campaign manager. Because he was a shoo-in, I was pleased to take on the responsibility.

To sum up, my 1946 agenda included 25 hours of academic life; a germinating political career; a full debate schedule; preparing for a trip to Norway; flying Navy airplanes at Port Columbus whenever I could make it; and a girlfriend I thought more of than all the other items put together.

Marg's schedule was worse than mine. Organization had to be the answer for us if we were to have any time together. At one of our quality-time meetings she dropped a bomb on me. She said that she was one of the leaders of the John Adams campaign to defeat my friend John Sagan for the student body presidency. Oh, oh. To top that she said that she had a couple of speeches Adams was going to give soon, and she would like for me to look them over and if possible punch them up a little.

I was not sure that I could be a campaign manager for one candidate, and a speech writer for his opponent, but in retrospect it seems like good training for real life politics. I was willing to try, because John Adams was one of the finest men I ever met. He was the son of an Indiana Methodist pastor. Early in World War II, soon after he had completed pilot training in the Air Force, he was shot down in his Flying Fortress while on a mission deep into Germany. He was a prisoner of the Germans for the remainder of the war, from which he emerged undernourished and gaunt. He entered Ohio Wesleyan in September of 1945, and established himself quickly as a superior, pre-theology student.

He graduated in my class of 1948, a Phi Beta Kappa with many other honors. He then graduated from Yale with a masters degree in theology. He served a number of pulpits in Ohio and Indiana before accepting the Methodist Church's invitation to head its national social action mission in Washington DC. For nearly 20 years John Adams was at the very heart of nearly all of the principal social and cultural revolutions of the 1950s and 1960s. I served as his lawyer for much of that period, and as his friend for all of it. I can tell you that he was fearless and selfless to a fault. His life was in danger many times and constantly he risked being arrested. Among his many other accomplishments, he wrote the funeral service for Martin Luther King, Jr. John died of cancer in the 1980s.

In late 1946 and early 1947, John Adams was nothing more than a candidate for the presidency of the student body at Ohio Wesleyan who didn't have a chance in the world of winning. I was glad to work over a few speeches for him because I honestly liked and admired him very much. Beyond all of that, let's face it, I would have done anything Marg Hanna asked me to do.

I continued to serve as John Sagan's campaign manager. As time went on it became obvious that the Adams backers meant business. In the end John Adams squeaked out a victory by just a few votes, which should have ended my political career right there. But a curious thing happened. One of John Adams' first acts was to ask me to serve as his "chief of staff," and to help him organize a new student government. My title was to be secretary of student affairs. As if I didn't have enough to do.

I managed to reduce my list of responsibilities by a bit of foolish behavior. Beginning in the late summer of 1946 I began to fly various Navy planes at Port Columbus about once a month. In October I checked out an SNJ, a trainer, and flew it much too low over the Ohio Wesleyan campus. My fraternity brothers didn't mind a bit, but the mayor of Delaware did. He got my tail number. I had to appear at a Navy hearing, and I was grounded.

About a year later I got a nice letter from the Navy advising that all was forgiven, and inviting me back to the reserve squadron. But it was too late for me. I no longer had any desire to fly on a now-and-then basis. It is hard to keep up proficiency in a high-performance, military airplane if you fly once a month or so. I not only declined the invitation, I asked for permission to resign my reserve commission. The Navy accepted. I think that it was my fortuitous resignation that kept me from being called to active duty during the Korean War. Nearly all my pilot colleagues who kept their reserve commissions were called up, in the early 1950s, for two years or more.

Also, I dropped varsity baseball from my list of things to do. Had it not been for those 25-hour semesters, I would have kept trying to be a starter on the team. I am sure I would have made it, but there just wasn't time for everything. The baseball coach, Bob

Strimer, remained my friend until he died in the Fall of 1999. At a banquet a few years ago, Coach Strimer introduced me as " … the most enthusiastic batting practice pitcher in the history of Ohio Wesleyan!" You could have a worse reputation.

I certainly did not drop debate. The speech teacher and debate coach was another famous name at OWU, Professor Roy Diem. In every sense he was a learned man. His theory was that you do not win debates with cute phrases and clever remarks. The winning is in the research and the outlining of the arguments. He believed in brevity and coming right to the point. Best argument first, next best argument next, that sort of thing. Even before Dr. Arneson invented my "pre-law" major for me, it was Professor Diem who began to encourage me to think about law school. He assured me that if I did not give it a try, I would be disappointed all my life. After 50 years of reflection, I know he was dead right.

Professor Diem had another idea which served me well as a lawyer. He believed that a good debater should be able to argue either side of any issue. He expected us to do just that on the inter-scholastic level. Sometimes he would not tell us whether we were for or against the resolution, until we were on the way to the debate. He believed that it is easy to argue points of view you agree with. What is tough, he would say, is to argue effectively when you are out of sympathy with your own argument.

In order to prepare the students who were going to Norway, Dr. Arneson had us over to his home one night a week for drilling in the Norwegian language. He was fluent in Norwegian, as he was in German and French as well. He believed that we would have a better understanding of the culture while we were in Norway, if we could master the native tongue. There were five students who were to make the trip, and a couple of them were genuine scholars who picked up the conversation in Norwegian in no time at all. And then there was me.

I think I might have been the entertainer in the group. From the time I was quite young I have had a good ear for mimicry and parody. It helped me a lot in music when I tried to sound like Harry James, and Morse Code came very easy for me, because I could "hear" it. As we all studied Norwegian together, and I will confess that I did not have a clue as to what was being said, I began to make up words and phrases which, so far as I know, do not exist in the Norwegian language. To a person who was not a native Norwegian, I began to sound like a native Norwegian. At first even Dr. Arneson was puzzled, and sometimes would encourage me to continue, hoping that any minute he might catch on to what I was saying. Finally, they all caught on, and I was nearly banished from the group.

As Marg's graduation loomed closer, it became difficult for us to imagine that we would not see one another at least once in a while. We tried to crowd in every minute together we could, but it was not easy. I was sorry that I sold my convertible because we could have had a little privacy if I had kept it. I even thought of buying another car, but never did.

I had a friend, Stuart Hoak, with whom I served in the Navy, who also now was a student at Ohio Wesleyan. Stuart was married and the father of an infant son. He and his wife were kind enough to let us baby sit a few times, and this was a cozy arrangement for us, especially after we got little Billy tucked in for the night.

We also spent several brief weekends at my home in Dayton, which was a treat for my mother and Matt, who quickly developed a love for Margaret. It was, and still is, impossible not to love Marg.

The academic year was then over. Marg's entire family came for her graduation. As was so typical of our relationship, I missed the whole thing. Two or three days before her commencement, I sailed out of New York on the SS Marine Jumper, for Oslo, Norway.

Shortly after Dr. Arneson committed me unilaterally to the trip to Norway, I met with him and explained that as exciting as it appeared to be, I simply could not spend any of my funds I had saved for graduate school or law school. I explained also that in order to graduate in 1948, I would have to earn academic credits during the summer of 1947, either at Ohio Wesleyan or at the University of Oslo.

Dr. Arneson, a man of great influence in the Norwegian-American community, asked for a few days to work things out. He promptly arranged a scholarship for me which would pay my tuition and expenses in Norway, and he assured that a committee at Ohio Wesleyan would review my transcript from the University of Oslo, and if I passed all the classes with a B or better I would receive the same academic credit I would receive if I remained in Delaware and took a normal, summer school academic load. I would have to be responsible for the cost of the transportation to and from Norway, and for incidental expenses. I could handle that easily.

The Atlantic crossing was very exciting. I made many new friends very quickly. The summer school program, a gift to the United States from the government of Norway for hosting and caring for the Norwegian royal family during the war years, was newsworthy enough that it was covered by *Life* magazine. The Life photographer, Yale Joel, was assigned a bunk next to mine and we spent many hours discussing his war time escapades which had earned him a number of journalism awards. He covered most of the big battles, and many of his pictures of prisoners of war were poignant.

Margaret Mead, the noted sociologist and anthropologist, also was aboard and led some of our discussion groups. The University of Oslo had several professors on the ship. They also led discussions and gave us some understanding of what, and with whom, we would be studying. There were more than 200

American students on the ship, and we came from more than 30 colleges and universities.

After five days the ship passed the White Cliffs of Dover, and a day later entered the Oslo fjord. American flags were flying on both banks of the fjord, and large groups of Norwegians gathered on the shores waving to us. A band greeted us at the dock with our National Anthem, followed by the much more appropriate "America the Beautiful."

In 1947 Norway was getting used to being free and independent again. The Germans had treated them very badly during the war. The country was literally taken over economically and socially. The Germans commandeered the Grand Hotel in the center of Oslo, and established it as the Nazi headquarters. Most freedoms were taken from the people. There were innumerable instances of brutal deprivation and torture as Germany attempted to learn all it could about Norway's "heavy water" experiments, which were vital to its attempt to build an atom bomb. Many of the professors at the University of Oslo were targets of these inhuman atrocities, and we soon learned that a profound hatred of the Germans still permeated the Norwegian culture two full years after the last Nazi left Oslo.

It was a time of patriotism and nationalism in Norway. During the war the royal family lived safely near Bethesda, Maryland as guests of the United States. Crown Prince Olav, who soon would be the King of Norway until 1991, became thoroughly Americanized. His two children, the oldest of whom, Prince Harald, now is the King of Norway, attended private schools and picked up a lot of useful information, such as the batting average of every player on the New York Yankees.

When King Haakon and his family returned from exile in early 1946, there was a vast outpouring of love and affection for all of them. When they passed through the streets the people would wave flags and cry. Freedom always has been precious to the Norwegians and it felt good to have it again.

During the ten weeks or so we American students were in Norway, we were treated like honored guests. It was as if we had personally cared for the royal family in Maryland. When it was noticed that some of us (not me) were having trouble adjusting to the smorgasbord, we were surprised one evening by being served hamburgers. When it became obvious that many of us (particularly me) were not able to absorb the lectures in the Norwegian language, the professors simply switched to English. It made very little difference to the professors or to the predominantly Norwegian students in our classes, whether the lectures were in Norwegian or English. This is something that is very difficult for an American to understand. Even harder for us to understand is that the switch could have been made to Swedish, German or French with equal ease. Fifty years ago Americans lived on a cultural island, and as nearly as I can determine that has not changed much over the years.

Our courses in the Norwegian language, culture, and history, were not strenuous. After all, you do not invite an honored guest and then flunk him. The professors were aware that some of us were expecting to apply for academic credit from our colleges, and I think they were particularly lenient with us. Compared to the load I had been carrying at Ohio Wesleyan, this was nothing but sheer pleasure.

We had lots of time for sightseeing in Oslo and traveling to other regions of the country. One weekend we took a train across the mountains to Bergen; on another we visited Rjukan, the heavy water facility in the mountains. One of my professors invited me to his summer home for a weekend. Another time we went to the quiet little village of Lillihammer, without an inkling that 47 years later it would become famous as the site of the 1994 winter Olympics.

Shortly before it was time for us to leave, Crown Prince Olav invited all the American students to a reception at his summer home, known as Skaugum. It was a lavish party. The American ambassador was in attendance, as was Anna Roosevelt, the daughter of our late president.

A diplomat from the American embassy pulled several of us aside and stated that the Crown Prince was going to say a few words of greeting to the American students in just a few moments. He wanted us to choose one among us to make a brief response. He added that the response should be in the Norwegian language because Olav would of course speak in English. Because all of the others were scared even more than I, I got tagged for this duty very quickly. All summer long I had been playing to the fullest my "talent" as a mimic, which had amused Dr. Arneson. Despite the fact that I was speaking utter nonsense, I think some of the Americans thought I might be fluent. I felt like running for the nearest exit but there weren't any.

Crown Prince Olav was magnificent as he thanked all of the Americans. From the time he was a little boy, he had been trained to make little witty speeches at gatherings such as this. He was elegant. As he spoke, I lost more and more confidence, knowing that at any minute he would walk away from the microphone and it would be my turn. I thought of several things I might be able to say, but I was sure that all of them would be trite and sound like pigeon-Norwegian. I was desperate even as I walked to the mike.

The Norwegian national anthem is beautiful both as music and as a poem. It is downright sonorous and vibrant in the Norwegian language and especially in its first line, which is: *Ja, vi elsker dette landet* ... which translates, "Yes, we love this land of ours ..." It speaks so softly of family and lakes and fields and things which are dear to Norwegians and peace-loving people everywhere. As I moved toward the mike I remembered something Professor Diem emphasized in our debate training. He said that we should try always to be the opposite of our "opponent." If he spoke quickly, we should speak slowly; if he were witty, we should be profound. It was clear to me as I arrived at the dais that I could never out-Olav the Crown Prince, certainly not in his native tongue.

After a long pause during which every American in the audience wondered whether I was going to faint, I began to recite with considerable passion all three verses of the Norwegian national anthem as we had done many times in our language drills.

"Yes, we love this land of ours ..." coming from an American was too much for the recently emancipated Norwegians. I noticed after a verse or two that Olav himself brushed a tear from his eye. Even if it were no more than a tear of laughter at my accent, it was a good day for the visiting team thanks to Professor Diem. Dr. Erling Christophersen, the director of the summer school, followed me and gave a much more appropriate, if less creative, "thank you" to the royal family.

The summer school ended much too soon.

I did not go straight home. The SS Marine Jumper was docked in Oslo, ready to bring us back; but I elected to adjust my ticket so that I could catch the next crossing, from Southampton, England in about 19 days. I bought a French bicycle from a Norwegian student and set out on my own from Oslo on a journey which was planned from day to day, and eventually took me to Stockholm, Copenhagen, through the American, British and French sectors of Germany, through Belgium and on to Paris, and then to London after a brief trip to Edinburgh and Glasgow. Of course I did not pedal that distance. I had a train ticket, and I might ride my bike for as much as an afternoon or an entire day before getting back on the next train. In 1947 it seemed that every train passenger traveled with either a bicycle, a dog or both.

When I arrived in London with a day to spare to catch the boat train to Southampton I was out of money. I was flat broke. I sold the bicycle in Glasgow for enough to catch the train to London. I didn't have a kroner, a franc, or a pound. Not even an ounce. I had a lot of memories and made a lot of friends along the way, but they were not the currency of the realm.

I checked into a modest hotel in London on the strength of a promise from the desk clerk that he would buy my two San Diego suits from me for enough to pay the hotel bill for the night. Around midnight he came to my room and said that while he had been sure that his brother-in-law would want the clothing, he now had to report that was not the case and he would not be able to buy my clothing. He wanted to know if this presented a problem for me.

It sure did. I had no alternative to dressing and going out on the town from pub to pub attempting to sell enough of my personal property to pay my hotel bill. In about an hour I sold my two suits, a wrist watch which had been issued to me by the Navy, and the black onyx ring which Jody Case had given to me. The British were tough negotiators in the middle of the night, despite the fact that I kept reminding them of Lend Lease and Bundles for Britain.

Because of my extra trip I arrived back in Delaware ten days late for the start of the fall semester. The Registrar was put out with me, but as usual Dr. Arneson was able to smooth his feathers. It did mean a lot of catching up, but I found all the professors most understanding. I think every one of them would have taken that extra trip if they had the opportunity.

In addition to being behind academically, I was way behind in my commitment to John Adams to help him operate his administration. We had done a little organizing in the spring, but now it was time to make things work. I was assigned a very nice office in the Temporary Union Building, known of course as the "TUB," and after I finished student government business, I found myself studying there because it was just across Sandusky Street from the college library.

I missed Margaret very much. While I was in Europe, she spent the summer working in Chicago for an institution known as "Students in Industry." Her industry was the Armour Company, where she packed bacon eight hours a day. In August she moved to Portland, Oregon and became a staff person in the downtown YWCA. She lived with her Aunt Nell, who was glad to have her. No gladness in me. I was sad to lose her. Portland seemed like a million miles away.

I began to notice an interesting thing in my academic life. Upon my return from Norway I was asked to give a 30-minute report to the student body at one of our chapel services. Several smaller groups also asked me to talk about the trip. Because of the extra exposure I was getting from student government, and the fact that a colleague and I debated the team from Oxford, England in another chapel program, I was beginning to be someone the professors recognized. My grades improved, although the quality of my work was no higher. Throughout my senior year I made nearly all A's. I was elected to both political science and debate honorary fraternities; and early in 1948 to Omicron Delta Kappa, a well-known national leadership honorary fraternity.

I was taking many history classes, which brought me into frequent contact with Dr. Henry C. Hubbart, the chairman of the department, and another faculty icon on a level equal with Dr. Arneson. Dr. Hubbart wrote a notable book entitled *Ohio Wesleyan's First Hundred Years*, which was published during my senior year. I complained a number of times to Dr. Hubbart because the grades I received from him were lower than I thought they should be. He always defended himself by saying, "You could do better, Hoskins."

One day just before I graduated Dr. Hubbart closed a class by asking "Mr. Hoskins, will you please report to my office immediately after this class?" With an enormous grin, he presented me with a copy of his book, with the inscription: "To Clayton Hoskins, who finally got an A with me. H.C. Hubbart." Early in 1999 I presented the book to Ohio Wesleyan, for its historic collection.

Earlier in 1948 Dr. Hubbart pulled me aside when we passed on the campus and said, "Hoskins, where is that Hanna girl I saw you running around with last year?" I told him that Margaret was graduated and now working with the YWCA in Oregon. Grimly, and in a near whisper, he said, "Don't ... let ... her ... get ... away, Hoskins!"

Many of the professors at Ohio Wesleyan were that human. In my freshman year I was taking a course in logic from Professor Loyd D. Easton, until recently a professor emeritus but then in his first year of teaching. One day he asked me if I had time for a cup of coffee. We went across the street to a little hole-in-the wall hangout, known as "The Dive." When Professor Easton walked in, it caused a bit of a stir. We took a booth in the back, and after the coffee arrived he leaned across to me and asked, "Just between you and me, how am I doing?"

He honestly wanted my assessment of how effective he was as a new teacher. I assured him he was absolutely wonderful, a true feeling on my part. I think he picked on me because as the world's oldest freshman and the world's newest professor, we were about the same age. Over the years Loyd and I remained friends; close enough in fact that he and his wife had no hesitation to drop in on us now and then unexpectedly. He remembered that I was in his first class, until the day of his death in February, 2000.

With due respect to the larger colleges and universities, I think there is no substitute for the personal touches you get only at a small liberal arts college such as Ohio Wesleyan. I realize that it poses as a "University," but it really isn't. I made friendships among the faculty, staff and student body which will sustain me all the days of my life.

Graduation day was a meaningful experience for me and for Mother and Matt. I have no idea how many students have made it through OWU in 29 months, but I did it. To cap off a great experience, I was elected president of the graduating class. I still hold that title 52 years later. In the spring of 1998, it was my pleasure to preside over our Golden Anniversary celebration.

The speaker at our Commencement was the Honorable Charles P. Taft, the mayor of Cincinnati. I don't remember a single thing he said. I do remember that when the Registrar handed me my diploma with a bit of a scowl on his face, Dr. Ben Arneson stepped out of the faculty section and was the first person to shake my hand.

He had that Christmas tree look on his face.

I have read the general genealogies on our family, and they are vague and uncertain. One of my cousins has chased the family back to an Ira Hoskins, who was born in Pennsylvania around 1800, and located in the vicinity of New Straitsville. Ira was the father of Samuel Harvey Hoskins; my grandfather was Samuel's son, and that's about all we know. I now look sadly back upon the questions I could have asked but didn't, when I was a youngster.

My grandfather, William R. Hoskins, and my grandmother, Ida Bainter Hoskins, and their eight children, circa 1910. My father, James William Hoskins, is at the far left.

Grandpa Clark was the lay preacher. He could not preside at funerals, weddings or at communion; but if you wanted him to say a few words as your mother's casket was being lowered into the warm, sweet earth you only had to ask him once. He was a kindly man, although outspoken on any subject. As a young man he was a blacksmith.

My grandfather, Josh Clark, and our oldest daughter, Jane, 1951

Ida Clark and Mary Chesser were hardly strangers. They had lived on adjacent farms on Asbury Ridge since the early 1900s. Neither of them had a home of her own in 1955. Mother and Matt invited both of their mothers to come live with them in Sacramento, for as long as they wanted to. Every day was a holiday. Sacramento was like heaven for them, and they didn't have to die to get there.

My grandmother, Ida Clark (on the left) and her life-long friend, Mary Chesser

The Josh Clark family spent the war years in Barberton, Ohio, which is a little city near Akron. Grandpa wanted to do something for the war effort, and when he learned that the rubber companies in the Akron area were in need of workers, he uprooted his family from Asbury Ridge and traveled all the way to Barberton. The rubber factory where Grandpa Clark worked made tires for Army ambulances, and my father, whom none of the Clarks had ever met at that time, was at that moment an ambulance driver in France, in the thick of the war.

James William Hoskins, my father, and the ambulance he drove in France, 1918

There was never a moment while I was undergoing aviation training that I was not thinking of some young, healthy Japanese youngster my age who was undergoing the same training somewhere in Asia. I convinced myself that someday we would meet in the skies over the Pacific, and one of us would not survive.

Aviation Cadet Clayton C. Hoskins, 1944

Gertrude Beattie told me several times that her roommate, Marg, was the girl for me. She introduced me to this beautiful young lady, Margaret Hanna, and I began to hear soft music playing in the background. There has never been a moment when I have not wanted to be with Marg, to talk with her, to entertain her and make her laugh, to protect her and to tell her of my love.

Margaret Eleanor Hanna Hoskins, at Ohio Wesleyan, 1947

Margaret was such a beautiful bride. We have many photographs to prove it. She was dressed in a gorgeous bridal gown, which today is packed carefully in a box in our attic. Marg had a special demeanor and bearing which announced to the world that she was ready for marriage, and expected it to be a lifetime commitment. Of course I felt the same way.

Mr. and Mrs. Clayton C. Hoskins, June 4, 1949

LAW SCHOOL AND FINDING A JOB

WHILE I WAS AT OHIO WESLEYAN I made the final decision that I wanted to go to a good law school. Dr. Arneson stressed the importance of attending a "national" law school where the spotlight is on the thought processes of the lawyer and not upon the mere reading of a few statutes of a single state. The problem with the parochial approach to the study of the law is that if the statutes are repealed or amended, your education is down the tubes.

With quality as my goal, and with Professors Arneson, Diem, and Hubbart as my sponsors, I applied to Michigan, Northwestern, Chicago, Harvard and Yale. In 1948 those five, along with Columbia and Stanford, were the best law schools in the United States. Every one of them admitted me, except Yale. My sponsors warned me that it was difficult to get into the Yale Law School unless your father and at least one of your grandfathers were graduates of that fine institution. Yale didn't say why I didn't match up to their high standards. They merely wished me well in my studies elsewhere.

At about the same time Yale was turning up its nose at my heritage, down in Hope, Arkansas a young man was just then coming into this world, who 22 years later would be welcomed at the Yale Law School despite the fact that his pedigree was as undistinguished as mine. President Clinton's father died even *before* he was born. A good argument can be made, but I prefer not to be the one who makes it, that if Yale had democratized itself 20 years earlier, I might now be a former President of the United States.

Among the four fine law schools which did welcome me, I selected Northwestern, for two practical reasons. Because the school was within walking distance of Chicago's Loop, I knew I would be able to find convenient employment with a law firm, or with the legal department of a corporation. My eligibility under the GI Bill was due to expire at the end of the first year, which meant that I was going to have to finance the last two years of law school with my own funds. That would require some part time employment. The University of Chicago, my second choice, would require a 30 minute bus or train ride to get to the Loop. The second practical reason I selected Northwestern was that Margaret Hanna was giving up on Portland after one year, and was intending to accept an employment offer from the YWCA in the center of Chicago's Loop. How very convenient.

During the summer of 1948 I was able to add to my law school funds, by working for the Air Force at a material depot in Dayton. My step-father, Matt, helped me secure the position, which paid at the rate of $2800 per year. I worked three full months, and saved most of my salary because I was living with my folks.

Law school started in mid-September. I lived in Abbott Hall, directly across a parking lot from the law school's academic buildings. Marg secured a small apartment near the University of Chicago, and entered the graduate school in the Human Development department. There were many windy, cold nights when I wished I had selected Chicago instead of Northwestern.

Law School was completely different from undergraduate school. Even the social life was different. There wasn't any. Because the tuxedo which I wore all through my days at Ohio Wesleyan was looking a bit tacky, I decided to start out at fancy

Northwestern with a new one. During the three years in law school, I never took it out of the box.

Our reading requirements were ferocious—80 to 100 pages a day. We studied by the case method, and most of the cases were interesting to read. The other required readings were mostly monotonous commentaries on esoteric points of law, written by our own professors or by senior professors from other leading law schools.

For at least half of the first semester I had no idea what the curriculum was aiming to accomplish. Although we studied cases endlessly, and in the greatest of detail, there seemed to be no attention given at all as to who won and who lost a particular case. The emphasis was on the thinking of the opposing counsel and of the judges who wrote the opinions. That significant point did not dawn upon me for a long time.

Until I learned better, I put too much significance on which side won or lost a particular case.

I had outstanding roommates and friends. Keith Ragan, the son of a prominent Illinois Methodist pastor and church administrator, and James T. Otis, a Harvard graduate from Connecticut, were both inspirations to me. Next door was Dale Bumpers, who would become the attorney general, governor and U.S. Senator from Arkansas. We began to study as a group, and this was helpful to me, because the three of them were much better students than I. Keith practiced in Phoenix with William H. Rehnquist, who would become the Chief Justice of the United States. Keith remains a senior partner of that firm, which he and the Chief entered at about the same time. Jim Otis practiced for more than 40 years with one of the distinguished law firms in Chicago's Loop. He is now retired and living in a home in western Illinois, which overlooks the Mississippi River.

Our faculty was equally distinguished. I was taught the law of Agency by John Paul Stevens, now Justice Stevens of the United

States Supreme Court. My Criminal Law professor was one of the inventors and developers of the lie detector. Another professor served on the United States Court of Appeals for many years. Another was Secretary of Labor in the Truman administration. It was an exciting time to be a student at the Northwestern University School of Law.

Early in 1949 I mentioned to John Hanna, Marg's oldest brother—the former Naval officer she was so worried about during the war—that I was going to need some employment before much longer. John was himself a law graduate of Northwestern, and was then counsel to a trade association of health and accident insurance companies. He spread the word among some of his friends, and before long I had an opportunity to work for the North American Accident Insurance Company, in the Rookery Building in the Loop.

The general counsel, Mr. Robert Neal, provided me with an office in the law department, and directed my work for the first few weeks. My responsibility was to qualify the company's many policies, for marketing in various states. The job paid $1.75 an hour.

In the 1940s, Congress passed the McCaron Act, which provided that the insurance industry would be regulated by the (then) 48 states, and not by the Federal government. As a result, if a company intended to sell a policy in a state, it first had to submit that policy to the state's insurance department for approval. The work was routine and consisted to some extent of mere record keeping. It was not unusual for this work to be entrusted either to a new employee or to a part time law student.

Northwestern's law school did not require class attendance in those days. It required that the student pass all the exams, and that was virtually impossible without regular class attendance. When I first started my job, I was careful to schedule the work so that I wouldn't miss any classes. This meant that on some days I might attend a class in the morning; then dash to the Loop and work for two or three hours; and then go back to the campus for another class or two; and wind up the day and evening back at the job. Mr. Neal wanted me to work at least 20 hours a week if I could.

After a few months I found myself rationalizing that it just wasn't worth it to dash back to the campus for only a class or two. More and more I began to cut classes. I was urged to work more than 20 hours if I wanted to, and I wanted to. I needed the money, and frankly I enjoyed the work with the insurance company more than I enjoyed law school.

I continued to participate in group study with my roommates and colleagues almost every evening, and they were very kind to let me look over their class notes. I tried to keep up with the required reading, but at the rate of 80 or more pages a day, it didn't take long for me to get way behind.

Despite the demanding schedule, I managed to pass all my courses at the midterm and at the end of my first year. My grades were not sensational. But they also weren't all that bad. Aside from the grades, I felt that I was learning something. I couldn't be sure but it seemed to me that I had a "knack" for the law. All I needed to be a better student was more time to apply myself to the task.

In spite of our two busy schedules, Marg and I managed to see one another as often as possible. Her job with the YWCA was most demanding. She was in charge of creating arts, crafts and other programs for the many young women who were working and living in or near the Loop. Her work involved many people, which meant many telephone calls and conferences with a wide variety of persons. The job took a lot of time and energy, including a considerable amount of night work. In addition to her employment, she continued her graduate studies at the University of Chicago.

In the spring of 1949, we decided that the only way we were going to see much of one another would be if we married. Of course the decision was more thoughtful than that, and it certainly was more romantic than that. For more than three years we both knew that there would never be any other person for either of us. In addition to being in love, we simply liked one another.

Margaret said "yes" while we were enjoying a weekend together with my folks in Dayton. We told Mother and Matt and they were delighted, and then we called Dad and Mother Hanna in Illinois to give them the news. They were pleased also, and Mother Hanna added a new wrinkle.

She wanted to know if I had come up with an engagement ring. When we told her there hadn't been time, she asked us to consider accepting her grandmother's engagement ring which for years had been laying in a bank vault. She made us very happy by saying that for months and months she and Dad Hanna had been hoping that we had marriage plans in mind. The thought of Marg wearing that special ring, gave an additional dimension of happiness to our engagement.

We planned a short engagement, which is the best kind. The wedding was Saturday, June 4, at Margaret's childhood church, the Methodist Church in Geneseo, the little Illinois village nine miles from the Hanna farm.

Mr. Neal was kind enough to give me an entire week off, and I arrived for the festivities the evening before the wedding. Mother and Matt were there, and he served as the best man. Marg's two brothers, John and Phil (both lawyers) were ushers, and her sister Elizabeth was maid of honor. Dad Hanna gave away the bride; and little Jaci Hanna, the three-year old daughter of John and Ruth, stole the show by proceeding down the aisle ahead of the bride, strewing rose petals thither and yon. Jaci is a grandmother today, and lives in Florida. I think she still likes to strew rose petals.

The night before the wedding, Marg's aunt, Nellie Hanna, who lived in Geneseo, gave us a memorable rehearsal party in the backyard of her lovely Victorian home. The morning of the wedding, Marg's two brothers took me golfing, in order to keep me from becoming a nervous wreck. For many years that golf game has been the subject of much discussion, and some criticism, because we lost track of the time and were still on the course until an hour before the music started. This produced several nervous wrecks, and the bride wasn't too happy about it.

Margaret was such a beautiful bride. We have many photographs to prove it. She was dressed in a gorgeous bridal gown, which today is packed carefully in a box in our attic. Marg had a special demeanor and bearing which announced to the world that she was ready for marriage, and expected it to be a lifetime commitment. Of course I felt the same way. We wrote our own vows, which did not include "obey" but did emphasize love and honor. Rev. Pattison, who presided, is still living. We had a nice letter from him on our 50th Anniversary in 1999.

The outdoor reception was at the Hanna farm. One of my cousins, who then lived in Peoria, came with his wife; as did our college friends, John and Marge Sagan. John was in graduate school at the University of Illinois. Aunt Nellie, who was better known in the Hanna family as "Lel," loaned us her Oldsmobile, and it was decorated by John and Phil in time for our getaway for an unforgettable, blissful week in Wisconsin.

Then it was back to work. A month or two before the wedding we decided that Marg's apartment near the University of Chicago wasn't going to be very efficient for either of us. More of her work was centered in the Loop, and I continued to hustle back and forth from the insurance company and the law school. We found a one-room basement apartment, with bars on the windows, within easy walking distance of the law school, and at a price we could afford. After we cleaned it thoroughly, built in some bookcases and painted everything Wedgwood Blue, it looked real cozy. Marg moved in a month before the wedding, and I brought in all my law books after the honeymoon. The apartment was located on North Michigan Avenue very close to the famous Chicago Water Tower. The 100-story Hancock Building sets on the site today.

I enjoyed my work at the insurance company during the summer of 1949, because I didn't have to worry about classes at the law school. As a result of that freedom from studying, I took on more responsibility and was given a raise to $2.00 an hour. I began to work a full, 40-hour week. This presented a gigantic problem when school started in September.

We had become comfortable with the extra money provided by the 40-hour week, but there was no human alive who could survive law school and that work schedule. After all, Northwestern was not a part time, or "night" law school. It was one of the best law schools in the United States, and it intended to maintain that reputation.

I tried it anyway. I worked my 40 hours during the days, attended the group study sessions with my former roommates in the evenings, and read most of the nights. Fortunately the law library never closed.

I was inspired to do the best I could because early in the Fall we discovered that we were pregnant. What a blessing. The joy of bringing a new life into this world overshadowed any inconvenience which might accompany the event. We both looked upon such things as our educations and our jobs as side issues of little importance. First on our agendas was the health of the baby and its mother.

In 1949 it was not the custom for a mother-to-be to work right up to the date of birth. This was doubly true if the expectant mother were employed by the YWCA to provide programs for young girls, most of them unmarried. Margaret immediately withdrew from graduate school; and we planned that she would resign her employment as soon as she became visibly pregnant.

There was yet another inconvenience. Our landlady was an honest, Irish woman. She could have come up with a lame excuse for kicking us out of our nest, but she didn't. She came right to the point. She said that because we had painted our room so beautifully and cleaned it up so thoroughly, she could now rent it to two persons for twice the amount we were paying. Had she known of our pregnancy, she wouldn't have had to be so honest.

We found a new apartment suitable for our modest budget. To get to it, we had to take the subway north for 60 blocks, and then catch a street car west for 40 more blocks. It was one room, but it was on the first floor and bars were not needed on the windows. We had to share both the bath and the kitchen with the family which rented the apartment, but through careful scheduling that was not as inconvenient as it now sounds. We were together and we were going to become parents. What else could matter?

Before many weeks passed, I found myself in the office of Dean Harold Havighurst, trying to explain why I had not attended many classes since school started in September. He was a formidable man, sober enough to make a good judge. In some ways he was not too unlike the Registrar at Ohio Wesleyan. The Dean and at least one of his brothers, a professor and author at Miami University, Oxford Ohio, graduated from Ohio Wesleyan. When I enrolled at Northwestern, I thought maybe the Dean might call me in and welcome me as a fellow alumnus.

He didn't. And he sure was not welcoming me as he confronted me in his office. He gave me a tongue lashing, the gist of which was that Northwestern would not tolerate anyone working full time while enrolled at the law school. "It just can't happen," he insisted. "You must decide whether you are going to work, or whether you are going to study," he added with a tone of finality.

I explained as best I could that I was performing in every respect except attending classes. I pointed out that I came to the law school every day, or night, for my reading; and that I studied with my colleagues almost every evening. I told him of my circumstances: GI Bill coming to an end; no backlog of money to speak of; going to be a daddy; etc. I might as well have been talking to a rock. He was convinced that the integrity of the law school required that none of its students works full time. That was it.

I explained all of this to Mr. Neal, who was understanding. We agreed that I would drop back to a 20-hour week, and schedule my work so that it would not conflict with classes. Mr. Neal also released me from a project he had given me during the summer. He had asked me to do some concentrated research on the McCaran Act, and to look into how the states were adjusting to their roles as regulators of the insurance industry. He said that he had some ideas himself on this subject, and that when I finished my research we would give thought to writing a joint law review article, or a paper for presentation at a future insurance conference.

I soon adjusted to being back in the shuttle business. Somedays I would go to the insurance company as many as three times a day. In all fairness, under this new arrangement I did find the classes at the law school more meaningful and interesting. My grades improved. Dean Havighurst was probably right, which didn't make him anymore sympathetic.

Marg enjoyed a number of baby showers given for her by the young ladies she was serving in her YWCA work. We quickly accumulated a collection of blankets, rattles, booties and toys which we stored at the Hanna farm because our little apartment was indeed little. In addition to our one room which served as our bedroom and living room, we had a very small un-insulated sun room, which formerly was a screened porch, where we ate until the bitter cold weather chased us inside. We had a little discussion with our landlady, this time an honest Polish lady, when our pregnancy became obvious. It was agreed that we would vacate the premises at the birth or shortly thereafter.

Despite our reduced income and the strains of employment and studying, we were not wanting for anything. It was one of the happiest times in our lives. We began to attend a Baptist Church near our apartment, and immediately made new friends there. We took in a movie now and then and did a lot of walking in the neighborhood. We visited John and Ruth Hanna in Glenview, the same little community in which I took my carrier qualification training in the summer of 1945. Life was not dull. We were full of wonder as Marg grew bigger and even more beautiful.

On May 12, 1950, baby Jane Eleanor Hoskins was born. To wear the "Eleanor" badge in the Hanna family is an honor. Her mother is Margaret Eleanor, and her grandmother was Lida Eleanor. She was the cutest thing you ever saw. The night before she arrived, Marg and I went to see the famous Gregory Peck movie, "Twelve O'clock High." It was too exciting for Margaret.

The next morning while I was trying to stay awake in a criminal law class, a secretary from the Dean's office, tip-toed in and said that I should get home as soon as possible because my wife might be in labor. What she *should* have said, was that I should get over to Wesley Memorial Hospital, which was only two blocks from the law school, because my wife *was* in labor.

Not wanting to trust the slow subway and bus, I took a cab to our apartment. A thousand thoughts were going through my mind. When I arrived, our landlady said, "What on earth are you doing *here* ... Margaret is at the hospital." By the time another cab got me back to where I had been, I became a father.

In other words it was the same old story, the plot of many a B movie: my baby was born while I was in a cab. That may not be the first time that has happened, but it was thrilling enough for me.

From the moment she came to us, Janie was a joy. I held her in the palms of my hands as she slept so confidently, and I just could not believe that such a miracle could happen. She was so perfectly formed. Her hands and feet were tiny and delicate, and it was obvious that she was totally dependent upon us. Caring for her was not an obligation either of us wanted to avoid. To the contrary, we hesitated to hand her to anyone else for even a minute. She was our first born, and she was beautiful.

We did hand her to Mrs. Koslow, our landlady, and after one peek there was no hurry for us to move out. Our apartment was not suited for a new baby, and of course we had agreed that we would vacate as soon as the birth occurred. Mrs. Koslow would not hear of it. She told us how wonderful it was to hear again the cry of a newborn child in the house, and she spent a lot of time in our rooms genuinely wanting to be of help. My mother came from Dayton to help Marg, and another bedroom in the house was prepared for her by Mrs. Koslow, without any charge.

Three weeks later, I completed my second year final exams, resigned my part time job at the insurance company, and accepted Dad and Mother Hanna's invitation to work on the farm during the summer of 1950. I knew nothing of the work on a modern livestock farm, but I had a willingness to learn because I was grateful that we would have a clean, safe place for the baby for the summer.

Dad Hanna insisted that I start out slowly, and for the first day or two I slept in until around 6 A.M. By that time he and the hired man, a young fellow who liked to play practical jokes on me, had completed a half-day's work. There were a lot of jobs that I could not do, such as handling the mammoth tractors without killing myself or someone else; but there were many simpler tasks that I could do quite well. I became a good hay man, and worked long, long hours in the steamy hay fields tossing the bales from the bale loader to the back of the wagon where they were stacked. I picked cherries, peaches and apples, and soon got to the place where I could do most of the morning and evening chores.

Marg was a big help to her mother, in spite of the care Janie required. The baby was a much admired infant by her mother, grandmother, miscellaneous visiting aunts and cousins, and the nearby farming community at large. Everyone Marg had known even remotely, wanted to come see the new off-spring. Jane never had a bath without the neighbors watching. If we had sold tickets we could have financed that third and last year of law school without any difficulty.

Within a month my body returned to that condition the Navy's athletic specialists left it six years earlier in Iowa City. I truly enjoyed the farm work. I learned to find jobs on my own without guidance. I took care of the yard work, and must have whacked a million thistles in the pasture fields.

The Hannas are an extraordinary family. Their ancestors arrived on the prairies of western Illinois late in the 18th century. They came from up-state New York, where they had located for several generations, after arriving from Scotland. They hoped to acquire and settle the beautiful, rolling land along the Mississippi and Rock Rivers. By the time they got to Illinois, that land was all gone. They had to purchase instead the endless, flat land which was selling for 50 cents an acre because it was less attractive than the river land.

Then came John Deere of tractor fame. He mechanized farming, so that it became possible to plow many furrows with one circle of the field. The prairie land, which was the Hannas' second choice, became much desired because the huge tractors could move at a greater speed on the flat surface. The soil was black and so fertile that you could almost run your hands into it before it was plowed. Gone were the 50 cents-an-acre days. The prairie land became some of the most valuable farm land in the United States.

Dad Hanna, a graduate of the University of Michigan, treated the land as if it were irreplaceable. He was a pioneer in farmland soil conservation, and a strong backer of farm organizations which promoted good farming techniques. He was a founder of the Farm Bureau in his county, and he served for years as an advisor to the department of agriculture at the University of Illinois. The leading farm journal of that day designated him a "Master

Farmer" in 1940. For more than 10 years he wrote a weekly column for the Chicago *Daily News*, which was called "A Diary of an Illinois Farmer." He and his families' identities were kept a secret all those years, and the various members of the family were assigned different names in the column. Marg was known as, you guessed it: "Jane."

Mother Hanna was the quintessential farm wife. Nothing happened on the farm without her knowing about it. She and Dad moved to the land at the time of their marriage in 1917, and that was it. She never left, even when she might be away for short periods. The farm and her family were her life. No one ever heard Mother Hanna complain about anything. She was the anchor. When Dad came in from chores at five in the morning, breakfast was ready. When he came for dinner, which was the noon meal, the radio was on with the dial set for the daily market reports. She took drinking water and food to all the workers in the hot, humid Illinois afternoons. If a salesman came while Dad was busy, he was shooed away by Mother. She helped Dad put in and care for the garden; she canned; she cleaned; she made sure the bills were paid on time; and that the children always did their homework. She had to be the one they had in mind when they named the farm "Seldom Rest."

All of this frantic activity on the big farm would not have meant much, were it not for the fact that above it all the Hannas were the nicest people in the world. Anyone in Edford Township would tell you that. No one wanted for anything if the Hannas knew of the need.

For Marg, Janie and me to live in that environment for even one summer was a rare treat. On August 1 our exciting time on the farm was enhanced by the wedding of Marg's sister Elizabeth. She married Lowell Hughes, a graduate of Ohio Wesleyan, who was soon to become a medical student at Ohio State. The wedding was somewhat a copy of our wedding 14-months earlier, except it was held in the evening and the reception was at the church rather than at the farm.

About three weeks before classes were to resume at the law school I went to Chicago to select several possible apartments for us, from which Marg and I together could make the final selection. I ran into a brick wall. For several frantic days I ran down every lead I could, and got nowhere. There seemed to be a void of any low cost apartments anywhere in Chicago.

Northwestern had a service which assisted students with housing, and it was of no help. I answered every ad in the Chicago newspapers and had no success. Each night I went to the Chicago *Tribune* office and waited in the lobby for the first edition of the next paper to arrive. I had a hand full of nickels, and immediately called every new ad appearing for the first time. No luck, day after day. I called at some of the larger apartment houses and asked if they knew of any units which were likely to become available soon. They didn't. I called the Realtors who managed large apartment complex, and asked the same question. I was put on waiting lists, without any enthusiasm or encouragement.

The tough part was having to call Marg each day and report no progress. We enjoyed the time at the farm, but we wanted to be our own family in our own home. We wanted to finish law school, and we wanted to do it together. We reviewed our budget and decided that we should look for more expensive places, even if it meant that I might have to go back to a part time job. I spent a second week in Chicago continuing to look, but nothing turned up.

Having no alternative, we decided that I would have to start law school while Marg and Jane remained at the farm. Of course I would continue to do all that I could to find something. When classes started I alerted all of my colleagues at the law school to our problem, and many of then tried to help by calling people they knew in the rental business.

Because I expected to find an apartment any day, I hesitated to commit to Abbott Hall, the law school dormitory, for an entire semester. They would not rent to me by the day or the week, and the hotels in the vicinity of the law school were much too expensive. So I accepted my old roommates' invitation to bunk in with them without registering at the Abbott Hall office. I slept in a different room each night, wherever there was an empty bunk and I was welcome. This went on for months.

In the late Fall, Marg's brother John, learned that he would be called back to active duty in the Navy, because of the Korean War. Ruth and their two children elected to go with John, who was soon to become a Lieutenant Commander, to his duty station on the east coast. They asked Marg and me if we would house-sit their exquisite four-bedroom home in Glenview, complete with a car in the garage which they would like us to drive now and then.

Would we ever. It was a God-send. We offered to pay them rent, but they refused, saying that having us in their house solved a substantial problem for them. It certainly solved an overwhelming problem for us.

Ruth provided Margaret with a two-page, tightly-typed set of instructions on how to take care of her house. It would remind you of the famous Beano lists put out periodically by the Navy: there will Beano this ... there will Beano that. After a preliminary paragraph or two, which set the stage in these words: "... anything I jot down here is meant to help you, and not to make you feel that I am trying to set up your life ..." Ruthie got rather specific with each room in the house: "The lamp shades are to be dusted at the same time you vacuum the furniture; for table tops use the large jug of polish ... it is wonderful for removing fingerprints; do not wipe the refrigerator all over, just in spots; you will notice that the windows get smoky; Clayt: we didn't get the car greased due to lack of time ..."

Margaret immediately went into shock. For the next few months, she insisted on following Jane around with a sponge, and the poor little kid was only seven months old. Marg or I were much more likely than Jane to destroy something. I tried to relax Marg by assuring that if disaster struck we would redecorate the entire house if necessary. That was somewhat an empty gesture, because in our financial condition we would have had difficulty replacing a light bulb. Obviously Ruthie had sensed that. Both of us understood Ruth's concern, which was entirely warranted. We found ourselves tip-toeing around in the middle of the rooms, trying not to touch anything.

The commute from Glenview to the law school was easy. In fact my Federal tax law professor lived a couple of doors away, and sometimes I accepted his invitation to ride to school with him.

Jane began to become a person. One Sunday we exercised John and Ruth's car by driving up to Racine, Wisconsin. We stopped at an ice cream parlor. Jane was eyeing my every move as I licked the delicious cone. I held it up close to her little lips, and she carefully stuck her tongue against the cold ice cream. It was the first cold thing she ever touched. Her eyes snapped open, and her tongue reached out for more, and more.

It took a little time for us to learn how to care for Janie. When she was three weeks old we took her to the Hanna farm by train, on a warm spring day. When we arrived Mother Hanna took one look at her, and said, "That poor little baby is going to smother." While we looked on, Mother Hanna unwrapped four baby blankets from the infant. After all, we wanted to keep her warm—especially while she had that darned prickly heat.

Law school was much easier in my senior year. I now understood the teaching methods. When I read a case I could see why it had been selected for study by the professors. I was not distracted by a part-time job, which meant that I no longer wasted time commuting to and from the Loop. Northwestern awarded two types of law degrees. If your point average was at a certain level you received an LL.B. degree. If you were above that level, and if you completed a few extra courses, you were awarded a Juris Doctor degree. Because of my big comeback in my final year, I managed to squeak out the doctorate.

We had no income, so we lived on the lack of expense. We had received some money as wedding gifts, which we planned to keep in a savings account. Upon second thought, we decided that now was the time to use some of it for my education. We were confident that once I got into practice, we could replace our savings and add to them.

I did not attend my law school graduation ceremonies. Ruth Hanna came back to re-claim her home while I was taking finals. To our great relief, and possibily somewhat to her surprise, she proclaimed that we were perfect housekeepers. Later in the summer, Ruth wrote to us and let us know that she was happy that we took such good care of their property. As she put it, "Those windows just sparkled!" What she didn't know was that if Jane had touched one of those windows, we would have put her up for adoption.

We were given a used Plymouth coupe by Dad and Mother Hanna as a graduation gift. It was owned formerly by Phil Hanna, so we knew it was reliable. Marg had it all packed, along with a rental trailer which we pulled behind it, by the time I took my last final. We rolled out of Chicago for my home in Dayton, and never looked back. If I graduated, I graduated. If I didn't, I didn't. Cutting the graduation ceremonies seemed like the thing to do, in view of my record of cutting classes. Secretly, I hoped the Dean became thoroughly frustrated while looking for me, as he handed out the Juris Doctor degrees.

The pressure on the law student does not end with his graduation. Now I faced the formidable Ohio Bar Examination, which was to be given next in late June. Almost all new law graduates take what is known as a bar exam review course, several of which are offered in most of the larger cities in Ohio. I elected to take one in Cincinnati sponsored by a man by the name of Gussweiler, a retired judge, who had excellent success with out-of-state law students.

Two days after we arrived in Dayton and "unloaded" on my folks, I headed for Cincinnati. I stayed in the downtown YMCA, and for three weeks, weekends included, I studied ten to 12 hours a day on the questions which had been asked on prior exams, and which probably would be asked on this one. Judge Gussweiler was unrelenting. He kept up a steady pitter-patter so we wouldn't lose interest, and he gave us all kinds of tips on how to write proper answers. In 1951 all of the test questions were essay type, and the pass rate was around 65 to 70 per cent.

The exam itself was given in Columbus, over a period of three days. I was physically spent, because we studied with Gussweiler right up to the night before the first day of the exam. Thanks to him, I was full of good information. Many of the questions looked enticingly familiar after I read them. I actually had more confidence at the end of the ordeal than I had at the beginning. On June 17, I wrote a letter to Margaret, from Cincinnati, in which I expressed my frustrations and feelings as best I could: "Right now my head is so crammed full of rules, cases, statutes, exceptions and theories ... don't get me wrong, I am not about to crack up. It seems humorous to me that I could get this worked up over a lousy examination. It even seems funny that I should be trying so hard to be a lawyer. I can live with myself, and forgive myself, for allowing myself to become so possessed by this silly business. I can tell you with all confidence that there is not the slightest doubt in my mind but that I will pass the darned thing. I say that not out of conceit, but because I respect the exam, and have prepared myself so carefully for it ... I will be very happy, but not at all surprised when the good news comes in August."

It took the examiners several weeks to grade the 800 papers, a fact of life I later understood when I became a bar examiner myself in the 1980s. This was a most anxious time for Marg and me. We had a lot at stake. I used the time looking for work, and that was equally discouraging.

I either wrote to or called upon most of the larger law firms in Ohio's larger cities. Except for good grades, my resume was so thin you could see through it. I received very few replies and even less encouragement. During the several interviews I had, the lawyers with whom I spoke reminded me of the aristocrats who turned me down at the Yale Law School. They wanted to know things like: are there any other lawyers in my family; and would I bring any clients to the office. Everyone of them congratulated me on my record, but said they were not hiring right now but would " ... keep my name on file."

In late July I finally found a kind soul, in Marietta, Ohio, who had an opening which was intriguing, if not very rewarding. Attorney Robert Hauser, a scholarly lawyer, had just completed a comprehensive book entitled *Hauser on Ohio Real Estate Law*, under a commission from West Publishing Company, a large law book publisher. He needed someone to index his book.

These days text books are indexed by computer. In 1951 the procedure was to go through the book, line by line, with four-by-six index cards in hand. We would note significant topics, names and facts. Subsequent page numbers were added to the cards, as the same topics, names, and facts later appeared in the text. It was demanding work which required considerable concentration. Mr. Hauser's book was four volumes in length. On the good side, it was like taking a graduate course in real estate law.

Most authors guarded against one person missing something, by having several index persons do the same work, which could then be compared and combined. Mr. Hauser had three other indexers, two law professors and an appellate judge, all of whom worked out of their offices. I worked in Mr. Hauser's office and coordinated the work of the others.

I also could "practice law" in Mr. Hauser's office on matters which did not require a license to practice. I could interview witnesses, deliver pleadings to the clerk of courts, proof read briefs, and the like. For all of this work, I was paid at the rate of $1500 a year. I was glad to have the job, and worked hard at it.

Marg, Janie and I moved to Marietta and regarded our new job as a long-time commitment. We found a three-room apartment above a garage a mile outside the city. It was very clean and airy compared to some of our digs in Chicago, and we actually bought a few sticks of furniture. Marietta was going to be our home.

In late summer the results of the bar examination were published in the newspapers. I lucked out with one of the higher grades in Ohio, and immediately Mr. Hauser's telephone began to ring with calls for me. Many of the same law firms which had no openings, or did not give me the courtesy of a reply, now wanted me to come for an interview. I think it was to my credit that I refused to visit any of them. Marg said it was not to my credit. It was just vanity.

I received one call which made my heart beat fast. Mr. John Durfey, senior partner of a top-rated firm in Springfield, called to say that he and his colleagues would like to talk to me about employment. He told me that he was one of my bar examiners, and that he had given me the highest grade he gave anyone. With Mr. Hauser's permission, I went to Springfield almost immediately, and I really liked the lawyers I met. At the end of a full day of interviewing, the firm of Corry, Durfey, Martin & Browne, offered me an associateship at $3,000 per year. That was one of the better rates for law grads in 1951, even in the larger cities.

I returned to Marietta and leveled with Mr. Hauser. I told him all the details, and assured him that while I wanted to accept the new offer, I would not abandon him after only a few weeks of association . I told him I knew that he had employed me for the long-term, which was my intent also. Because Marg and I both were grateful to him I was willing to honor our understanding.

He would not hear of it. He encouraged me to accept the new opportunity. He was acquainted with several partners in my new firm and assured me that I was joining an honorable band of counselors. He wrote a letter to Mr. Durfey in my behalf, which was a kind thing to do.

On October 1, 1951 I started my association with Corry, Durfey, Martin & Browne with high hopes and considerable enthusiasm. I was finished with my formal education at long last. It seemed to me that I had been a student forever. Sometimes it had not been easy, but it was always worth it.

I was ready to put it all to practice. I was soon to find that would not be easy either.

LEUKEMIA FOR BEGINNERS

I THINK WE NEED A BREAK from my day-to-day escapades. It has been a long trip through college and law school, not to mention marriage and parenthood. Let's shift gears a little bit and talk about a form of cancer known as leukemia. Of course you will never get it.

That's what I thought. In February of 1999, nearly 50 years after the start of my adventures in the practice of law, I was in California and Arizona covering two golf tournaments for a British golf magazine, for which I am the American correspondent and monthly columnist. My lawyering days were long over. Commencing in the mid-1980s I could see that the strenuous life of the lawyer was beginning to be too much for me. In my prime I could gain weight during a ten-day trial. In 1984 I finished a three day trial, and could not remember the last two days. I retired at the end of 1986 while I could still tie my own shoes, and became a golf writer.

As I watched the PGA Tour players from the fairways in 1999, I began to realize that I was not feeling well. At first I thought I had the flu, but then it seemed to me that the sensations were more deeply within me. Marg was on the trip, and we decided that we should come home and get a little medical advice. Our little baby Jane, whose birth was featured in the last chapter, is now practicing medicine in Seattle. She encouraged us to seek help. Believe it or not we are now in our mid-seventies.

Our family doctor is, in the best sense, a curious man. Dr. Shailesh Patel was born and educated in India. With only a blood report before him, he suggested that I should put myself immediately in the hands of The Arthur G. James Cancer Hospital at The Ohio State University. Whoops. That is the sort of thing that only happens to someone else.

It is not easy to describe leukemia in simple language. The professionals have trouble doing it, although they try. It is believed by most oncologists that leukemia victims will respond to treatment quicker if they have a basic understanding of what is happening to their bodies.

The reason we have blood is to transport oxygen, nutrients and chemicals to cells throughout our bodies. The blood also assists with the removal of toxins and other waste materials from our bodies. There are many components in the blood, but the important ones are the white cells, the platelets, and the red cells. In the healthy body there is a balance among these components, which enhances the responsibility of each.

The white cells are vital to the immune system, and are the main defenders against infection and disease. At the outset of my cancer, my immune system was so weak that my doctors wanted me to stay away from people as much as I could, because I was likely to attract a bacteria, virus, fungus, or other infection with which I could not cope. Some friends and neighbors who wanted to support me found it strange that visits were restricted to a quick five-minutes. Close friends understood, as did persons who were familiar with leukemia personally or from caring for a victim.

The platelets are essential for clotting of the blood. The ideal range for the platelet count, in thousands, is between a low of 130 and a high of 400. Mine was too low early on, and I recall that the doctors were very pleased when about a month into my treatment my count hit 164. What the oncologists did to help me reach the acceptable range is a mystery to me. Frankly, I doubt if they could explain it to me. It happened, and everyone seemed to be pleased that it did.

The red cells, simply put, are the remainder of the blood. Each of these three components of the blood is classified further by the doctors. For example, the white cells consist of monocytes, granulocytes and lymphocytes. This is not the end of it: the lymphocytes consist of T cells, which control the functions of the white cells; and of B cells, which make and release antibodies, which in turn help remove infections from the body.

If I go into this explanation much further I will be in over my head, although I have spent days reading books and searching deep within my computer for information. Going further also will run the risk of telling you more than you want to know.

I have gone this far to demonstrate how incredibly complex this disease is. I have not as yet mentioned the other body system which is as important as the blood system to an understanding of leukemia. That would be the lymph system. Stay with me for a minute more and I will give you LYMPH IN A NUTSHELL.

The lymph system *is* the immune system. It is a complex network which runs throughout the body. A milky fluid called lymph circulates within this network. Lymph is mostly lymphocytes, which if you are still awake, you will remember are one of the three subdivisions of the white blood cells. The blood system and the lymph system are therefore linked by the lymphocytes.

As the lymph circulates in the lymph network it tends to become trapped in some of the glands in the body, thus forming lymph nodes. The nodes often are found under the arms, and in the pelvis, neck, and abdomen. As the lymph passes through these nodes, foreign and toxic substances are filtered out by the antibodies, which you may remember are a product of the B cells of the lymphocytes.

Lymphoma is the name given to a tumor which may develop in the lymph system, often in one of the nodes. While technically it is a tumor, the doctors are quick to explain that it is not like the tumors commonly associated with cancer, which often develop in one or more specific organs of the body and can be treated by surgery and radiation as well as by chemotherapy.

The cause of lymphoma is not always clear to the doctors, but the latest research is relating it more and more to hereditary or chromosonal abnormalities. When I asked my oncologist how on earth I got my lymphoma, if that is what I have, he confessed he didn't know for sure. But he added, "It is entirely possible that it was destined at the precise instant of your birth." If you are not a Presbyterian steeped in predestination, that possibility may come as a shock.

I have been describing "leukemia" as best I can, when in fact I may have "lymphoma." A recent immunophenotypic analysis conducted by The James Cancer Hospital reported that my condition is " … consistent with a lymphoproliferative disorder." The same report said in the next line that this " … is similar to … mantle cell lymphoma or a typical chronic lymphocytic leukemia."

In the beginning of my illness, our family doctor concluded that I had what he referred to as CLL, or chronic lymphocytic leukemia. I think that yet today if you were to ask Dr. Patel what I suffer from, there is a possibility that he might say leukemia. The specialists, however, draw a tighter distinction between leukemia and lymphoma. Ask them what I have and they might answer MCL, which means mantle cell lymphoma, and they might add quickly that my MCL is not to be confused with SLL, or small lymphocytic lymphoma, which for a time they thought I had.

In the final analysis it might be a case of paying your penny and taking your choice. Notwithstanding this uncertainty, you have to give the oncologists a lot of credit. The chances are that they were the kids who came up with the best science projects in high school. They probably were top-notch students in college, and A-plus students in medical school. They were enthusiastic students throughout their residency in internal medicine, which was followed by a fellowship in oncology. That represents at least 14 years of expensive, formal study beyond high school. For many oncologists the education trail does not end there. Many of them specialize further and become an oncologist/pathologist, an oncologist/radiologist, or an oncologist/pediatrician. There are additional categories of specialization, all of them requiring more years of concentration and formal study.

This professionalism shows up in their work. In this day and age I don't think any cancer patient should be treated by his family doctor, or any doctor who is not certified as an oncologist. I have been treated primarily by Dr. Christopher Rhoades, of the James staff. From the first day he insisted that I call him Chris. He gave me his office and home numbers, and even his pager number. He made it clear that no question in my mind was too dumb to ask. Before long I discovered that none of my questions was too technical or esoteric for him. Seeing me when Dr. Rhoades can't is another oncologist from James, Dr. Kelli Cawley. She is equally informal, and well-informed. In the more recent stages of my illness I have been treated by two additional James oncologists, Dr. Michael J. Stanek and Dr. Pierluigi Porcu, both of whom we like and respect.

All of these outstanding physicians work as a closely coordinated team, in association with three or four highly trained and kind-hearted oncology nurses. It is comforting to Marg and me to notice how all of them remember my case, month after month, without looking up anything. My chart, actually a large three-ring binder, is more than six inches thick. Both the doctors and the nurses can look at one of my current blood reports and contrast it with any of my former blood reports without consulting the earlier report. Each report is two solid pages of numbers listed opposite funny sounding categories like "nucleated RBC" and "segmented neutrophil." I think they all have minds like rocket scientists.

Although CLL, MCL and SLL are related closely, in the minds of the specialists there are clinical and morphologic distinctions which can lead to different prognostic and therapeutic options and implications. For that reason my diagnosis was very slow in coming. I thought the doctors would *never* make up their minds on what kind of a beast I had within me. They gave me so many tests: a bone marrow biopsy, several CT scans of different areas and organs of my body, several x-rays and other imaging scans, and even a stress test to make certain my heart was strong enough to endure the type of chemotherapy I might need. I was getting two complete blood workups each week, while awaiting the diagnosis.

The word came down finally from the James mountain that it was likely that I had mantle cell lymphoma (MCL), but we could call it leukemia if we wanted to. The team at James quickly put together and prescribed what should go into my chemotherapy recipe in order most effectively to discourage the cancer cells in my blood. It was referred to as COP, with each letter standing for a different drug in the formula. I was warned that if COP didn't work I would then get an even more toxic jolt known as CHOP. I also got all the standard warnings about chemotherapy, ending with " … none of which may apply to you."

Before I knew it the big bags of COP were hanging menacingly above my head and the poison was dripping relentlessly into my body. I am not going to tell you about my reactions to chemotherapy because of that vacuous remark: " … none of which may apply to you." Smart as they are, the oncologists can not predict how every patient will react to chemotherapy, or even when the reaction may come if it does. I have had three sessions of chemotherapy, and suffered three different reactions. None of them was pleasant, and one of them put me in the hospital for eight days. But I lived through all of them. I might have an altogether different reaction if I have to take chemo again. Or I might have no reaction at all.

If you are faced with chemotherapy the best advice I can give you is to submit to it bravely and with confidence. It is not nearly as tough on you as it is on those pesky little white cells in your blood which are reproducing wildly and killing off all the other good stuff in your blood.

In July, four months after my leukemia was diagnosed, Marg and I were told that the amount of cancerous activity in my body was at such a low and stable level that my immune system could cope with it. In translation: my body was free of cancer, "free" of course being a relative term. There were times during the four months when I was not sure who was winning. My weight dropped forty pounds. My muscles atrophied. I had no strength, or appetite or zest for life. I couldn't stand up straight, or walk safely without a cane. My skin was too big for my body, and looked like it had been left out in the rain.

I could never have made it without Marg. Those many years ago when we wrote our wedding vows and left out "obey," we left in "in sickness and in health." She never forgot it. She would not let me give up. She prayed for me, and with me, and encouraged others to do the same. She fed me, or at least tried to. She suffered along with me. Thanks to her, and to medical science, the worst is behind us. I am now into physical therapy to rebuild my body and I have more zest than you can imagine. But that is a whole different subject, and of course we have no way of knowing how long our good fortune will last.

If I make it all the way back to normal health, which I think I will, I will be a better person. Life means more to me now. I am more tolerant of persons who move slowly or have painful faces.

I have a greater desire to cheer up people who appear to be under stress.

I think that if I am driving down the Interstate, and I come up behind a tractor-trailer, and I can't go around it because some character is driving beside me in the passing lane, and he has been driving in the passing lane all the way from Erie, Pennsylvania or somewhere, and he won't drop back, or pass the truck, and he won't get over, and all I can do is slow down so I won't crash into the rear of the semi. Well, if that happens, I think … well … I think … I think I want to give that situation a little more thought. Cancer may not have made me *that* merciful. But I am more compassionate now, within reason. I intend to stay that way.

All of which is not to say that I am glad I got cancer, or that I want anymore to do with it. I don't even want to write anymore about it. I am sure you have heard enough.

It is time now to return to the practice of the law, a subject I know something about.

THE PRACTICE OF LAW

In 1951 THE PRACTICE OF THE LAW in a small city of 80,000 was one of the best ways in the world to earn a living. You did have to earn it, and for a new lawyer it was not a living that would soon make you rich. What made it such a pleasure was the trust of the community. If you were a lawyer in those days, you were somebody.

I was the seventh lawyer at Corry, Durfey, Martin & Browne. As the low man on the totem pole, I caught all the work no one else wanted. It has worked that way in law firms for as long as there have been law firms. That aspect, perhaps unpleasant, is offset by the fact that if you are associated with a firm you have more legal work than you can handle from the day you first walk into the place.

That is not so with new lawyers who start their own offices and practice alone. My former colleague at Northwestern, Senator Dale Bumpers, said that his telephone did not ring for weeks on end, when he started his practice in Arkansas. A new doctor can start a solo practice next door to a new lawyer, and people will line up the first day to place their bodies in the hands of the new doctor. They wouldn't think of placing their property in the hands of the new lawyer.

There may be good reason for this. The lawyer does not get

clinical training in law school on the level enjoyed by the doctor in medical school. At Northwestern, we had a legal aid clinic and I spent a few days on duty there. My exposure was nothing compared to the medical student, who may start seeing patients, with an experienced doctor, as early as the second year in medical school. If the doctor is certified in a specialty, he has at least three years of post doctoral training, much of it clinical in nature. A lawyer can get an A in his course in real estate without ever seeing a deed or a mortgage. He has no residencies or fellowships. He may clerk in a law firm during his second and third years of law school, but if he does that clerkship is as much designed to give the firm an opportunity to look him over, as it is designed to give him serious clinical training.

The young lawyer learns from the other lawyers in his office. The older lawyers know this, and are very patient. After all, if the new counsel screws up, the senior lawyers will be included in the malpractice suit.

My chief mentor at the Corry firm was John Harper, Esq., a sharp attorney with about three years of experience. He graduated from Ohio State's law school with very high grades. At that time Ohio State was not considered a national law school, but John would have excelled at any law school. One of the nicest things about him was that he was overjoyed that I was hired, because now he would not get all the grunt work. He wanted to see me fully trained as soon as possible. I wanted that too.

In a firm as small as ours I worked with all of the lawyers. If one of the seniors challenged me with something I knew nothing about, John Harper was always there and willing to help. He took me to the courthouse and introduced me to the judges, other elected officials, and as many of the employees of the principal offices as we could find during several trips. He took me to the banks and real estate offices and introduced me. He showed me where various public and private buildings and offices were located, and identified the movers and shakers at each place.

One of John's most important responsibilities was to show me how to check the title to a tract of real estate. The procedures for acquiring a marketable title varied from county to county in Ohio in 1951. In Clark County there was nearly a total reliance upon an opinion letter from a lawyer to the buyer, certifying the condition of the title. Rarely did we use title insurance, which is the way the title often is guaranteed these days. The lawyer's examination of the title remains the lynch pin, nevertheless, because the title insurance company relies upon the lawyer's opinion letter.

Title searches are as much art as science. They also are a large part of a law practice in smaller cities. They are the bread and butter which pay the overhead. Title searches are never performed by senior lawyers.

I hated doing them. I must have grumbled about doing them without knowing I was doing it. Little Jane told her mother one day: I dink I go down wiff daddy today, and hep him chek his tytals.

I have never met an ambitious lawyer who enjoyed searching a title. The fact that I was in the courthouse checking a title was proof that I was a junior lawyer. If you did them early in the morning, your hands and clothing were dirty the rest of the day; if you waited to do them in the afternoon, you ran the risk of going to sleep. The work took me into the dustiest portions of the Probate Court as I made sure that all of the taxes were paid, and that all of the next-of-kin were timely notified, in an old estate proceedings which might be 40 or 50 years old. I had to check every deed in the chain of title to make certain each had two witnesses, was notarized and contained the correct legal description for the real estate. If the property were purchased by John Doe it had to be sold by John Doe, and not by Johnny Doe or J. Doe.

This drudgery was not taught or even mentioned at Northwestern's law school. I was taught how to merge two banks, or how to prepare a brief for filing in the Supreme Court. Checking a title was for the lesser lawyer, the one who did not attend Northwestern.

I was now less than a lesser lawyer. At my firm, I was the least lawyer. I checked about three or four titles every day of the week. I was earning my entire weekly salary by mid-morning of every day. We represented the First National Bank of Springfield, which made a ton of real estate loans. In addition to checking all those titles to make sure the Bank would have a clear title if its mortgage were foreclosed, I presided at the closing of those loans. I prepared the closing documents, and went over each of them with the borrowers so they would know what they were signing.

The good thing about all that title work was that I met a lot of local citizens at the loan closings. The key to developing a law practice in a small city is meeting people, and making a good impression upon them. I tried to be helpful to them, as I explained the documents as thoroughly as I could. Now and then one of them would ask, "you don't happen to prepare wills, do you?"

I sure did. During the time I was with the Corry firm I prepared hundreds of wills, maybe as many as a thousand. For years after I left Springfield, I would receive notices from the Probate Court asking me to verify my witnessing of a will, or less often appointing me an executor of an estate. I was surprised at how often I could remember the decedent, and the very day the will was executed.

There was one Last Will and Testament I won't forget, even though it never was written. A woman called for an appointment to prepare a will. When she arrived I could see that she was in an advanced state of anxiety. A lawyer soon learns that most of the people he deals with are a bit distressed. If they weren't concerned about something, they probably would not be consulting a lawyer.

This lady was beyond distress. She was on the edge of rationality. Her opening words to me were, "I want you to write up a will for my husband, because I am going straight home and kill the S.O.B."

She had my attention. I explained carefully that under Ohio law a wife can not make a will for a husband. If he wanted a will he would have to consult with the lawyer of his choice. I didn't tell her, but at that moment I hoped that his choice would not be me. Then I noticed that she had a very large purse on her lap, and that she had one hand in the purse. It was obvious that she didn't like what I was telling her.

New lawyers often make a lot of mistakes. In my early years I closed the door to my office while I was with a client. I thought the privacy might promote honesty, and also it occurred to me that if I were giving bum legal advice, it might be better if no one heard it. As I watched the lady with her hand in her purse I made a mental note to leave my door wide open from now on, assuming of course that I lived through this adventure.

She held me in my office for more than two hours. Why none of the other lawyers or secretaries came to my door during that period is a mystery. A couple of times I suggested to her that I wanted to make a telephone call, and in a threatening way she suggested that she would rather I did not. I was trapped and I knew it.

She mentioned the name of a psychiatrist who was caring for her. By luck, I happened to know the doctor. I asked if she would have any objection if I called him, and was pleased when she said that I might. I told the doctor that one of his patients was in my office, and I would be grateful if he would come and confer with her. When I mentioned her name he said, "Oh *her* ... by the way, does she have a gun on you?" I replied that I thought so, and I found his next statement something less than reassuring. He said, "Don't worry a thing about it ... she may even shoot at you, but if she does she won't hit you!"

The psychiatrist came and took her away. I was a free man. And a wiser one.

John Harper also was anxious that I learn our firm's Municipal Court practice, which pleased me because I loved the work. At any given moment our office would have dozens of cases pending in what amounted to a small claims court. They all involved tiny amounts of money, and routine issues. Over the years I learned that a client never regards his own lawsuit as routine or unimportant. I might have a $200 law suit coming for trial, in which our client would expect me to interview everyone in town at least once, and to research the case all the way back to the Magna Charta.

I had a lot of competitive gusto for these little trials, and hated like the Dickens to lose one of them. I think that might have been due to my debating background at Ohio Wesleyan. I fell into the habit of keeping track of my won and lost record. That was another bad idea springing from my lack of experience. Fortunately, I no longer kept score when, later in my career, now and then I might try a case where several hundred million dollars might be at stake. Scorekeeping, at that point, would have been dumb. In complex litigation there often is no clear line between winning and losing.

There was a laugh a minute in the Municipal Court. I tried a case involving aluminum storm windows, when they first came on the market. When the case was over, the judge called me to chambers and said, "All the way through that trial something was bothering me ... *Why* would anyone want storm windows made of aluminum? You wouldn't be able to see through them."

I caught on to the small-town practice quickly. Within two or three years, I graduated to an occasional trial in the Common Pleas Court, usually when one of the senior lawyers would ask me to sit with him at the trial table. The quality of the advocacy was much higher than the Municipal Court. The problem was that so long as I was the lowest lawyer on our list I had to check those titles, and run those traps in the Municipal Court.

One evening Mr. Durfey asked me if I would deliver a note and a mortgage to the members of the official board of a rural Methodist church just outside the city. Marg and Jane went along to enjoy a little ride in the country, and Jane had her PJs on in case she got sleepy.

When we arrived at the church it seemed a little odd to me that the parking lot was nearly full. When I went in the church I was greeted by a nervous gentleman who wanted to know why I was late. I told him that Mr. Durfey had said seven-thirty, and I was right on time. He said, "No, no, it was seven o'clock ... by the way, what is your name again ... follow me, we are ready for you."

I followed him to the altar, and was flabbergasted as he clapped his hands, called everyone to order and said, "Ladies and Gentlemen, I am pleased to present to you Attorney Clinton Hodgkins of John Durfey's firm, who will now explain to us the legal aspects of our building campaign!"

Just as Professor Diem, my old debate coach, had saved my life at Crown Prince Olav's party in Norway, he did it again. He drilled into us time and again that if you are not prepared, you should always rise to the occasion by never letting anyone know you are not prepared. I remembered that, as I thought to myself, "These people are expecting a good speech, and I might as well see to it that they get one."

I thanked them for waiting so patiently for me to show up. I told them how sorry Mr. Durfey was that he couldn't make it, and added that in all probability *he* would have been *worth* waiting for. Ha, Ha. All of that took five minutes, at least. I then gave them a pep talk on how important a building campaign is to the life of a church. Another five minutes. I then pulled out Mr. Durfey's note and mortgage, and was pleased to see that the lender was the First

National Bank. I knew those documents backwards, and proceeded to explain each of them in detail. For good measure I threw in a lecture on Ohio mechanics lien law, and summed up by telling them that when they closed their loan I would be there as attorney for the bank, and to make certain that Mr. Durfey made no mistakes. Ha, ha. End of speech. Any questions?

When I returned to the parking lot, Marg and Jane both were sound asleep and the left rear tire of my car was as flat as my speech must have been.

The next morning Mr. Durfey came to my office, which was highly unusual. All he said was, "I hear you did a good job at the church last night ... thanks again for helping me out." The fact that *he* came to *my* office was the only "apology" I got, or needed.

Marg and I met so many nice people in Springfield. We rented a second floor apartment on North Limestone Street. It had a small back yard for Janie, and an attic which she could explore on rainy days. We joined the downtown Presbyterian church, and before long were both involved in a variety of congregational programs.

In October of 1952, Mother and Matt surprised us with the news that they were moving from Dayton to California. He was doing well as a civilian employee of the Air Force, and the move was a promotion for him. For us it meant no more frequent visits, and it was a sad day when they headed west. Looking back it was a good move for both of them. Los Angeles was exciting for them, and they enjoyed entertaining visiting relatives from Ohio, including us when we could make it. Getting ahead of my story a little, I made frequent trips to California when I began to represent the Union Oil Company of California in the l960s.

In no time at all it was 1953, a very exciting time for us. We decided early in the year that we should buy a home of our own, to greet our new baby due to arrive in July. After endless traipsing through house after house, we finally selected a Tudor home on Kewbury Road in the north end of Springfield. It was on a dead-end street and was a cute little place. It had three bedrooms, all on the second floor with the bathroom. On the first floor there was a modern kitchen with a separate breakfast room, a good size dining room, and a nice living room across the front of the house. There was a large basement which we learned had a bad habit of flooding during the monsoon seasons.

The house cost $15,000, a small fortune for us. From our savings we scraped together a down payment of $5,000, and the First National Bank gave us a loan of $10,000. John Harper closed our loan, sparing me the necessity of explaining the terms of the loan documents to a very nervous Margaret. John said he was glad to do it, and added the old bromide: "The attorney who represents himself, has a fool for a client."

The day we moved in was a happy one, although we were flat broke again. The law firm had given me a couple of annual salary increases by this time, but every penny counted for a while. We had no furniture in the dining room, very little in the living room, and none at all in one of the bedrooms. This gave Janie a good choice of where to play. The back yard was a show place, because the prior owners were accomplished gardeners. We inherited a courtly rose garden which we never learned how to keep debugged. One of our first purchases was a lawn mower.

Laura Ann Hoskins came to live with us at our new home, on July 26, 1953. From the first look at her, our hearts melted. Janie loved her too. We prepared Jane for this new arrival, by describing the newcomer as a new doll for her. She held us to the promise, and some of our first pictures of Laura show her tottering precariously on the little lap of her big sister.

The night Laura was born was a little out of the ordinary. Gert Beattie, the Ohio Wesleyan friend who first introduced Marg and me, was now married and living in Arizona. She and her husband were traveling through Springfield on the way to her folks' home near Cleveland. They arrived to look over our new house, shortly before Marg went into labor. They wound up watching Janie most of the night, while we went to City Hospital to pick up her new doll.

In those days fathers were not welcome in the delivery room. We thought that was a silly rule, and early in the pregnancy we reached an understanding with our doctor that I might be present with Marg. He agreed a bit reluctantly, but he did agree. When we arrived at the hospital for the big event, we learned that the nurse on duty in the delivery room did not know of our agreement with the doctor.

The nurse was a formidable person, at least six feet tall. She told me in no uncertain terms that under no circumstances was I going into that delivery room. Marg wanted me with her. For months we had been counting upon my being there. I pleaded with the nurse that I had permission, but she wouldn't listen. I finally had to appeal to her sense of logic. Had we gotten into a fist-fight she would have won.

I asked her if it were not a fact that her instructions provided that if a father wanted into the delivery room, she was to tell him that he could not enter. She said that was right. I asked her if anywhere in her instructions she was authorized to block his entry, if he threatened a lawsuit. She said that her authority did not go that far. "All right," I concluded, "you have followed your instructions, and if you try further to keep me out of the delivery room I will sue you." She helped me into my hospital gown.

I had my camera with me, and got some terrific slides, which Margaret keeps under lock and key.

Laura was an angelic child from the moment she was born. She was so incredibly cute, so tiny, so beautiful. The hospital staff tried to tell us that it was gas pains, but we knew that she was smiling at us an hour after her birth. Today Laura is a second grade teacher in a school system near Akron, and the mother of two teenage daughters. She is as solid as a rock: intelligent, patient with others, sweet and loving, thoughtful, generous almost to a fault, and in every possible way a good citizen of the world and of her neighborhood. We hope her character is in part due to the fact that her father was present in the room when she was delivered by natural childbirth, a rare event in 1953.

It was nice to have two kids. Jane called Laura "Lulu," and after a year or so Laura called Jane "Zanie." Jane was always protective of her sister, and spent hours talking to her and showing her the world. Jane would "read" to Laura from some of her books she had memorized. Marg read to both of them endlessly, and that had a lot to do with the fact that both girls were honor students in high school and in college.

My work at the office was becoming burdensome. By my third year or so, I was comfortable with about everything which came along. The lawyer in general practice is no stranger to diversity.

Truck drivers called me day and night. The drivers carried my telephone numbers in their cabs, and if they had a wreck I heard from them. I would call George Wisler, a good natured local photographer, and we would rush to the scene. I interviewed witnesses, while George took pictures. In the wee hours he always offered to take my picture, to "prove to John Durfey that you were not sleeping on the job." One of my favorite memories is of Marg standing by our bed in the middle of the night, and saying into the telephone, "Roadway Express Company? Roadway Express Company? There is nobody here by *that* name!"

As I became acquainted with more people, I began to pick up assignments from my friends and neighbors. I had great hope that the firm would expand so that I could escape the title searches, but year after year it did not happen. I finally got to the place where I had to ask the Clark County Recorder if I might have a key so that I could work in her office at night.

I became involved in the work of the Community Welfare Council. The mission of the CWC was to oversee the operations and budgets of the 40-some private and public welfare agencies which shared the money gathered each year by the United Appeal. The CWC was organized by Dr. F. James Schrag, the chairman of the department of sociology at Wittenberg University. Jim and his wife, Lois, became our lifetime friends. Jim was the first president of the CWC. In 1954 he asked me to succeed him in that office, and I could not see any reason to refuse because I was certain that we were performing an honorable and necessary service to the community. I was president for four years, and it was a very happy but busy time for me.

I was active also in bar association work and church work. I even dabbled a little in politics, serving as the campaign manager for the Honorable C. William O'Neil, a native of Marietta and a candidate for attorney general. Mr. O'Neil was elected, and later in his career he became the Governor of Ohio. Even later, he was elected Chief Justice of the Ohio Supreme Court. Before he was elected Attorney General, with my modest help, he was Speaker of the Ohio House, thus making him the only person in the history of Ohio to head all three departments of government. I found it exciting to have a friend in high places.

In 1955 Mr. Homer C. Corry, our senior partner who had been with our office continuously since 1913, died quite suddenly. I thought that his death would prompt the partners to hire a new associate, but it didn't happen until more than a year later in 1956, my fifth year with the firm. The young man who was hired to take my place at the bottom of the stack, was a lifetime family friend of one of our senior lawyers. He had been practicing for about a year in Texas, and was wheedled into coming back to Ohio to help us out. I doubt if he had any intent to start at the bottom.

Marg and I concluded that the firm didn't care whether I moved up and away from the grunt work. I was pretty good at it, and in that sense was of considerable value to the firm. John Harper shed the routine stuff after three years; but after five years

I was at most getting rid of only part of it with the arrival of the new man. I could not grow as a lawyer until I could escape the daily title searches and the other routine, monotonous work which did not appeal to the others. When I learned that the new man was being paid the same as I, because of his prior, but brief, experience at the Texas bar, I knew that it was just a matter of time until I would have to look for other employment.

The new man took part of the title searches, and that helped a great deal. I even gave him my key to the Recorders office, which I doubt if he ever used. The extra time allowed me to try more cases in the Common Pleas Court; and I argued several matters in the Court of Appeals. I began to do a little more corporation work, for which I think I had a special talent. I helped organize several small businesses, and when wage and salary controls came on the scene, I became the only lawyer in our office who knew anything about the new regulations. I got to argue one of the firm's cases in the Ohio Supreme Court, and that was a treat.

1956 surely was not entirely a down year. On April 8 our family increased in size one more time with the arrival of James Matthew Hoskins, who was named after my father and my stepfather. When Jane and Laura were born, I took one look at them and wouldn't have traded either of them for anyone in the world. When Jim made his appearance, the thrill was entirely different. This was my son. I now had a buddy who would understand my male attitudes and thoughts. He would not want to play tea party, he would want to play catch. When he had to go at a restaurant, I would be the one who took him. If he fell off his bike he would not cry. He would just get back on so he could fall off again.

Don't let anyone tell you that girl babies and boy babies are the same. One is not better than another. They are all gifts from heaven. But gosh, are they different. With all three of our kids, we have followed the "rosebush" school of thought. If they were dashing into the street and could get injured seriously, we stopped them. If they were merely falling into a rosebush, we let them go ahead and learn a lesson. It seemed to us that Jim was falling into a rosebush every hour of the day.

The girls were cute and sweet, and willing to forgive. Jim was solemn, even sedate; and likely to take a swing at you if you got in his way. Janie took Jim in stride, although he was an annoyance sometimes. On the other hand, Laura looked upon him as a trespasser. Once when Jim was sitting in his playpen and looking in the other direction, Laura sneaked up behind him and was about to crease his skull with a cast iron model of a John Deere farm tractor. Marg grabbed the tractor in mid-air. On another occasion, Laura tried to pull him off the bed when he was unattended for a second.

Jim would never have expressed himself in that way. If he wanted to square things with Jane or Laura, he would simply back up a few steps and plow into their midsections, like a fullback attempting to make a first down.

There never has been a day in our lives when Jim and his sisters have not made us proud. As a kid Jim was a terrific little athlete. In high school he came to us and asked if he could switch schools, because he had heard that the academic program at the new school was better suited for him. When it was time to select a college he chose Lawrence University in Appleton, Wisconsin, a nearly perfect choice for him. Upon graduation he joined the Peace Corps and spent 27 months in a lonely village in Senegal, attempting to show the African people how to grow enough food to last an entire year. After he returned home, he earned a masters degree in rural sociology and now is employed by The Ohio State University.

Jane, the doctor; Laura, the teacher; and Jim, the research expert, are the closest of friends. It makes us happy to see them looking out for one another. They are in near daily contact by telephone or E-mail, and they are tightly knitted in every sense of the word.

Despite my growing disappointment at what I regarded as a lack of support at times, I maintained a genuine respect for each of my colleagues. John Durfey was a gentleman in every sense. In 1956 he was elected president of the Ohio State Bar Association, which gave our firm a statewide presence. Oscar T. Martin, next in line, posted some of the highest grades ever recorded at the Harvard law school. He was a tremendously over-worked lawyer, simply because he was so good at it. Many a night I would leave at nine or later, with Oscar still at it. Bitner Browne also was a Harvard lawyer and scholar. He was the second-best trial lawyer I ever worked with. After I left the firm, Bitner was elected president of the Ohio Bar. Anson Hall, an associate when I came to the firm was made a partner in about 1955 or so. When he was a young boy he lost his left arm at the shoulder, in a tractor accident. He was a kind-hearted man, who treated me well. Because he had been the lowest ranking lawyer for even longer than I, he understood my problem. There wasn't much he, or I, could do about it. I have described John Harper previously. He always pulled for me. He is fully retired now and living a quiet life in Springfield.

One of the most exciting clients of the firm was a gentleman of Greek ancestry, who came to the United States in 1903 without a dime to his name. I think it would be better if I not mention his name, and merely refer to him in pronouns. At the time I knew him, he was the owner of an ice cream manufacturing business, which he built from the ground up to become a multi-million dollar business. When Mr. Martin could no longer find time to take care of his legal work, I caught the assignment.

Soon after my new client arrived from Greece, he got a job as a short-order cook in a local restaurant. He saved every penny he made, and within a few years bought the restaurant. A few years later he bought a second restaurant, and soon he owned a chain of lunch counters and restaurants. In 1913 he discovered how to flavor ice cream, which until that time was all vanilla. He experimented with lemon, and then with strawberry, without much success. When he succeeded with chocolate, a new industry was born, and he became wealthy.

When I began to do his legal work he may have been the richest man in town. We became good friends, because we admired each other's work ethic. At Christmas he always provided our family with Greek pastries, which he made himself.

One of his most serious legal problems was providing for the continuity of his business after his death. I worried about it for months, and could see no obvious solution. He had no family in this country. He ran the enterprise day and night, as a one-man company. He even lived above the factory in a modest apartment.

When I learned that he had a nephew in Greece who had just graduated from a Greek university with a graduate degree in business, I suggested that he give some thought to bringing the lad to Springfield and teaching him the business. He liked that idea, and arranged for the nephew to come to Montreal for an interview. He chose Montreal because he wanted to keep the nephew far from the business, until he could size him up. After a day or two he came back from Montreal, and I could tell by his long face that things had not gone well. He didn't go into detail, but he told me this much.

He said, "I think my nephew is a Socialist. He tried to impress me with a book he is writing which is entitled *The Distribution of the World's Wealth*. He should not be concerned with the distribution of the world's wealth. What he should be concerned with, is the acquisition of his share of it." I never heard anymore about the nephew.

He finally decided, on his own, that he would leave his business to a faithful secretary, bookkeeper and general office manager who had worked for him for 30 years. He concluded, I think from the *Readers Digest*, where so many Americans get their legal advice, that if she were his spouse, he might save some payroll taxes. We prepared a prenuptial agreement, which was to be signed the day of their marriage, and before the start of the honeymoon. It was at that point that it became clear that the marriage was a commercial transaction. The bride did not go on the honeymoon. As he put it in his delightful accent: "She'sa not going ... just'a me."

There were other interesting clients which made my nine years in Springfield so much fun. I knew every other practicing lawyer in the city. We all ate together virtually every day at a round table at a downtown hotel. You had to develop a thick skin at that table, or you could not survive. I was referred to as the "Dispose-All," because the other lawyers insisted that my firm gave me all its garbage to handle. There was just enough truth in that to make it funny to everyone but me. In 1958, I was designated the "Outstanding Young Man of the Year" by the Junior Chamber of Commerce, and the lads at the round table couldn't believe it. They had a thousand comments and questions about how I must have bought that honor, and how much I must have paid. "Not much," they concluded.

It was because of these fun times, and all of our loyal clients and friends, that it was hard to turn in my resignation to Mr. Durfey and prepare to pull up stakes and move. Of course we could not keep everyone happy, and there were some disappointments.

I represented a local businessman, who went out of his way to make certain with me that I honored the attorney-client privilege. I remember saying to him that talking to me was "just like talking to a priest." He then began to tell me in great detail how his son was involved in a number of thefts of government checks from US mail boxes in the community. I turned white. Because I did not represent the son, anything I knew about the youngster was *not* privileged. I am certain the father never understood why it was necessary that he and I together take all of the information to the United States Attorney. I doubt if he ever again trusted a priest. Certainly he never trusted a lawyer

I was serving as a trustee for a valuable tract of real estate which was for sale in downtown Springfield. A local lawyer called me and made a generous, oral offer, which I accepted. Before he could get a written offer to me, however, another buyer came to my office and presented me with a written offer. The written offer was higher, and as a fiduciary I was required to accept the highest offer. Under Ohio's statutes, an offer involving an interest in real estate must be in writing to be enforceable. The first lawyer knew the law, and knew that I was applying it correctly. But his view was that with him, a deal was a deal. His word was his bond. He swore he would see me in Hell. He passed away soon after that, but of course I have no idea where he wound up after death. If I do see him again, he will never understand.

I left the firm in June of 1960, after giving notice late in 1959 of my intention. I spent months looking for the right position. The world was full of opportunities for a lawyer of my age, and with my experience, but Marg and I could not find anything with which we both were comfortable.

At least two other small law offices in Springfield asked me to join them when my intent to leave the Durfey firm became known. Another good-natured lawyer, whom I had stitched-up pretty good in a couple of trials we had against one another, came to my office and said that if I needed any money to support my family until the first payday at the new job, I needed only to ask.

Camaraderie within a profession can not reach a higher level than that.

In mid-June of 1960, I became the new general counsel of a high-tech electronics company in Columbus, Ohio, known as Industrial Nucleonics Corporation.

This position would provide me with many professional challenges, which pleased me; and because the development of peaceful and industrial uses for atomic energy was a worthy purpose, the new job pleased Marg.

It was the job we had been looking for.

THE DOMESTICATED LAWYER

Industrial Nucleonics Corporation was founded on May 12, 1950, the very same day our Jane Eleanor was born in Chicago while I was in a cab. The founders were two brothers from Louisville, Bert and Roy Chope, and their close friend from Illinois, George Foster.

If the three of them were not geniuses, they were very close to it. They all had baccalaureate degrees, with honors, in electrical engineering. The Chopes studied at Ohio State, and Foster finished his schooling at the University of Illinois after studying before the war at Harvard. In addition, Bert had an MBA from MIT, and Roy a masters in physics from that same distinguished institution. With the war now over, and their educations completed, the three young veterans were about to become pioneers in the peaceful and industrial exploitation of a new form of energy. Radiation is a mysterious phenomenon of nature, whose dangers were largely unknown in those days. Perhaps as a result of careless handling of radiation substances, including isotopes, two of the three founders of Industrial Nucleonics died at early ages from cancer. And they died rich.

When the war ended, much of the government research in and around Boston dealt with radiation. The three young engineers became privately employed in the Boston area. Bert Chope and George Foster worked for a new, high-tech company known as Tracerlab. Roy Chope had other employment which was equally exciting.

Tracerlab developed several products, none of which was making much of a splash in the market place. Bert and George were not high enough in the company to influence the management, but they both were restless because Tracerlab was not exploiting a prospective product known as the beta gauge, which had come to the attention of Tracerlab.

Bert Chope and George Foster sent several memorandums to the Tracerlab management, extolling the virtues of the beta gauge, which at that time was little more than a concept. No one knew whether it would work or even if it could be built. The purpose of the beta gauge, assuming its existence, was to measure customers' products, without touching the products or in anyway changing their molecular structures.

The beta gauge is about as hard to describe in simple terms as leukemia. The contraption, if it could be engineered, would consist of an isotope, which for safety's sake would be triply encapsulated. A stream of low-level nuclear energy, primarily electrons, would be released by the isotope, and allowed to escape through a fail-safe door in the three capsules. That energy then would pass through the product of the customer to be measured. The customer might want to know the thickness of his product, or its weight or size. After the energy passed through the product, it entered an ion chamber placed on the other side of the product being measured. The rate at which the energy entered the chamber was a function of the mass of the product.

The ion chamber converted the nuclear energy to low-level electrical energy. The electrical energy had to amplified to be of any use. That was accomplished by passing the energy through a sophisticated circuit which was either invented or perfected by Roy Chope. After it was amplified, the intensity of the signal could then be calibrated so that the thickness or other measurement could be read on a dial. In later years after the beta gauge was refined and developed, the read-out might be an impulse sent to a computer, or an impulse sent to a feed-back mechanism, which automatically adjusted the customer's machinery in order to keep the desired measurement constant.

When it became apparent to Chope and Foster that Tracerlab was not interested in developing the concept of the beta gauge, they decided to look into the idea themselves. The problem was they had no money.

Foster came from the north shore of Chicago, and while he had no money he had family friends who did. Bert and Roy Chope were given the job of organizing the new company, to be known as Industrial Nucleonics Corporation, or simply IN, and George took it upon himself to dig up the seed money.

Thought was given to incorporating in either Illinois or Kentucky, the home states of the founders. But because they could not agree on which of those two states, they selected Ohio. Bert and Roy both remembered Columbus from their years at Ohio State. They also remembered that it was the home of the Battelle Memorial Institute, the nearest thing in the Midwest to a "think tank." It was at Battelle that the technology behind the Xerox copying machine was developed.

Bert and Roy Chope parked their car on Capitol Square in Columbus and went to the Secretary of State's office and asked how to form a corporation. It must have been a slow day, because instead of telling them to hire a lawyer, a nice lady in the Secretary of State's office gave them the necessary forms, and some helpful hints on how to proceed. For one thing, they learned that they had to have a typewriter. They also had to know such baffling data as how many shares they could authorize for the minimum filing fee, how many classes of shares to create, whether there would be stock restrictions, how many shares would be issued, the corporate purpose, and who would be the directors and officers.

Foster's job of digging up the money to get this shaky enterprise off the ground was equally daunting. He worked at it for weeks, without any success. Nothing could discourage any of these tigers for long, and before May ended the Chopes had Articles of Incorporation on file, and George found a Chicago financier, a well-known mortgage banker, who was willing to roll the dice for about a half-million dollars. That would not be enough, but it was a start, and the founders were sure the investor would protect his initial investment by coming up with more when it was needed.

The investor retained an experienced Chicago corporation lawyer, who nearly retched when he saw the Articles of Incorporation which Bert and Roy had typed themselves in the back seat of their car. They had copied most of the language out of a 50 year old Pennsylvania law book on corporate forms, none of which they understood.

The lawyer redid the entire incorporation proceedings, and among other things protected his client. The founders had no lawyer to protect their interests, but they had their seed money, which is about all they wanted. They were sure they could make a beta gauge which would function.

The first gauge was made in the small apartment where the three founders lived. The gauge was rudimentary, to put it kindly. The ion chamber, for example, was fashioned out of a tin can. The isotope, which would fuel the device, was more or less borrowed from a private research laboratory in Columbus; in truth, scrounged might be a better word. This was electronic and nucleonic research and development on the cheap.

The weird looking product worked, and the investor came up with more money to design and build proper prototypes. By the time the founders hit the ripe old age of 30, they were millionaires. The investor did well too.

When I joined IN, in 1960, the tenth year of the company, the founders were in their mid 30s, which was my age also. George Foster, a born entrepreneur, left Industrial Nucleonics in 1958 under cordial circumstances, in order to start up a new company of his own. George liked to found companies, but he did not like to operate them. Bert Chope ran IN with considerable enthusiasm and an iron hand, and brother Roy was in charge of product development.

IN needed a lawyer who knew something about litigation, because IN and its founders were up to their ears in a law suit which Tracerlab filed in the US District Court in Boston. The gist of Tracerlab's case was that these three whippersnappers had stolen their property and used it for their own gain. On the surface that argument had a ring of truth to it.

The defense was that Tracerlab had no intent of developing the beta gauge, even though Bert and George had called it to their attention and suggested that it was a winner. IN argued that while the commercially successful beta gauge, which it developed in Ohio, might be conceptually based on Tracerlab's meager proprietary data, the engineering that made the device work was developed by IN with IN money. There was nothing in Tracerlab's file which showed how the ion chamber could be built or made to operate; very little about the amplification circuits; and nothing about the feed-back devices. IN also argued that Tracerlab did not sue until years after the IN beta gauge became commercially successful, and that was too late under the doctrine in Equity known as *laches*.

IN applied for and received several US Patents on its beta gauge, in the mid to late 1950s. Even before Tracerlab filed suit it bought an IN gauge on the market, copied it and began to build one similar to it, which later it sold at a lower price. IN filed a counterclaim alleging patent infringement and antitrust violations. What we had, when I arrived, was a lawsuit and counterclaim which would make the blood of an ambitious lawyer run hot.

When I read the pleadings in the Tracerlab lawsuit I thought I was in heaven. This was not Municipal Court practice. This was bigger than any case ever handled by my former employer in its 80 year history. This was why I went to a good law school. I had checked my last title. Little Jane would no longer have to feel sorry for me.

Not everything was rosy. I had to adjust to corporate life. A private lawyer is a prima donna. People select him because they want him to be their advisor and advocate. They rarely try to second guess him, and seldom do they try to tell him what to do. He proceeds as he thinks he should. The employees at IN never heard of me. They didn't care whether I was the company's lawyer or not. They had played no part in selecting me as counsel. I certainly was not representing them in a personal way. They only wanted to cover their own flanks, to put it politely. They would tell the company lawyer only what they wanted to, and they cast everything in a way calculated to protect their past and to enhance their future.

To some extent the experienced in-house corporate lawyer follows the same scheme. He soon learns that if he gives the management nothing but bad news, they will close those big wooden doors to their offices and stop dealing with him. They do not want to be told they can not do something. They want to know how they can do legally, whatever they wish to do.

One of the hardest things for me to come to grips with was the monthly report. As a well run company, our management expected everyone in the company to prepare a monthly report setting forth the status of everything happening in his office. I was handling a huge law suit which was a potential company-breaker, and I was not about to tell the whole world what the strategy was in that litigation. For one thing, to do so would destroy the attorney-client privilege.

I was reporting to a vice president of administration who did not give up easily on this, or any other of his corporate responsibilities. He said I had to file a report. I said I wouldn't. Bert Chope, the president of the company, said he had to back his vice president. I told him that if he lost his lawsuit he wouldn't have a vice president or a company. We finally reached a dimwitted solution. I agreed to file a monthly report, but we put no time limit upon when it had to be filed. When I left the company after about 53 months, I was 53 months late in filing my first monthly report. To this day, some 36 years later, I receive a Christmas card each year from a former senior officer of IN, upon which he scrawls, "When are you going to have that first monthly report ready?" The strange thing about all of this horse hockey is that everyone at the company was satisfied with this silly arrangement, including me.

IN had several hundred employees when I joined, and more than a thousand when I left. I was about the only corporate officer with a liberal arts education. Many of the engineers had Ph.D degrees, either in nuclear physics or electrical engineering. Nearly everyone, including the salesmen, had masters degrees in business, engineering or both. The level of education was very high.

The legal department, which I headed, consisted of one other lawyer and two patent attorneys. The other lawyer helped with the drafting of documents, the preparation of corporate minutes and reports, and similar work. He had less experience than I, and looked upon me as a mentor. The patent lawyers looked upon me as an ignoramus, and most of the time they were right.

The patent lawyers were themselves ignoramuses, when it came to the subtleties of managing litigation. Until I arrived they were in charge of the Tracerlab case. When I came aboard and changed most of the strategy, I was looked upon as an interloper. Fortunately there wasn't anything they could do about it, and anyway the company was generating so many patent applications that they had little time to cause me trouble. In time we all became friends, and when my strategy began to show good results we worked together as a unit.

My strategy was simple enough. First, I encouraged all of the employees who knew something about the founding and the early days of the company, to write a confidential memorandum to me telling me everything they knew. I assured everyone that only I and our trial lawyers would have access to these memos. If they thought that the three founders were thieves, I wanted them to say so, and explain why. Second, I encouraged everyone to stop trying to be of help in winning the case, and to get back to their normal work. I explained why litigating a significant law suit is an art; and assured them that when I needed help, which I was sure I would, I would ask for it. Third, I began to cooperate to a much larger extent with our Boston trial lawyers.

Before I arrived, IN retained the Boston law firm of Hale and Dorr. James D. St.Clair, Esq., a senior lawyer in that firm and the best trial lawyer I have ever worked with, was assigned to our case. I went to Boston immediately, and was shocked to learn that St.Clair was considering resigning, because he did not have the freedom he needed to handle the case. Bert Chope had even suggested that Jim St.Clair should file a monthly report.

St. Clair was a nationally known trial lawyer. He was at the elbow of the celebrated Joseph Welch, when the two of them represented the Army in the widely publicized "Army-McCarthy Hearings" in 1954. Mr. Welch achieved immortality among trial lawyers, and many Americans, when he looked Senator Joe McCarthy squarely in the eye and said, "Senator, have you no shame …"

Jim St.Clair was sitting next to Mr. Welch in those famous TV moments. On my first of many trips to Hale and Dorr, I visited Mr. Welch's office which was preserved as a shrine. In 1974, Jim St.Clair again became widely recognized throughout the United States, when he became the personal trial lawyer for President Nixon.

St.Clair confided to me on my first visit that personally he liked the Chope brothers, but from his point of view they were pains in the neck. "They want to try their own law suit," he complained, "and they want me to work exclusively on their case and do only what they tell me to."

We got that mess straightened out in a hurry. I had private meetings with Bert and Roy, and after a heated discussion or two we agreed that except for myself no one in our company, including the two of them, would have any personal contact with Hale and Dorr, unless the contact were initiated by the law firm. I was to be the collection agency for all bright ideas, and I was to be the lawyer who decided what went to Hale and Dorr and when it was to go.

It was natural that this strategy was widely misunderstood throughout the company, and especially by the Chopes. I pleaded with them to try it out anyway, and when it began to show good results after less than a year, there was no further resistance to it. I had to demonstrate that I was not trying to build an empire for myself, upon the turf of someone else.

Tracerlab was not my only responsibility. In 1962 Bert Chope decided to initiate a stock option plan to compensate all the officers and employees who were in key positions. He had about 120 persons in mind, many of whom had been promised the opportunity to own stock when they accepted employment with IN. In my case, the probability that I would become a shareholder was dangled before me. I realized that the stock could be valuable some day, but as the breadwinner in a family of five, I was more thrilled with the fact that my starting salary was significantly higher than my earnings in Springfield.

Because the participants were so numerous, the stock option plan was a "public offering." This meant that we had to file a registration statement with the Securities and Exchange Commission in Washington, and to it had to be appended freshly certified financial statements, and a dozen other ponderous exhibits. This was a mammoth undertaking, and the work was far too specialized for me. The project had to be coordinated with a financial printer, and there were none in the Columbus area equipped to handle such a stock offering. We hired a prominent Chicago law firm to do the work, and I supervised the endeavor from Columbus.

The offering of options was made in 1963, and Marg and I received a generous opportunity to buy IN stock. We bought all we could afford, and sold the shares after I left the company for about 13 times our purchase price. Looking back, I can see that we never again had any financial worries from the day we sold that stock. We were not rich by any means, but we had all we needed for the remainder of our lives.

Early in 1964, I knew that ultimately I would have to leave IN. I was having no major professional problems. The litigation was slogging along in fine style, but never fast enough to satisfy the Chopes. Both sides were taking depositions and my responsibility was to prepare our witnesses. I collected the documents which were germane to each witness, and went over the testimony with him. I gave the usual cautions about not volunteering facts, and stressed the importance of being impeccably honest.

In the spring of 1963 we filed a motion in the US District Court for a summary judgment, and St.Clair was kind enough to let me come to Boston and present part of the oral argument. We won, but within weeks our judgment was appealed by Tracerlab to The United States Court of Appeals for the First Circuit. Again, with Jim St.Clair's encouragement, I presented part of the oral argument on appeal. It seemed like a long way back to my cases in the Springfield Municipal Court.

Our judgment was reversed, which was very hard for me to explain to the Chope brothers. They always regarded the Tracerlab litigation as a personal attack upon their honesty. When the First Circuit reversed, Bert and Roy wondered why St.Clair and I had not called "character" witnesses in their behalf. Of course, on such an appeal we called no witnesses at all.

My problems arose out of my personality. I was not cut out to be a domesticated staff lawyer at a corporation. This was no reflection upon IN, or the good people who worked there. Other lawyers love this kind of steady, reliable employment. They can have it. I like the swashbuckling life of the private lawyer. I prefer to fuss with lawyers and judges, rather than with electrical engineers.

Marg and I and the children liked living in Columbus. Soon after we left Springfield we had an opportunity to return. Mr. John Durfey died of a heart attack within months after I left his firm. Mr. Oscar T. Martin, the head of the new firm, Martin, Browne, Hull & Harper, sent me a handwritten letter inviting me to come back. I would be a partner and would earn the same salary I was being paid at IN. After careful thought of all the consequences, Marg and I decided not to look back. We have never regretted that decision.

In the summer of 1960 we bought a house on two acres near the west bank of the Scioto river, five miles outside the city. The day we moved in we were again flat broke, and in debt more than ever. My earnings were decent, and it wasn't long until we were making two mortgage payments each month. We enjoyed the opportunities of the capital city, and yet lived in a quiet atmosphere in the country. Today the city extends beyond our property for 15 miles, and the neighborhood is no longer quiet. We sold the house in 1990.

We became very close to Richard and Grace Gantt, who lived near us. Dick needed a job and I introduced him to Industrial Nucleonics. Before long he was operating one of IN's most sophisticated milling machines. Grace adopted us. Without her help, Marg could not have earned her masters in sociology at Ohio State. The Gantts moved in when we travelled without the children. Dick fixed everything that either rattled, squeaked or refused to go on or off. Our kids turned out well because they did not want to disappoint Gracie and Dick.

When we concluded that corporate life was not for us, we decided to try to find something in Columbus because we liked our home and lifestyle. All three children were doing well in school, and the thought of leaving their friends was something they preferred not to talk about.

Our dilemma was solved in the summer of 1964, when I received a telephone call from a senior lawyer in a well-known Columbus law firm. He and a couple of his partners wanted to have dinner with me to talk over the possibility of my joining their firm as a partner. I was surprised they ever heard of me. Someone at IN had spoken of me to one of their partners. They checked further, including some inquiry in Springfield, and decided to ask me to dinner. I visited their offices, which were swanky compared to my austere facilities at IN. The share of profits which would be mine was impressive, and I was about to accept their offer, when it dawned on me that I owed some professional responsibilities to IN. They had treated me quite well, and here I was about to abandon them.

I decided that I would discuss the realities of leaving with Jim St. Clair. He had become my mentor, and friend. A couple of times I stayed at his house during my many trips to Boston. We often played golf together in Columbus and in Boston.

St. Clair was kind, and said that my leaving IN would increase his burdens. He thought, on balance, that I had to do what was best for me and my family. He suggested that I discuss the situation with John Eckler, Esq., a distinguished Columbus lawyer who was a member of the board of directors of IN. I had worked closely with Mr. Eckler and several other lawyers in his firm, from the time I arrived at IN.

Mr. Eckler was beyond all question the finest lawyer I ever met. In a later chapter I intend to tell you quite a bit about him. He was a moral philosopher. His understanding of my problems at IN was thorough and complete. More than once, over the years, he had gone directly to both Chopes when I could not make them understand why we had to do something, or stop doing something. They often would listen to John Eckler when they would not listen to me.

When I tried to reach Mr. Eckler, I learned that he was vacationing in Canada. Senator John W. Bricker, former governor of Ohio and former US Senator, John's senior partner, gave me his address, and I sent a letter outlining the offer before me, and asking for his advice.

I received a telephone call immediately. Mr. Eckler told me bluntly that under no circumstances was I to accept any employment from anyone. "You," he said loudly and clearly, "are going to become a partner in my law firm just as soon as I can work out the details." A couple of days later I received a letter from him in which he confirmed his telephone call. Based on the call and letter, I respectfully declined the other offer of employment.

Upon his return, Mr. Eckler explained to me that the problem was how to break this news to Bert Chope without losing a client for his law firm. Mr. Eckler's firm had represented IN since about 1958. At the same time I was straightening out the relationships with Jim St.Clair, I was strengthening the relationships with Mr. Eckler. I insisted that we copy Mr. Eckler with all the evidence and correspondence we sent to St.Clair. Even my confidential memorandums to Jim St.Clair, which I was not distributing to anyone at IN, were sent to Mr. Eckler. I thought that we should have the benefit of Mr. Eckler's thinking on all we were doing. The attorney-client privilege was preserved, and in the event of my sudden death, there was another lawyer in addition to St. Clair, who would be up to speed and ready to go. Mr. Eckler was pleased with this procedure.

The position which John Eckler took with Bert Chope was that I was going to leave anyway, and it would be better if I joined his firm because then I would be available if needed. He suggested that I could continue to manage the Tracerlab litigation from my new office. The two Chopes agreed readily to this arrangement. They were happy with it. My leaving was nothing personal. We remained friends until their deaths. But without me hanging around and picking at everything, they could do things the way they wanted to. They could even insist that St.Clair file a monthly report, if they wanted to. To their way of thinking they must have been doing something right without all of my interference, because their combined wealth approached $100 million. Hard to argue with that.

I made my final career change, as a lawyer, in November of 1964, when I became a partner in the Columbus law firm of Bricker, Evatt, Barton, Eckler & Neihoff, which a few years after I came aboard, mercifully shortened its name to Bricker & Eckler.

BUT FIRST ... GOLF

I AM ANXIOUS TO TELL YOU OF MY PARTNERSHIP in one of the finest law firms in Ohio, but first I want to tell you of my lifelong passion for the greatest game ever conceived by the human mind. For a few minutes, now, I speak of golf.

No one knows for sure when golf first was played, or where. There was a game with a similar name played in the Netherlands prior to the 12th Century. A ball was hit with a stick, but the joy was in the hitting. The goal was not to put the ball into a hole in the ground. Without putting, which is about half of the game, that could not have been golf.

My guess, shared by many historians, is that on a moonlit night on one of those verdant Scottish hills which roll gently southward from St. Andrews toward the Firth of Forth, a lonely shepherd was bored stiff. Without knowing what a treat he was providing for future generations, he took a swing at a rock with his crook. The rock holed out in a sheep bunker. Golf was born. There has never been a bored shepherd, or golfer, since that sweet and silent night.

There are few sports like golf. It is not a team sport. You are on your own. If you win you get the glory. If you lose, you can't blame anyone else, except maybe Mother Nature or the Weather Man. I have no desire to start a political argument here, but I feel compelled to report that virtually all PGA Tour players are

Republicans. They are not looking for social security, and they hate all forms of taxation. They just want to be left alone so they can play golf.

There is a myth that golf is the game of rich people. Most golfers do keep their car payments current, and few of them are being pursued by bill collectors; but they are not rich. There are upwards of 16,000 golf courses in the United States, and anyone who wants to, can play on about 13,500 of them. You also can play on most of the other 2,500 if you are staying at the resort or spa where they are located, or if you can afford the outrageous greens fees charged by a few of them.

One of the most famous golf courses in the world is Pebble Beach Golf Links, in California. It is wide open to everyone; but the catch is that for the past ten years the greens fee has hovered around $300 per player per round. If you go there with three guests, and use caddies, you have pretty well kicked away $1500. Arnold Palmer, and some other well-healed investors, bought the place in 1999 for $850 million, and the rumor is that the greens fee soon may double. You better hurry.

I became addicted to golf in the late 1930s when I caddied for my mother. She was a member of the Hocking Hills Golf Club south of Logan, in southeastern Ohio, where we lived. I enjoyed my life as a caddie, but unfortunately I snickered once too often and got fired on the spot.

The county prosecuting attorney Mother worked for was Mr. Gerald Lanning. When he learned I was available, he let me caddie for him. He knew I wouldn't snicker at his game, because my mother's livelihood was at stake. He paid 25 cents a round. Big money. By the time I reached junior high age, I wanted to play myself. Mother let me use her clubs, which were about the right size for me. Jumping ahead a little, when we found that Mother was suffering from cancer shortly before her death in 1993, I refinished her old fairway wood in my hobby shop, which I maintain in our home. I had it shining like it did when it came out of the MacGregor factory 60-years earlier. She was thrilled to see it again. She insisted on taking in out in the yard for one last mighty swing. Before she made it swish she said, "Now, don't you snicker."

You had to play baseball in my home town to keep from being run out of the county. This interfered with my available time for golf, but I really liked it. The best golfer in our high school was my friend, Ray Lohr. When I began to think my game was coming along, Ray would just demolish my confidence. I never gave up, because golfers never give up. We always are able to find some reason when we have a bad round, and we always are ready to try to do better.

To give you an idea of the extent of my addiction, when I was in law school, and Marg and I were awaiting the birth of our first baby, our funds were just about gone. One day as I was riding a Chicago street car west on Irving Park, on the way to our one-room apartment which we could scarcely afford, I noticed a golf shop was having a sale. I got off at the next corner, and walked back. I found that for $35 I could buy a matched set of top-of-the-line MacGregors consisting of three woods, eight irons and a wedge. Because I hesitated for a second, the merchant threw in a new golf bag with matching head covers.

I called my brother-in-law, John Hanna, who is twice the golf fanatic I have been most of my life, and asked him whether I should spend the $35 at such a critical time. He said I would be an idiot not to.

Margaret understood. I assure you that at this moment somewhere in this world there is a golfer who is trying to figure out how to explain to his wife that he just bought a new $500 driver. Prices have gone up a little, but the malady lingers on.

I didn't play much in college or law school. When St. Peter hears how busy I was at that time, he will forgive me. St. Peter is a scratch player, you know. So were all the Apostles. You can read the Bible from cover to cover, and you will not find any evidence that the Carpenter From Nazareth did not golf on Thursday afternoons.

I played up a storm anytime I was at the Hanna farm. We had a course nearby called Blackhawk, and I was there so much that some people thought I was on the maintenance crew. I played in Springfield too. I was working day and night you may remember, but I managed to visit Snyder Park golf course at least once during the week, and once on the weekends.

When I joined Industrial Nucleonics it was golf that helped me keep my sanity. Several of the IN employees were good players, and they took me to the Ohio State golf courses, where many of them had playing privileges and could bring a guest. I traveled constantly, and almost always took my clubs, if I were going to be gone for more than a day or two.

Very soon I will be telling you about my first days at the Bricker law firm. You will learn that my schedule was overwhelming. Because I was approaching 40, and had not been exercising on a regular basis, I was beginning to acquire that bodily spread which, as any doctor who plays golf will tell you, can be controlled best by golfing on a regular basis. It's a good way to control a hot temper too.

The life of the lawyer in private practice affords more opportunity for indulging an addiction such as golf, than does the life of the domesticated, corporate lawyer. The vice president of administration at Industrial Nucleonics, to whom I reported because I couldn't avoid it, was against all forms of exercise except jumping at incorrect conclusions. Ironically, he was of Scottish ancestry, but his family must have lived in the bottom of a hole rather than high in the glens. He understood neither golf nor golfers, and was oblivious to our special needs. One of the reasons he and I never got along well was that I never "sneaked" away to play golf. I always enjoyed watching his jaw drop open in amazement, so I always told him right to his face when I was leaving for the course. If he were not around, I left a note for him: Gone Golfing, Have a Good Day! In contrast, no one at the Bricker law firm cared a bit whether I golfed or not. They knew I would take care of our clients, and after I did I was a free man.

I found that a few of our clients enjoyed playing golf at Muirfield Village, and it was fun to accommodate them. There wasn't a lot of smoozing of clients. Never did I take anyone golfing in order to woo him as a client. The probate judge invited me to his club one afternoon, and I would have been a fool to disappoint him.

It is a myth that golf provides an environment for big-time deal making, and for developing clients. I am speaking with some authority when I tell you that is poppycock. Never in the history of this honorable sport have two tycoons stood side by side in a sand bunker and one said to the other, "Let's merge." Never has a merchant prince said, "Nice shot, will you be my lawyer?"

When newly emancipated women began to enter the world of business and professional life in the 1970s and 1980s, they often used this myth to try to convince private golf clubs that they should not be placed at the bottom of the waiting lists for admission. Sometimes they even threatened litigation. The admission committee members were all male golf nuts, and they knew that their greatest fear was that all of their clients would be stolen away by the woman lawyers, while the men were out playing golf. So they let the women into the golf clubs by the hundreds, in order to keep an eye on them. It wasn't the fear of lawsuits that brought about this cultural revolution.

Having taken a good-natured swipe at womanhood, I should dispel yet another golfing myth. During the more than 60 years I have been hanging around golf courses on a regular basis, I have not once been the victim of slow play by a woman golfer. I mentioned Muirfield Village Golf Club near Columbus. If you know golf you know that for 25 years it has ranked near the top of the best courses in the United States. We have many women players, and they are a delight.

I hope the day will come when golf in our country will be a family sport, as it has been in Scotland for several hundred years. Grandmothers play in Scotland, and they play well. As our emancipated women grow older, and perhaps wiser, the same thing should happen here.

After I had practiced with the Bricker firm about six years or so, we began to handle the estate of the late Charles Nicklaus, the father of Jack Nicklaus. A contemporary of mine, William Leighner, an experienced probate lawyer, had the primary responsibility. Because the estate had some significant corporate law problems, Bill asked me to give him a hand now and then.

This is how I met Jack Nicklaus. That friendship led to my getting some assignments from Jack's vast and growing empire. Upon the Nicklaus recommendation, I became the attorney for a PGA Tour player, John Cook. This may have caused the Western Golf Association in Golf, Illinois (how's that for a classy name for a village?) to ask me to become a director. Then the United States Golf Association invited me to become a Committee Member. When Chris Perry, another fine Tour player heard about all of this, he sought some legal advice, and later appointed me his PGA Tour Player-Manager, a responsibility I still enjoy.

Before you could say "Has Anyone Seen Hoskins This Afternoon?" I was a player of sorts, a lawyer for players, and a golf administrator. These activities brought me into contact with many of the golfing powers of our country, and eventually led to my becoming a golf writer, after I retired from law. The whole thing was a domino effect, started by the death of the unfortunate Mr. Nicklaus, who died much too young.

I have noticed that many people have a kind feeling about the lawyers who handle their parents' estates, assuming of course that the estates are handled well. That was the case with Jack Nicklaus. Bill Leighner handled everything smoothly, and fortunately I didn't mess up anything. As a result, we made a friend. When I went to PGA Tour events in the 1970s and thereafter, Jack would see me sometimes in the galleries and give me a friendly greeting.

One year at the Masters, I was standing in a huge gallery, most of whom were badly wanting a Nicklaus autograph. He saw me and came over for a visit while the green ahead of him cleared. After Jack played on, a particularly ebullient fan slapped me on the back and said, "Well, if it is the best I can do I will settle for an autograph from a friend of Jack Nicklaus." It is the only autograph I ever gave.

There was another occasion at the Masters, this time after I became golf writer, when Jack broke my heart. We were all standing around in the rain waiting for him to tee off on the tenth hole. The area was full of little kids with autograph books. I had watched him come in on the ninth hole, and because I have been pretty close to his game for years, I knew that something was not right. After a few moments I went into the clubhouse to see if I could round out my education, and bumped into Jack. He confided that he had a very sore back, and was withdrawing from the tournament.

My heart was broken because there was not a way in the world that I could make a dime out of this bit of sensational information, which the entire world of golf would know within five minutes. Golf writers remember lost opportunities like that.

Being close to Jack Nicklaus always has been a treat. I have driven around North Palm Beach with him in my car, and watched the motorists wave and toot their horns. I have sat on the turf just outside his swing zone and placed balls on a tee for him, hour after hour, while he practiced. I sat in Younger Hall at the University of St. Andrews and watched him become a Doctor of Laws. My step-father, Matt Chesser, used to try to kid me a little by putting down Nicklaus. He would refer to him as Fat Jack, as did some members of the media when Jack first began to stick it to their idol, Arnold Palmer, on a regular basis. Finally, Matt went with me to a tournament, and I introduced him to Jack. That night I overheard Matt telling my mother: "He is the nicest man you would ever want to meet … Clayton really *does* know him … He is just like any other regular fellow …" I never heard another word around our house which belittled the greatest golfer ever to swing a club in the entire history of the sport.

I attended a professional golf event for the first time in 1957. The galleries were very small in those days, and we walked right out on the fairways with the golfers. There was no PGA Tour then, as we now know it. The touring professionals were a division of the PGA of America. The PGA still exists as a strong influence upon professional golf, but primarily for the benefit of the club pro. It has much less to do with touring professionals, than does the PGA Tour, a separate entity.

My first professional event was the American Golf Classic, which was sponsored by an impresario from Chicago, Mr. George S. May. He became famous, and forever dear to the hearts of the Tour players, by offering a first prize at his tournament of $50,000. To put that number into focus: in 1957 there were 32 official events, and the total of those purses was $820,360. That averages out to a total purse for each event of about $25,600. The winner often got 20 per cent of the purse, or about $5,000. It is easy to see why Mr. May was a hero in the eyes of the pros, men like Sam Snead, Ben Hogan, Jimmy Demaret, Bob Toski, Julius Boros and the up and coming Arnold Palmer, the leading money winner for the first time in 1958.

The leading money winner in 1957 was a much less famous player, Dick Mayer. He won George S. May's $50,000 while I watched. That same summer he won the US Open at Inverness in Toledo, Ohio. Despite his success, his earnings in 1957 were a little more than $65,000. In 1999 we had four tournaments in which the first prize was a million dollars. That's for each tournament, mind you. That record will be broken in 2000.

In 1957 there was very little TV at golf tournaments, but there was radio. George S. May's event was covered by a program known as Monitor, on the NBC network. I happened to be standing a few feet away, as the Monitor sportscaster was interviewing Mrs. Dick Mayer. He asked all the standard questions including the inevitable, "How does it feel to have your husband win $50,000?"

Mrs. Mayer startled the world of golf, and her husband too I will bet, with an answer that was the headline on every sports page in America the next morning. She said, "Well, it would be nice if we could keep all of it, but we have to share it with the others."

My eyes popped open, and I was not to become a journalist for another 30 years. The NBC announcer knew he had a scoop. With a few more quick questions, he developed the story that Dick Mayer and several other prominent players had formed a syndicate, and agreed among themselves that they would share the prize if any of them won it. Mayer got to keep $12,500 instead of $50,000. Fortunately, this arrangement did not violate any state or federal law, and there was no PGA rule against it at that time. Politicians and pundits pontificated about this evil, for the next few weeks.

About 30 years later, just as I was starting to write articles for golf magazines on a regular basis, I was playing golf in San Diego. I saw a sign in the pro shop at Torrey Pines, which said that the 1957 US Open champion, Dick Mayer, was available for lessons. I didn't call him about lessons, but I did try to reach him because I wanted to know exactly what he said to his wife as soon as she got off the radio. I learned that they were now divorced, so I dropped the subject.

My life in golf has been full and satisfying. Except for the year my mother died, I have been to every Masters since the late

1970s. I had access to four badges in the early days, and owned a Cessna 210 which could get my friends and me to Augusta in less than two hours. We dropped into Bush Field, parked right next to Arnie's big jet, rented a car for the week, and contributed mightily to the Georgia economy.

Augusta was a sleepy little, dusty village posing as a small city when I started going there. The Masters was a big event to golfers, but nothing like it is to everyone today. My impression is that it is now out of hand. When the Masters started in 1934 it was not popular with the public. Badges for the week were five dollars, and they couldn't give them away. A couple of years ago, Marg and I were leaving the course late in the day on Thursday, the first day of the tournament. We were approached by a gentleman who offered us $4500 in cash for each of our badges. Keep in mind, there were only three days of golf remaining. I have heard that badges now bring $7500 for the week.

I no longer have access to any badges. The gentleman who gave me his for many years died, and his badges died with him. I have a permanent media badge issued to me by the PGA Tour, which will get me into any other golf tournament in the world. It is not worth a dime at the Masters. The fact that I am the Player-Manager for contestants in the Masters, also is not worth a dime. My eleven years of service to the USGA as a committee member, is worthless. Sometimes magazines I write for have arranged media credentials for me, and many of my friends often provide a badge for a day or two here and there. Without fail, every year I send off a letter to the nice folks who conduct the Masters. I cite my contributions to golf and plead for a badge, which I am willing to buy. No luck. There just are none, unless you want to pay the outlandish prices to the scalpers. I know of cases where contestants, actually playing in the event, have been unable to get enough badges for members of their families.

Years ago I was taking some depositions in one of our major, southern cities. The attorney on the other side was a kind of a prissy fellow who would remind you of "Frasier's" brother Niles Crane. During a break we started talking golf. He didn't really know much about golf. If you have been around awhile you can spot a wannabee golfer. If he is a golfer he will ask about your USGA Index, not your handicap. He will have a right hand more tanned than his left, because of wearing a golf glove. This guy was a big talker. I was flabbergasted when he made the outlandish statement that he was a member of the Augusta National Golf Club. I remarked that I would have to see some proof of that. Sure enough, he had a current membership card, one of the few I have ever seen. It was right then and there that I decided that Augusta National, and the Masters, were not keeping the proper company.

There was a time when the galleries at the Masters were the most knowledgeable in the world. They were quiet, orderly and did not yell "nice shot" while the ball was still in the air. Those days are gone. Many of the people attending today have inherited their badges from their parents and grandparents. They do not have the understanding of golf their ancestors had. It has become a social event. I am told that the Super Bowl, the World Series, and the Final Four suffer the same fate. A man who owns a bank and wouldn't know Tiger Woods if he patted him on the back, has a far greater chance of attending the Masters, than does a high school teacher who loves golf and can tell you Tiger's shoe size. Or a guy like myself.

Things have changed around Augusta too. I have stayed at the same motel over the years. In 1975 the daily rate was $18 to $20, every week of the year except Masters week, when the price was jacked up to $34. Today the exact room goes for $175 a night, four-night minimum, no refunds. No wonder the galleries are boisterous. They are mad at being had.

I think the best tournament in the world today is The Open (known in the US as the "British" Open) when it is played in Scotland. When it is played in England, there usually are traffic and parking problems. There can be some of those in Scotland, but the people around Troon, Turnberry and St. Andrews have so much experience in conducting tournaments that they seem to know how to overcome most of the problems.

The 1997 Open at Troon, won by the American Justin Leonard, was the best run golf event I have attended. My son Jim and I did not have a convenient hotel. In fact it was 25 miles away. But when we got within 10 miles of Royal Troon we were ushered into different traffic lanes depending upon the kind of badge we had. I drove all the way to the media car park without touching my brakes. Leaving was as easy.

The other two "major" tournaments, The US Open and the PGA Championship, are becoming more and more inconvenient to attend because of the enormous galleries. The United States Golf Association conducts the US Open at a different golf course each year. It takes about 2000 to 2500 well-trained volunteers to make any tournament a success. The USGA wrote the book on how to conduct a tournament, but the problem is that they are staffed with volunteers who may not have worked previously on the course where the tournament is being played. In Olympia, near San Francisco, in 1998, I noticed that the volunteers got better each day. On Sunday they were veterans.

At Royal Troon I struck up a conversation with a volunteer on the fourth hole. He was as knowledgeable about golf as a person can get. He told me that he had worked the fourth hole at every Open played at Troon since Tom Weiskopf won in 1973. That is a big advantage over the volunteer who shows up at a US Open to help park cars, and has never seen the parking lot.

It would be impossible to overstate the importance of the USGA to our sport. Nearly everything directly, or indirectly, good about golf is due to the influence of the USGA. In some quarters they are looked upon as stuffed shirts, but that attitude is taken mostly by persons who are unaware of the mission of the USGA. The stuffed shirts do not serve to make golfers happy.

Their goal is to keep golf pure. In conjunction with their counterpart in Scotland, The Royal and Ancient Golf Club of St. Andrews, they write and enforce the Rules of Golf. It always has seemed significant to me, that the first section in the Rules deals with etiquette and courtesy on the course. No other sport will admit being that genteel.

I am impressed as well by the fact that, except for a small staff, every official at the USGA receives no compensation, and pays his own way. I served as a member of the Junior Amateur Championship Committee of the USGA for a little more than 11 years. During that time I was the USGA official in charge of conducting the junior qualifier tournament in central Ohio. Because we were playing at Muirfield Village, our tournament was well attended. We usually attracted close to 400 of the best junior golfers in the country, who came to our event from 15 to 20 states. The next largest USGA junior qualifier in the US attracted fewer than 100 young golfers.

The fourth "major" each year has the toughest field, because all of the players are professionals. For a few years the PGA Championship suffered because the staff at the PGA was not selecting sites which could handle a major tournament. Any golf tournament is better attended if it is played near a large population center, and it suffers most if it is played at a venue which may be famous, but inaccessible and isolated from hotels and motels. In recent years the PGA officials have wised up and played at Medinah (Chicago), Winged Foot (New York City), and Riviera (Los Angeles). In 1996 the PGA Championship was played at a course in Louisville which the PGA owns, known as Valhalla. The fans showed up from all over the middle west, including the hills and hollows of Kentucky and West Virginia. As a result, the PGA is returning to that Jack Nicklaus-designed course again in the year 2000.

The fact that golf is on a roll, and never been more popular, gives me great pleasure. The success of the sport does cause any dedicated golfer to wonder where everyone is going to play in the coming years. The membership at most good private golf clubs is filled and there are long waiting lists for admission. One of the best clubs in central Ohio is the Scioto Country Club, where Jack Nicklaus learned the game as a youngster. Scioto has been overshadowed a little by the proximity of Muirfield Village Golf Club, but Scioto is a special place. It hosted the US Open in 1926, and the Ryder Cup matches in 1931. A partner in my law firm who wanted to become a member at Scioto waited more than 20 years for his name to float to the top of the list.

The jam at the public courses is much worse, because there is no 20-year or other final end to it. It just goes on and on. Reservations are booked weeks in advance, and if you do not have a reservation, you must get in line at the first tee and wait for a no-show. If you drop by a well-cared-for public course any time before noon, you are likely to see several dozen golfers waiting for just one cancellation. In the late afternoon the lines may get longer, because many public courses lower the greens fees in the evenings. Most public courses, even those which are not particularly well maintained, are in use from before sun up until total darkness. This is the case even in bad weather.

So the question is: where are all the millions of new golfers going to play? Are we going to say that a person who has been waiting for admission for 10 to 15 years, at a private club, must give way to another person who can make a good case for discrimination? Are we going to tell a golfer at a public course, who has been standing in line for three or four hours, that he must stand aside for a new golfer who wishes to learn the game?

Building new golf courses, perhaps twice as many as we have now, is not going to thrill the environmentalists, many of whom believe that our existing courses are using too much land and water. Finding a compromise with the environmentalists may be possible, and could be the answer. Several years ago, Nicklaus came up with the idea of developing a golf ball which won't go so far, so that a golf course could be built on fewer acres. Maybe that is the answer. Some kind of a simple handicap system which will determine who can play on certain courses, or at different times of the day, may be the solution. Bigger and better practice facilities, where new golfers can go to learn the game before they actually play on a course, is worth thinking through. Further attempts to get people to play faster are essential. In the end golf may be saved by a combination of many solutions.

Much of the current frenzy came with Tiger Woods, who joined the PGA Tour in the summer of 1996. Never in the history of golf has a player brought so much talent, not even Nicklaus or Palmer. Winning one of our national amateur championships conducted by the USGA, is a singular achievement. Jack Nicklaus became famous for winning the US Amateur Championship twice. He never won the US Junior Championship. Palmer never won the Junior, and he won the Amateur just once.

Tiger Woods won the Junior Championship three times in a row, and the Amateur Championship three more times in a row. Soon after he became a professional, he began to dominate the PGA Tour just as he had amateur golf. He won the 1997 Masters by 12 strokes over whomever came in second. In 1999 he won his second major tournament, the PGA Championship. He has earned in excess of two million dollars in prize money each full year he has played. In 1999 alone, Tiger Woods won six tournaments, and earned more prize money than Jack Nicklaus earned in his entire career, one of the longer careers in the history of the sport. Woods has earned more since he joined the tour in late 1996, than Nicklaus and Palmer together earned in their combined careers, which date back to the 1950s. Before he hit his first shot on the Tour, at age 19 and a half, Woods booked at least $60 million in product endorsements. The exact amount is unknown, and some experts who are privy to this type of information, insist that the figure may be closer to $100 million. Most of his endorsement contracts are short term, and it is predicted that when they are renegotiated in a few years, he will become the first athlete, in any sport, to command a Billion dollars in product endorsements. That is not a misprint.

A good case can be made that Tiger Woods should not have turned pro so young. In June of 1996 he finished his second year at Stanford, one of our distinguished institutions of higher education. What an opportunity it is for a youngster to have the chance to study at such a place. There are Stanford students who are not eating regularly, so that they can afford to study there. Woods was on a full ride, four year scholarship. The ages from 18 to 22 are so critical for any young person, and particularly so for a college student. This is the time when the world opens up. Not only is the mind sharpened, but so is the total person. Woods missed a big part of this, in order to became wealthy beyond all belief. Perhaps that was enough for him. I expressed these sentiments in a piece I wrote in 1996 for a golf magazine, and the editors received many letters from readers. The gist of every letter was the same: how could anyone expect Tiger Woods to turn down that kind of money? Another reader came to the point more directly: what would that SOB, meaning me of course, do in the same circumstances? I honestly do not know what I would do. I think I was the only SOB (read: golf writer) who thought Tiger should think it over; but then of course I am also the only golf writer who has served as a trustee of a liberal arts college continuously since the year 1963.

My major reason for hoping that Tiger Woods would wait a year or so before turning professional, was my fear of what his presence would do to golf. My worst fears came true. People who never heard of golf joined in the frenzy. Golf writers called it Tigermania. To me it was a disaster. An 89-year old friend, an Episcopalian clergyman who suffers from emphysema, called me and proclaimed proudly that he was going to "take up" golf. He thought it would please me, to hear of his decision. Take up golf? What on earth for? He would need two caddies, one for his bag and one for his air tank. It makes no sense.

The people who managed Tiger Woods, when he joined the Tour, made no sense either. The event was tainted with racism. Woods is not an African-American in a pure sense. His father is, but his mother is not. Nevertheless, the advertising agency handling him, made a big thing out of his minority status. We were bombarded with TV spots, and full page ads, which showed underprivileged children, most of them African-American, all proclaiming "I am Tiger Woods." Woods appeared at a press conference and highlighted the fact that despite his talent and success as an amateur, there were many golf courses where he would not be welcome.

Except for the talent and success part, I could have made the same statement. But I wouldn't do it—not even to sell over-priced sneakers.

With Tigermania came an unparalleled interest in golf on television. There is a distinct possibility that eventually TV could ruin golf. This comes as a surprise to people who know only TV golf. The fact is that what you see on the tube is, at most, an imitation of golf. If it were a sincere imitation it could be forgiven; but it is money-driven, and completely divorced from an intent to be faithful to the sport.

TV golf should be honest. The men on camera are good people, and they know golf from long experience as players and lovers of the game. Behind the scenes for each telecast is a producer, and while I don't know as many of them as well as I do the on-camera personalities, my guess is that they are sensible persons too. Behind the producers there are legions of ambitious network officials, many of whom have degrees in marketing. These marketeers are dominated by the sponsors. The sponsors want to sell, sell and sell, and put on a good show. To these salesmen, Golf is less a sport and more an entertainment vehicle.

So we see a lot of Tiger Woods. If he is winning, which is most of the time, he is on constantly. If he is not playing well, he is on camera much of the time explaining why he is not playing well. If he is not in the tournament, we get a lot of commentary on why he is not in the tournament; and endless clips from the last tournament which he was in.

The announcers must produce drama. If there is any on the course, they show it, along with a replay or two. If there is no drama, they create some. Every hole is described in all of its horror. Two-foot putts are said to be four-foot putts, because there is less drama in a two-foot putt. Every shot is "the most difficult shot in the history of the sport." There will "never be another shot like that one." There is " … very little green to work with," they tell us over and over. The rough is too thick. The greens are too fast. The landing areas are too small. This is the most; that is the greatest. What is the USGA trying to do? For heavens sakes don't go to the bathroom, you might miss something sensational Tiger is about to attempt.

There are other, less obvious, marketing ploys at work during the televising of a tournament. As an example: the current scores for every player in the tournament are available to the producer at all times. But he won't show them. There is a status board on the tube, with room for the seven best scores. That is referred to as Page One. Sometimes the producer will flash on Page Two for an instant, and if our reflexes are quick enough, we can learn the scores of the next seven players, for a total of fourteen players.

Those are fourteen players out of the 150 who are playing on Thursday and Friday, and the 70 players and ties who are playing on Saturday and Sunday. The marketing reason why only seven or fourteen scores are shown, is that the sponsors are tempting you to keep watching. If you learn the score of your favorite player, you may turn off the TV.

There is another trick associated with this. If the last player on Page One is, for example, three under par, and Page Two is not shown, you will come to the logical conclusion that there are no other players at three under. You may find to your consternation, when Page Two finally is shown for a second or two, that your favorite player also is three under. There just wasn't room for him on Page One. Dirty Pool.

The justification for all of this chicanery by the ratings-driven network officials, goes like this: what the heck, most people only want to know how the top players are doing; and anyway every now and then we run all the scores on a banner at the bottom of the screen.

The fact is that sometimes you have to wait as much as 45 minutes for that banner, and that is exactly what the marketeers want you to do. Don't touch that dial. Near the end of the tournament, the banner is run less frequently.

For persons with experience in attending golf tournaments, the TV show is not harmful, because they can laugh at it as they measure it against reality. The person who knows only TV golf, is getting a jaded view, and nine times out of ten doesn't even know it.

I know nothing about basketball, football or much about modern baseball, but I watch all of them on TV. Based on what I know about television golf, I am sure that I am being hoodwinked in those other sports. That bothers me.

There really is no need for a journalist to go to a tournament these days if he does not want to, or is on a limited budget. The Golf Writers Association of America has a website, which presents everything a writer needs. Interviews with the players are on the Internet within a few minutes of the time the interviews are conducted at the tournament site. All of the scores, which are updated every minute or two, are available for all players, not just the leaders, including hole-by-hole summaries. Biographies and stats on the players are available, along with maps of the course.

Considering the traffic and parking problems and the cost of Dove bars, there is a great temptation for a golf writer to stay home and enjoy life.

I have resisted that temptation. I like to feel the turf underfoot, and the breeze in my face. I like to berate the kid selling the Dove bars. I like to speak directly with a player, and watch his facial reaction. I used to do the same thing when I was cross-examining a witness in a law suit. I like to take what they say and contrast it with what they said previously. I like to rebut their arguments with a statistic they overlooked. Needless to say, so I need not say it: lawyers make good golf writers.

Despite all the pressures to kill it, golf will live on. It isn't a sport, you know, it is a Way of Life. Augusta is not a city in Georgia. It is a Mecca in Georgia. Jones and Hogan and Old Tom Morris are not dead players, they are Saints. The Rules of Golf are the Ten Commandments. St. Andrews is the Vatican.

Because of my illness, I have not played golf for many months. My son Jim plays enough for both of us. Genes, I guess. I have been thinking lately about how I used to take him golfing with me when he was little. I would carry him on my shoulders from shot to shot. I will have to get myself in shape, in case Jim offers to carry me. I think he might do it.

Any day now, I will take my shag bag out in the back yard and do exactly as I did as a 15 year old. I will pretend that I am playing in the US Open. I can hear the voices of the TV commentators: The rough is too high. The greens are too fast. What is the USGA trying to do? Just watch this next shot.

Now *that* is living.

BRICKER & ECKLER

Soon after Thomas E. Dewey and his running mate, John W. Bricker, lost the 1944 campaign for the presidency to Roosevelt and Truman, Bricker decided to return to private life and found a new law firm.

He was 50, and his life to that point had been spent in politics. The campaign with Dewey had taken him to every part of the United States. The political loss to a popular president, in the middle of a war, did not constitute a mark against him. The Republican Party was grateful that he put up a good fight. He had been a good sport about the whole thing. He had wanted to be the presidential candidate rather than the vice presidential candidate, but when it became obvious to him at the Republican convention in 1944 that Dewey was the man, Bricker accepted the second slot gracefully, and tried very hard to win.

Bricker and Dewey were never close friends, before or after the campaign. They were excellent politicians, so they put up with one another without any outward displays of discontent. To his closest associates, Bricker confided that he thought there were fundamental political mistakes during the campaign, most of which were made by Dewey's handlers, whom he called "that New York crowd."

Bricker was unaccustomed to making political mistakes.

When he was very young he was defeated for a local office, but he came back from that quickly, and served on the Public Utilities Commission of Ohio until he was elected to the office of Attorney General. That office was his springboard to the governor's office. When he became Governor Bricker, Ohio was deeply in debt. By the time he was running with Dewey, there was a large surplus. He was known in every county seat in Ohio as Honest John Bricker.

Bricker was a conservative Republican, not unlike Senator Goldwater when the Arizonian ran for the presidency 20 years later. It was Bricker's reputation as a right-winger, that made me think twice before becoming his law partner in the fall of 1964. The last thing I needed was a senior partner who might tell me what to think, and when to think it. I should not have worried. In the 25 years I practiced with Senator Bricker, he never attempted to impose his point of view upon anyone. I think he might have been a "compassionate conservative" a couple of generations ahead of Governor George W. Bush.

Bricker's new firm was known as Bricker, Marburger, Evatt and Barton. His three partners were not as famous as he, but all of them were well-known Ohio politicians with considerable experience in the real world of law and government. Ralph Marburger, who resigned amicably from the firm and died before I became a partner, was a veteran utilities lawyer. William Evatt had been chief counsel to Attorney General Bricker, and Tax Commissioner of Ohio during the administration of Governor Bricker. Robert Barton had been a practicing lawyer in Columbus, before he joined the Bricker administration as the top administrative secretary to the governor. It was commonly known that in that job, he practically ran state government for several years.

The new partnership rented space in Columbus on the 33rd floor of what was then known as the A.I.U. tower, a 45-story building in a city where the average height of the downtown buildings was closer to a dozen to 20 stories. In 1928 and 1929 my mother worked for a brokerage firm on the 28th floor of that same building. In our family scrapbook there is a clip from a 1928 newspaper, reporting that the elevator stuck in the A.I.U. tower, trapping three secretaries for several hours. Mother was one of those. It might have been her 15 minutes of fame.

The new Bricker law office opened shortly after the presidential campaign ended in November, 1944, and it prospered immediately. In truth, it took off like a rocket. Everyone wanted to retain John Bricker. He was six feet-four inches of national hero to Republicans from coast to coast. Many of them were the heads of national companies, who wanted to express their gratitude to him for a job well done. He was an extraordinarily handsome man, who made friends easily and worked hard to keep them. During the campaign his picture appeared on the cover of *Time* magazine.

The major problem Bricker, Marburger, Evatt & Barton had in its first days and weeks, was how to keep up with the success. They soon had to become selective in taking on new work. They earned a reputation quickly for turning out high quality work, and for getting good results for their clients. Except for opening the doors of government to his clients now and then, Bricker did not himself practice much day-to-day law. To my knowledge, after his run for the Presidency he never again drafted a legal document or made an appearance in any court. He was too busy with speaking engagements throughout the country; with meeting his friends who wanted to become clients, and those who were clients. Much of his time was spent keeping all of his fences mended, so that he could run for the United States Senate when he was ready and the time was ripe.

Shortly after the end of World War II, the new firm was ready to take on a new lawyer. They had several young men under consideration, when the best candidate of all came for an interview. He was LCDR John A. Eckler of the naval reserve, who still had his officer's uniform and battle ribbons on, when he made an appointment with Governor Bricker.

John Eckler graduated from Ohio Wesleyan in 1935, a member of Phi Beta Kappa and president of the student body. Some 12 years after his graduation, when I was assisting John Adams, then president of the student body, in the organization of student government, I checked some old files and came across a 50-page manual written by Eckler and entitled "The Organization of Student Government." I had no way of knowing that I would one day be his partner, and that this was merely the first of many times when he would make things easy for me.

Soon after his graduation, John Eckler married a classmate, Mary Rickey, the oldest daughter of the famed baseball mogul, Branch Rickey. John joined the St. Louis Cardinals, at that time Rickey's team, and was assigned to one of its farm clubs in upstate New York, as a player-development manager and scout. In the fall of 1936 he enrolled at the law school at the University of Chicago, from which he graduated with the class of 1939. He posted some of the highest grades ever recorded at that prestigious law school. One of the articles he wrote for the Law Review was on the subject of the law of baseball. He was elected to Order of the Coif, the highest academic honor a law student can achieve.

Prior to the war John Eckler practiced law with a large firm in Chicago. He joined the Navy in 1941 as an Ensign. He spent years in various combat zones in the Pacific, and his career was highlighted with his becoming the commanding officer of a submarine-chaser in 1944.

After the war John and Mary decided that they would not return to the Chicago law firm. He read a story in the newspapers about John W. Bricker and his new law firm in Columbus. Eckler was born in Elyria, Ohio, and became familiar with Columbus while studying in nearby Delaware. He fired off a letter to Bricker, and immediately got an invitation to drop by the office.

In Eckler's day, and mine as well just a few years later, there was no recruiting by law firms on the campuses of law schools. There were no second-year clerkships for law students. The new lawyer was expected to find work by calling on firms, and letting it be known that his services were available. He did not ask for work. That would have been considered begging. He merely inquired of the lawyers he was interviewing whether they knew of any law offices which were expanding, or of any solo practitioners who needed help. Not many corporations maintained their own law departments. Most public jobs with prosecutors and the courts were filled through politics.

John Eckler remembered that his opening words to John Bricker were, "I am thinking of moving my practice to Columbus. Do you think there is room for another lawyer in Columbus?" Years later, he confided to me that he certainly would not have needed a moving van to move his practice.

John Bricker had less of a memory of precisely what was said at that first meeting. Mostly he remembered a good feeling, as he listened while this war hero expressed his hopes and aspirations. Right on the spot without clearing it with the other partners, Bricker invited Eckler to join the firm as a salaried associate. John accepted then and there, without first discussing it with Mary. Not a word passed between the two men as to what Eckler's duties would be or what his salary would be. They simply liked one another. Bricker was a baseball fan, and the thought of having Branch Rickey's son-in-law in the office pleased him. The fact that the young man was an honor student from Ohio Wesleyan, which had given Bricker an honorary doctorate while he was governor, was icing on the cake. Eckler said he was not worried about details like salary, because he knew that Bricker was an honorable man.

These two honorable men practiced law together for 40 years, and for much of that time there was no written agreement between them. When the firm got so big it needed a written partnership agreement to satisfy the younger lawyers, Bricker and Eckler both signed it. They might have read it. But they didn't pay much attention to it. Their's was a matter of trust. With them a handshake was as good as a bond.

John Eckler was just what Bricker, Marburger, Evatt and Barton needed. He was a scholar, but more than that he was a born leader, and a doer. He had a knack for organizing, and for doing the right thing at the right time. He was quick and accurate. His capacity for work staggered the imagination. The firm represented the Pennsylvania Railroad, and John tried most of the railroad's jury trials, after Bob Barton guided him through the first two or three. John said years later, that the trial load for the railroad turned his hair white overnight.

The largest local client of the office, and the one with the greatest potential for growth, was the John W. Galbreath Company. John Bricker and John Galbreath are the two most famous persons ever born and raised in Mount Sterling, Ohio. They were very close all their lives, and they both lived well into their 90s. They liked to leave the impression that they were inseparable as youngsters, and that they went to college together in the same buggy. This is a bit hard to swallow since they went to separate universities. The inconsistency never kept them from repeating the story. When Bricker was running for vice president, the Republicans arranged for a ticker tape parade down Broadway in New York City. Bricker invited Galbreath to ride with him. According to Galbreath, Bricker turned to him as said, "It sure is a long way back to Mount Sterling, isn't it?"

John Galbreath owned a modest real estate office in Columbus until World War II came along. Significant government and military contracts, during the war years, allowed him to expand, and to learn how to put together large real estate deals.

Within 10 to 15 years after the war he built huge office buildings in most of the principal cities of the US. Many of these large projects were owned by Mr. Galbreath, or members of his family. He built the largest residential real estate development in the world in Hong Kong, and the second largest in Saudi Arabia. He owned a mortgage company which serviced FHA and Veterans loans. He became wealthy, perhaps worth as much as $300 to $400 million at a time when a dollar came much closer to being worth a dollar. He owned the Pittsburgh Pirates baseball team; and on two separate occasions his horses won the Kentucky Derby. Mr. Galbreath maintained his home west of Columbus on a 3000-acre horse farm. He owned another horse farm in Lexington, Kentucky of almost equal size; and the two farms were operated as a unit under the name "Darby Dan Farms." He had a private zoo on his Ohio farm.

John Eckler was with Mr. Galbreath every step of the way, during the early days of the building of this empire. Eckler did not handle every transaction, but he was aware of them all and made certain that Galbreath was well represented by local counsel.

In the fall of 1946, just two years after the firm was founded, Bricker was elected to the US Senate. Eckler was in the process of easing into his new office in the law firm, as Bricker was putting together his Senate staff. Bricker took it for granted that Eckler would go with him to Washington as his chief of staff, and was amazed when Eckler hesitated to do so. It was the closest the two men ever came to misunderstanding one another.

Eckler hesitated to go to Washington, because he and Mary wanted to stay put in Columbus. During the war, she had followed him from city to city when the Navy would permit it, and they longed to start a family. They were both 32, and were just about to develop roots in the Columbus community. The thought of serving as the top aide to a Senator intrigued Eckler, but he was not about to ask Mary to move again.

After some extended discussions, Bricker and Eckler reached a compromise. Eckler would go to Washington as the administrative assistant to Senator Bricker, but there would be a two-year limit to the appointment. Senator Bricker was happy with this solution because he was certain that Eckler would develop Potomac fever, and would stay beyond the two years. Eckler was happy because it gave him a taste of national politics. Mary was happy because John was happy.

John and Mary found a modest apartment in a building near the Capitol. Another tenant was the newly elected Congressman from California, Richard M. Nixon and his wife Pat. One of John's new friends was a young lawyer from New York City, Mr. William Rogers, who recently had joined the Justice Department. In time he would serve as Attorney General of the United States, and later as the Secretary of State in the Eisenhower administration. Dean Rusk, also to become a Secretary of State, lived nearby and was one of John Eckler's new friends.

Life in Washington was stimulating. Senator Bricker loved meeting with people and making speeches. He did not like the routine work, such as setting up appointments, preparing and enforcing budgets, hiring and firing in the office, and keeping up with the details of pending legislation. Eckler caught all of that duty. Eckler also had the responsibility for meeting with angry constituents who wanted something done immediately. Over time he became a tremendous negotiator. He knew the federal government intimately, and the people who worked in all of the departments, agencies and bureaus. Eckler knew what was going to pass in each house of the legislature, and which laws were going to be vetoed by President Truman.

Every now and then a situation would come along which John Eckler could not handle. It would be a problem without a handle. It might be two large contributors to the Bricker campaign who were arguing with each other, or perhaps wanting the same thing.

Eckler would do all that he could to get the parties together, and finally would recognize that he was getting nowhere. This was a matter for the Old Man.

Senator Bricker enjoyed the impossible situations. Bricker's years in politics would come to the surface, and he would almost instantly suggest an obvious solution that was acceptable to both sides. Bricker would never use threats, or make outlandish promises in these difficult impasses. He would simply draw upon his long experience in government, and usually call to mind a similar deadlock that came up years ago in some county in southern Ohio, when the sheriff and the county commissioners were fussing with one another.

John Eckler was a fast learner, and in his second year at the job he had to refer less and less to Senator. He was thoroughly enjoying his work. He was dealing with the heart of government, and with famous people. It was life in a fish bowl, but his job was made easier because of the temperament of John Bricker. The Senator never took any step without first clearing it with Eckler, his loyal and talented administrative assistant. Bricker became dependent upon Eckler. He honored that dependency by always taking Eckler into his confidence.

At the end of two years everyone adhered to the two-year agreement without a whimper. John Eckler hated to leave, but he did. Senator Bricker was not sure how he could get along without Eckler's counsel, but he let him go. Mary stayed out of it, but she longed to get back to Columbus. Eckler did not plead with Mary; the Senator did not plead with Eckler. It was a matter of honor. A deal was a deal.

One thing that may have motivated Senator Bricker, was his knowledge that Eckler was badly needed back at the law firm. The firm had taken on no new lawyers, and Bill Evatt and Bob Barton were working themselves to death. They were superior lawyers, but they were not skilled in management. Neither of them was prepared to lead the firm into the growth which lay before it. They wanted Eckler back in the firm, and they explained that fact very carefully to Senator Bricker, each time he returned to Columbus.

Upon Eckler's return to Columbus in 1949, things began to happen at the firm, still known as Bricker, Marburger, Evatt and Barton. A Cincinnati lawyer, Richard Neihoff, was asked to come with the firm. To induce him to do so, the name was changed to Bricker, Marburger, Evatt, Barton & Neihoff. Mr. Neihoff was neither a partner nor an associate of the firm. He was a wealthy man married to an even wealthier wife. Among her assets, Mrs. Neihoff owned the A.I.U. Tower, and thus she was the landlady for the law firm.

The arrival of Neihoff, while a bit nebulous in form, was a sound idea in substance. Neihoff got a ready-made place to practice with a minimum capital outlay, and the firm made its landlady so happy that she did not raise the rent for many years. Neihoff was a licensed lawyer, but he did not practice much. He rarely assisted with any of the firm's work. Mostly he handled his and his wife's private investments, and on more than one occasion he referred substantial clients to the Bricker firm. To those advantages, could be added the fact that Mr. Neihoff was a splendid gentleman, who was easy to get along with. He was still with the firm when I joined.

John Eckler was not a partner, upon his return to the practice. He continued to be a salaried lawyer until the middle 1950s. I never heard him complain about the long wait to be made a partner, but I did hear him comment one time, rather dryly, that he thought he might have been the highest paid salaried lawyer in the history of law firms.

Without being a partner, he became the leader of the firm. He was never one to strive for recognition, he just enjoyed it when it was heaped upon him. Between the mid-1950s and the early

1960s, Eckler's single-handed efforts brought six new lawyers into the firm: John Selby, Richard Pickett, William Chadeayne, William Leighner, and two sons of founders, Bob Barton and Jack Bricker. His two seniors, Mr. Evatt and Mr. Barton, were absorbed in their own substantial practices, and they were no more interested in recruiting new lawyers than they were interested in offering a partnership to the man who was keeping their firm afloat.

All of the record keeping functions of the firm, including bookkeeping, writing of checks, and ordering of supplies, was delegated to Mrs. Nellie Henry, who had been Bricker's secretary when he was governor. I have heard the following story from so many different people that I believe it to be true. Nellie was on duty in the governor's office on his very last day in office. As the second hand moved toward noon, and his last seconds in office, she went out to the telephone switch board. There were about three dozen telephone calls in progress, evidenced by the telephone wires which were plugged into the various holes on the board. At the stroke of noon, Nellie gathered up all the wires and pulled them out of the board. "Let the damned Democrats take care of things now," she said.

Nellie prepared the firm's partnership tax returns, which she shared with no one who was not a partner. Nellie kept the books with a stern look, and a no-nonsense attitude. On one occasion she escorted an IRS auditor out of the office when he questioned a couple of items on a tax return. She said he was nothing more than a " … Democrat up to no good." It took several weeks for Senator Bricker to mend that fence, and at the same time avoid a full field audit.

In the election of 1958, Senator Bricker was soundly defeated for a third-term in the Senate, the only election of any consequence he ever lost. He might not have lost that one, had he followed his own intuition.

The post-war period was a time of constant strife between labor and management. This was the period in which the Taft-Hartley Act became law, and President Truman tried to take over the steel industry. Unions were attempting to negotiate "closed shop" provisions into their industry-wide contracts. These provisions provided that a new employee had to join the union whether he wanted to or not, as a condition of his employment.

Closed Shops were considered by most Republicans, including Senator Bricker, to be as dangerous to our society as polio, which was running rampant while Dr. Jonas Salk was working furiously on a new vaccine. Several large industrial states enacted what were known as "Right To Work Statutes," which provided that any closed shop clause in a labor contract was unenforceable.

The leaders of the Republican Party in Ohio strongly supported efforts to enact such legislation in Ohio, and when Senator Bricker heard about those attempts, he protested to the party leaders. His view was that it would be wiser for Ohio industry to refuse to accept closed shops during negotiations, even if it meant long, costly strikes. He feared that any political party which supported legislation against closed shops would be inviting organized labor to unify against that party's candidates.

The "Right To Work" movement in Ohio killed the Republican Party from the top to the bottom of the ticket. The Republican governor and attorney general, both popular officials until 1958, went down. Bricker went down. Large city mayors lost, and so did most county officials in union strongholds. It was a Democratic landslide which cleaned house, and changed the character of Ohio government for a decade. Bricker had won big in 1952, when he ran for his second term during the first Eisenhower campaign. Ike was re-elected easily in 1956, and everyone thought that all of the Republican candidates, especially the incumbents, would be safe in 1958.

Bricker was very disappointed, mostly with himself for falling for the Right To Work debacle. But he didn't say much about it publicly, because he honestly thought that the day would come soon when the GOP would invite him to run again. He could not visualize Ohio politics without John W. Bricker leading the Republican ticket. Politicians tend to think that way, when they have held important national offices, and are only 64 when they are ousted.

Bricker's only choice was to return to Columbus and his law firm. During his 12 years in the Senate, the firm had sent him his share of the profits from the practice. The other founders were smart enough to realize that many, if not most, of the firm's significant clients resulted from Bricker's magnetism. They knew that if he left the firm or even if he retired, much of the client base could dissolve.

In truth, Bricker was not nearly the rainmaker in 1959 that he was in 1944 when the firm was founded. He was now politically damaged. Many of his cronies in the national companies who once wanted him as their lawyer, were now retired. High-office holders throughout the country who were once loyal to him, were now out of office. It was not widely known, at the time, that Bricker had advised against the Right To Work movement. To the contrary, he was considered to be a leader for the movement, and he caught a lot of the blame for the political calamity.

The new star in the firm was John Eckler. He had been back in Ohio for about ten years when Bricker returned involuntarily. Eckler had served as the youngest president of the Columbus Bar Association. He had taught Constitutional Law for years at a night law school in Columbus, and made many friends among the current lawyers whom he had taught. He had appeared regularly on a Columbus public opinion radio and TV program which dealt with world, national, and local issues. He was a first class litigater, and a lawyer with a solid reputation as a formidable negotiator. Everyone had a good word for John Eckler.

About the time Bricker came back to the office, the name of the firm was changed to Bricker, Evatt, Barton, Eckler & Neihoff. Eckler was welcomed as a full partner, earning the same substantial income as the others.

If Senator Bricker ever sensed that his importance to the firm was diminishing, it was not because of any lack of respect accorded him by Eckler. Until the day Bricker died in 1986, Eckler treated Senator with dignity and the deference due a distinguished American. Eckler never addressed Senator Bricker as "John."

When I came to the firm the Senator had been back for six years. It had now become clear to him that the Republican Party was not going to call upon him again. He enjoyed being the titular head of the law firm, but he knew who was in charge.

The Bishop's mantelletta rested firmly, but always lightly, upon John Eckler's shoulders. Strictly speaking he was not a founding partner. In fact he founded the firm I was willing to join. He nurtured it, gave it vitality, shaped it, and provided the leadership it needed.

Not a bad contribution. When I walked into the firm's offices in November of 1964, I felt honored to be a part of what would soon be Bricker & Eckler. It was an altogether new career for me, one which would span the next quarter of a century.

MOTHER AND MATT

I HAVE NOT SAID MUCH ABOUT MY MOTHER, Ada Grace Clark, or my step-father, Matthew P. Chesser, because I have had in mind devoting an entire chapter to them. This seems like a good place to do that, because we need to catch our breath before jumping back into the practice of the law.

You may remember that Mother and Matt were married in Dayton, shortly before I graduated from high school. They had marriage in mind for years, but put it off for a reason they both regarded as sensible. The Carnegie Hero Fund Commission awarded Mother and me a medal, and a monthly check, in honor of my father's act of heroism. The award provided that we could keep the medal, but the monthly check would end at my high school graduation or if my mother re-married, whichever first occurred.

The monthly check kept us alive. It made the difference between our living with the assurance that we would have shelter, clothing and food, and the reality that without that money we might have to give up as many as two out of three of those necessities.

There was another complicating factor which contributed to their long courtship. In 1937 Matt contracted tuberculosis, a disease which in those days often proved fatal. His younger sister died of TB in 1935. Before he became ill, he owned and operated a company which he modestly named "The United States Greenhouse Construction Company of America, Ltd." When you hear that name, or see it on a letterhead, you conclude that it must be nationwide in scope; perhaps the kind of an enterprise which would want to retain John W. Bricker as its lawyer.

The company was not incorporated, and it consisted of Matt, a couple of his brothers and a friend or two, all of whom repaired greenhouses around central Ohio. It expanded after its initial success, and built a number of new, fancy greenhouse on the estates of wealthy people. The upscale greenhouses at Henry Ford's home near Detroit were built by TUSGCCOAL It grew to the place where Matt had two separate work crews, one of them working in Ohio and the other in Washington DC

The business did not make Matt rich, but it provided him and the others with steady work during the Depression, and that in and of itself was an accomplishment. The tuberculosis ended the company. The others tried to keep it going, but Matt was the sparkplug and leader.

Matt beat the odds and survived. He could not go back to building greenhouses, because it was too strenuous for him. He sold automobiles in Columbus for a year, and in 1940 landed a job in the war effort, as a civilian employee of the Air Force. He was a lowly administrative assistant at first, but by the time he retired in 1968, he was highly paid by Air Force standards. At one time he was in charge of the world wide maintenance and support of the Lockheed Constellation, one of which was the "Columbine," better known as Air Force One in the Eisenhower administration.

I did not get invited to Mother and Matt's wedding. I have no idea why not. They simply went to the courthouse by themselves, obtained a license and were married on March 28, 1942, Matt's 34th birthday. It did not seem peculiar to me at the time, and I was so occupied with my school activities that I did not give the matter any thought. There is the possibility that they decided on that quick procedure, in order to spare me from any stress regarding my father's death, 15 years earlier.

Shortly before the marriage, Mother and Matt bought a house on Emmons Avenue in Dayton. Mother and I moved in a few weeks before the wedding, and Matt joined us when they were married. For the first time in my life since I was a toddler, I had a father living in the house with me.

Our relationship was exceptional for step-relatives. Never did Matt try to demand my respect. He had it anyway, and knew it. Never did he make suggestions on how I should conduct myself. He let me live by my own standards, and did not encourage me to live by his. I was a high school musician of better than average talent, who was making good grades, and he always complimented and encouraged me. He never disciplined me, or suggested that my mother should. Most important of all, for all of his life Matt was kind to my mother, and grateful to her for sharing her life with him. His attitude toward my mother, made him my friend.

Mother and Matt were frugal. The depression years had taught them to be. The new house, a two bedroom bungalow in a good neighborhood, cost them $4200 at a time when a top of the line Ford sedan was under $450. If you multiply the current price of a Ford by about nine times, you will be near the current value of Mother and Matt's first house, which still seems to be in a good neighborhood. They sold my mother's car to make the down payment, and mortgaged the balance. This was the first time in the life of either of them that they had a debt. They did not care for debt. The note to the bank was paid off and the mortgage canceled in 1945, while I was still in the Navy.

All their lives my folks lived as if they would be out of work tomorrow. Every purchase was given careful consideration, and they always used cash. After Matt died in 1986 I tried to get my mother to accept the credit card her bank offered her. I explained all the convenience it would provide, and that there would be no debt expense, if she paid in full within 25 days of receiving the monthly statement. Rather than costing her anything she would actually get a "float" on her money. "Nothing doing," she insisted. "If I have the money I will buy it, with cash."

When my mother said "cash" that is what she meant. We took her to a furniture store in the little city in California where she had lived for 20 years, so that she might select a new chair for her living room. She picked the one she wanted, and told the clerk that she would go to her bank and get the money to buy it. He assured her that the store would accept her check, and she was genuinely surprised that they would do that. She told me on the way home, "I'll bet they don't deliver the chair until that check clears." That kind of an attitude about money is hard to believe in this day and age.

Getting married was exactly the right thing to do for Mother and Matt. From the time my father died suddenly, Mother had to make all the important decisions alone. She relied a little on my Grandpa Clark, and her older brother, Ray Clark, until his death in 1940. For the most part she just figured things out for herself.

One of her decisions did not set well with the Hoskins side of the family. She used my father's life insurance money to complete her education at a business school in Columbus. Her thought was that having secretarial skills would assure her of steady work. Some of my father's relatives thought that she should save the money and give it to me when I reached manhood, or use it to sustain me along the way to it.

My father's death was hard on the Hoskins family. My grandfather, William Hoskins, took it in stride reasonably well, but my poor grandmother, who was not in very good health, went into shock at the time of the tragedy and never recovered. She died in

1941. As they put it in those days, she "went out of her mind." Others among my father's siblings, and their families, handled his death in different ways. Some of them had as little as possible to do with Mother and me. Their attitude seemed to be that they better stay away from us, because we might need some financial help, and they were already strapped. Others, notably my dad's oldest brother, Porter Hoskins and his wife Hazel, were always solicitous of our well-being and eager to help us. The youngest brother, Ernest Hoskins, was the friendliest of all. He came to our house all the time as I was growing up. He almost always gave me a quarter. At his death he left me a valuable diamond ring, which I wear now and someday will leave to my son.

Matt had been kicked around by life too. I mentioned his tuberculosis. Chronic unemployment was another problem. Most men suffered from that condition in the late 1920s and the first half of the 1930s. He left school after the eighth grade, because there was no high school available.

My mother faced the same problem, but her parents, Josh and Ida Clark, had enough funds to send her each week by train to high school in Logan. She lived with a family in Logan named Clark, which was not related to us. The Nathan Clark family, which took care of mother in Logan during the week, lived at one time on the property later occupied by the Chesser family on Asbury Ridge. Every Sunday evening my grandfather would take Mother to Starr, Ohio in his horse and buggy, and she caught a train for the 18 mile trip to Logan. On Friday evening she made the return trip, and Grandpa would pick her up in Starr.

When Mother and Matt married, their lives were enhanced. Mother worked for a firm of certified public accountants in Dayton, and later for an orthodontist, and was paid well. Matt was getting started in his Air Force career, and his income was a little more than hers. More important than the money, of course, was the fact that they had a companionship which they both needed.

In 1952 they made an important decision. The Air Force indicated to Matt that he had a bright future, but that in order to take full advantage of it he would have to move to a new position in Los Angeles. Matt knew that such a move would be difficult for my mother, because she was just getting used to being a grandmother to our daughter Jane. Laura was on the way. It would be difficult for her to move away from me too. I was her only child and she had mothered and fathered me from my infancy. She loved Marg like a daughter. We lived in Springfield, where I practiced law, and that was an easy drive from Dayton.

Wisely, Mother and Matt did not bring us in on the decision whether to move. They merely announced it, about a month before they left. They sold their Dayton home without any difficulty, and after the moving van pulled away on Holloween night, they came up to Springfield and stayed with us before heading for California early the next morning. It was not easy to see them go, despite the fact we knew they made the right decision for them.

Life in Alhambra, a suburb of Los Angeles, was very exciting for them. Mother was 49 and Matt 44, and the change of scenery helped them escape a mid-life crises. They bought a small house, and took in all the sights of southern California. For several years before they moved to southern California, they enjoyed a little mid-winter vacation by going to the Rose Bowl Parade. Those trips were always hurried, and included only the parade, and not the football game. Now they lived in that California wonderland, and had all the time in the world to look it over and soak it up.

After about two years, just as they were taking in all the sights for the second or third time, the Air Force asked Matt to move once again. His new job would be at the McClellen Air Force Base near Sacramento. There was no hesitation on this move. So long as the new destination was in California, they were ready to go. Sacramento opened up a whole new menu of places to visit. Not the least of these was the beautiful valley of the American River, north and east of Sacramento in the former gold-mining country, which now was filled with ghost towns. They became avid fishermen, and invested a substantial amount of time in the sport.

Mother worked in Los Angeles for a savings and loan company, but when they moved to Sacramento she decided to retire from the business world. It was obvious that Matt's work was transitory, and probably would remain that way in the future. His salary was substantial now, so that there no longer was a need for her employment.

The joys of living in the Golden State were marred a bit by the plight of my Grandma Clark. Grandpa Clark died in 1952, and Grandma was all alone in the world. She wrote us a nice letter telling us about Grandpa's last days. "Last Wednesday," she reported, "he had a bad spell." The two of them had been cleaning wall paper in the living room. "I quit," she continued, "to get dinner, and he ate a hearty meal and sat down at the radio to listen to the news." When my grandmother checked on him, Grandpa couldn't talk and his legs were numb. Their youngest child, my Uncle Dwight, was called, and Grandpa was taken to the hospital in Nelsonville. He was in and out of the hospital for the next few months, and died there.

After the death, the farm on Asbury Ridge was too much for Grandma to handle alone. She was terrified during electrical storms, which are a part of normal life in Ohio. As a newish lawyer, I prepared the deed and helped my grandmother with the sale of the farm where I grew up.

For several years Grandma Clark lived here-and-there with her sons in Ohio, and with my family and me in Springfield for a time. She really missed my mother, her only daughter. Mrs. Mary Chesser, Matt's mother, was a widow also. Ida Clark and Mary Chesser were hardly strangers. They had lived on adjacent farms on Asbury Ridge since the early 1900s. Neither of them had a home of her own in 1955. Their late husbands, William Chesser and Josh Clark, were highly-opinionated Englishmen by heritage, and they rarely saw eye-to-eye on anything. The two women forgave them, and the bickering of their husbands had no effect upon their lifelong friendship.

Mother and Matt invited both of their mothers to come live with them in Sacramento, for as long as they wanted to. The two elderly ladies had rarely been more than 50 miles from their homes and families. My mother came to Ohio and escorted them to California, and for years they had the times of their lives.

Every day was a holiday. For decades the two ladies had worked from sun up to sun down, caring for their families in a rural setting. They baked their own bread, churned their own butter and presided over large households with very little money and virtually no conveniences. In addition to looking after their families, the two ladies looked after each other. While they were living as neighbors in the Ohio countryside, my grandmother wrote to us that " … Mrs. Chesser just brought me over a good hot dinner … a can of good hot coffee and a can of vegetable soup … isn't it wonderful to have such good neighbors?"

Sacramento was like heaven for them, and they didn't have to die to get there. After less than a year Mrs. Chesser asked Matt to bring her back to Ohio so that she might live for awhile with her oldest living daughter. After my grandmother's death, Mrs. Chesser returned to California for a second visit, and stayed there until she sensed that her life might be coming to an end. Mother and Matt brought her to Ohio by automobile, stopping along the way at the summit of Pikes's Peak, and visiting the Garden of the Gods. She died within a year, in 1969.

Grandma Clark came back to Ohio once, too. I escorted her back to Ohio briefly in 1957 so that she could attend the funeral of her youngest son, Dwight, who died of cancer. It wasn't long before she wanted to return to Sacramento. "They treat me so nice out there," she told us time and again.

Matt was transferred in 1960 from McClellen to a small facility near LAX, the Los Angeles International Airport, where the

Air Force was conducting research and development of missiles. Grandma went along with the move, but she never enjoyed living in Los Angeles. Her health failed quickly and she died in the spring of 1962, nearly 10 years to the day after Grandpa Clark's death.

My grandparents were among the last of Ohio's pioneers. The generation ahead of them settled on the Ohio land which had been, in turn, cleared by the generation ahead of them. Their first home on Asbury Ridge was built by the early settlers, and it was old when they got it. The Chesser family, just north of them, lived in a log cabin built by the generation which cleared the land. In 1918, my grandparents built a new house, which was the nicest one in the immediate neighborhood. It had no electricity and its running water ran only because of gravity. It did have a bathroom, which was the marvel of the community.

Mother and Matt genuinely missed "Mrs. Clark and Mrs. Chesser," as they always called the two grandmas. Mother often remarked that after their deaths the house seemed empty. For amusement, they bought a house trailer which they took on weekend trips to get out of the hustle and bustle of Los Angeles. They hauled it back to Ohio several times to visit us, and each time insisted they would never do it again.

In 1965, after I had been with Bricker & Eckler about a year, we all met in Estes Park for a vacation. We booked two cabins side by side at Park's Pine Haven, and spent about 10 days getting reacquainted. Jane flew to Los Angeles ahead of our vacation, and traveled with her grandparents to Colorado in the house trailer. In 1967 Laura got her turn. She traveled from Ohio back to California with Mother and Matt in the trailer. Jim never made it.

Matt retired from Air Force employment in 1968, with a generous pension. He was ready. He had found the work confusing. He was not one to complain, but if you got him started he had lots of tales of the red tape and waste which seem to be a part of government life, and which always offended his frugality. The Air

Force constantly was reorganizing, and he rarely knew from time to time whom he was reporting to, and who was reporting to him.

After retirement there was no reason to live in crowded Los Angeles. On one of their travels with the trailer, my folks came across a picturesque little city high in the mountains east of Chico, in northern California, by the name of Paradise. After a couple more brief visits there they decided to retire in Paradise, something I guess many people strive to do.

In 1969 they sold their home in Los Angeles, and bought the nicest house they ever owned, in Paradise. It was on the edge of a forest, on a couple of acres. It had a separate guest house in the rear, which the relatives from Ohio, including us, occupied several times. After a year or two, they decided that Paradise was a little more remote than they had anticipated, and the climate was a lot cooler than they expected.

In 1971 they made their last move. They relocated in Vista, California, which is inland from Oceanside, in the North Country of San Diego County. Their house was on top of a hill, on a street called Tiger Tail. Vista was mostly avocado groves as recently as the 1950s. The farmers dug service roads through the groves, in order to plant and harvest the crops. When the village and city developed, the streets were built on the original service roads. The result is that when you are in Vista you never know whether you are going north or south. You just go up and down and around.

Vista was a city of about 19,000 people when my folks moved there. Today it is knocking on 80,000 or more. Probably no one knows exactly how many.

Matt died on Tiger Tail in 1986, and my mother in 1993. They are buried in the same grave, near Oceanside. You can see the Pacific from their resting place.

Mother and Matt were more than just persons who grew up in Ohio, had more than their share of struggle, married, moved to

California for the happy life, and wound up with a view of the ocean which only their spirits can see. For our family they were our vitality. It is because of them and their examples that we can accept our own travail with a measure of equanimity. They were living proof that you don't have to have much money to find peace. They taught our kids to tie their shoes. And much more than that.

Marg and I have been back to Oceanside to visit them a couple of times since they died. Their home has sold twice since I settled Mother's estate. So we have no welcome mat out for us where the avocados used to grow. It is just as well. The image of our parents on Tiger Tail is a happy one, and the image is enough.

Let's see. I was about to join the distinguished law firm of Bricker, Evatt, Barton, Eckler & Neihoff, was I not? From now on why don't we just call it Bricker & Eckler?

BACK TO THE GOOD LIFE

THE TWO THINGS WHICH STICK IN MY MIND as I remember returning to the private practice of law, are the variety of interesting work which awaited my arrival, and the very nice persons who welcomed me. There were some real characters at Bricker & Eckler, and the cases they were eager to hand to me were intriguing.

Bill Evatt sometimes wore his hat in the office. It was an ancient felt Stetson, not unlike the one LBJ wore when he was not in Texas. It was larger than a regular hat, but not a 10-gallon capacity. Bill's hat had not been cleaned and blocked in recent years, and it looked like some sandlot team had been using it for home plate. If he walked into his office in the morning with the hat on, and the telephone was ringing, he would take the call and forget to take off the hat. Other days he just felt better if it were on.

After I had been in the office a day or two, Evatt asked me to drop by his room. I just assumed he was going to give me an assignment or two, which is what all the other senior partners were doing. At the end of my first week, I had 13 cases to handle. I will tell you about some of them in a minute or two. Mr. Evatt did not want to give me work. He wanted to explain to me in some detail why it was that from the year 1803, our year of statehood, the entire government of the State of Ohio, including all the acts of the legislature and all the decisions of the Supreme Court, were illegal and not worth the paper they are written on. If you did not know Bill Evatt and his rich contributions to state government, you might conclude that he was in need of psychiatric help. As the former first assistant to the attorney general and former tax commissioner of Ohio, he was as well-grounded in Ohio law as any lawyer. He insisted we were illegal from the beginning.

Bill Chadeayne (Cha-*Dayne*), one of my contemporaries in the firm, told me later that Evatt made his explanation to every new lawyer, and believed that it was his duty to do so. Chadeayne and I agreed that assuming that Evatt's analysis might be correct, there wasn't a lot we could do about it.

Evatt and I became as close to being friends as a man of 40 and a man of 72 can pull it off, without being father and son. He was a walking encyclopedia of law, as you might expect, but also he was remarkably well-informed in many other fields. He was like a *World Almanac*. He was curious about everything. He wanted to know how a Navy pilot could navigate at night over open ocean, and what it was like to land on a carrier. He wanted to know what Industrial Nucleonics was up to, with its much ballyhooed "peaceful exploitation of nuclear energy." I must have explained a dozen times how a beta gauge works. He had convinced himself that we were building the hydrogen bomb.

In his early years Bill Evatt lived in Cincinnati, and was a violinist in the Cincinnati Symphony. When our 11 year old Laura decided that she would like to play a viola, I asked Bill where I could buy a cheap one until we could determine whether she was serious. I had in mind spending up to $100, but only if necessary.

Bill spent days running down a "decent" viola for Laura. He first explained, in detail, why buying a cheap viola was a huge mistake, and would in fact cause her to lose interest. He called dealers in New York and elsewhere; and finally insisted that I invest, as he put it, in an extraordinary instrument which a dealer found for us. He gave me all the technical data on the viola, including the fact that it was worth more than the asking price of $1350. In today's dollars that would be around $7000. I think Laura played it for a year or two. I have no idea where it might be today. In a bank vault, I hope.

Evatt was not the only character in our firm. Bob Barton was a trial lawyer, one of the best in Columbus. I never visited his home, but other members of the firm told me that it was like a lavishly furnished museum. I heard that there were five sofas in the living room.

Mr. Barton was glad to see me arrive, and gave me an estate to handle, which had been kicking around the office for years. It had no assets to speak of, just legal problems. The case was so old that the widow could only vaguely remember the name of her dear, departed husband. After dozens of trips to the probate court and nearly that many to the widow's home, I reported to Mr. Barton that I was prepared to file a final accounting, and was ready to send a bill for services rendered. He thanked me for what he regarded as an achievement, and added that he didn't think we ought to bill anything at all because it had taken us so long to do the work.

That was typical of Bricker & Eckler in 1964. The firm was unorganized. Not disorganized, mind you, just unorganized; and uninterested in making much money. Lawyers like Bricker, Evatt and Barton considered it to be a badge of honor that a lack of formal structure existed. There were no firm meetings, or hourly rates assigned to various lawyers. Statements were not sent to clients on a regular basis. The work came in, it was assigned to whomever had time to handle it, and when it was ended there was a feeling of relief. It would be billed sometime in the future when the firm needed money for some reason, or when Nellie Henry had time to prepare the statements. Both Barton and Evatt might go for as much as a year without preparing any statements to their clients. Life was a lot easier without a bunch of rules and regulations. Sufficient unto the day was the emergency thereof.

It was not that our founders were unfamiliar with organization. Bob Barton had run the State of Ohio as Governor Bricker's top assistant. Surely he must have noticed that people around him seemed to be on some kind of a schedule. As the Governor of Ohio, you would think that John Bricker would have to be organized enough, at the very least, to know when he should go to the General Assembly and deliver the State of the State address.

Those lawyers, nearly the last of a breed, believed they were engaged in a profession. They looked upon the lawyers, the clergy, the educators and the medical doctors as the only bona fide professionals. What set the four professions apart, was the fact that they did not work for money, and what they did was creative. They scoffed at certified public accountants, who sometimes referred to themselves as engaged in a profession. Bill Evatt would say, "Show me a creative accountant and I will show you an accountant who will soon need a lawyer." Barton said that the reason why so many buildings collapse, is that the engineers think they are in a profession.

Such an innocent attitude today would cause a hard working lawyer to starve to death. In 1964 the lawyers could afford to be independent. Despite their carefree attitudes, each of the senior men at B&E earned the equivalent in today's dollars, of just short of a half-million a year. Them was the days!

I grew up in this cavalier environment, and of course I adopted it. Who wouldn't? I enjoyed it. Who wants to go to a lot of meetings? As the others did, I also shied away from total specialization. I came to the firm as a person who was supposed to know something about corporation law, and complex corporate litigation. So I handled most if not all of that type of work which came along, and counseled the other lawyers in those matters from time to time. But I did not fully specialize, until we had sufficient manpower to make it possible. A lawyer can not specialize in a small firm, unless the entire firm is specialized. Our firm was a general practice firm.

If a client asked me to prepare a will, I did it. If he needed a corporation, I organized it. If his corporation was sued, I defended it, including the appeals. If it was taxed unfairly I negotiated with the IRS, and sued them if necessary, always hoping that they would not audit my own tax return. John Eckler said one time that if you wanted to sue your dog, I was the man to see.

Nearly every lawyer in our office worked that way. It never dawned on any of us that by working only in a narrow specialty we might make more money. If we had thought of it, we would have rejected such a commercial thought.

The greatest portion of the firm's work was performed by John Eckler, John Selby, Dick Pickett, Bill Chadeayne and Bill Leighner. All five of them worked long hours, and were totally dedicated to being lawyers. The two associates, Bob Barton and Jack Bricker were willing enough, but both were in their learning years.

I have mentioned several times that I came to Bricker & Eckler as a partner. I did and I didn't. John Eckler had carved me loose from Industrial Nucleonics without losing IN as a client. It took keen negotiating skills on his part to pull that off. The Chope brothers were as intelligent as Eckler, but they were not as smart. As a part of his deal with them, he gave them his personal assurance that my starting salary would not be greater than my earnings at IN; and thus, in their eyes, I was not making the switch for monetary reasons, a concept most important to them. The second part of his assurance to them was that I would be a salaried employee and not a partner. I am not sure why this was important to them, but it seemed to be. John did not disclose any of these conditions to me, until after I came to the firm. A part of being a good lawyer is not disclosing everything you know, except to your client.

The way he put it to me was, "Oh, by the way ... we aren't going to announce your partnership with us until the beginning of 1965. I want to keep faith with the Chopes, and I told them that you would be our employee making the same salary they paid you. But don't worry about it ... trust me ... we will fix you up come January 1." In my early days of practice, I learned never to believe the person who says, "trust me." But John Eckler was different.

In November and December of 1964, I was given regular payroll checks at my Industrial Nucleonics pay rate, which was $20,000 a year (or about $105,000 in today's money). Promptly on January 1, 1965 my partnership was announced; my share of the profits of the firm was expected to yield $35,000 a year (today, about $175,000) and the firm gave me a Christmas bonus, which was calculated to be the difference in the two incomes for the two months I worked in 1964. Fortunately the Chopes did not audit our books, although I doubt if Nellie Henry's bookkeeping system would have made any more sense to them than it did to many of us in the firm.

She did not have a "double-entry" system. We were lucky to get one entry.

To give you an idea how loose her system was: If a lawyer were going on a business trip to New York, for example, he would go to Nellie and ask her for perhaps $200 in cash. At the end of the trip if he had $100 remaining, he would return them to Nellie with a chit which read "Expenses to NYC, $100." That would be the way she entered the transaction into her bookkeeping system, as soon as she got around to it. She was accurate to the penny, and a very honest person; but if you tried her system today you would wind up in the Federal pen.

I mentioned that B&E's offices were on the 33rd floor of the A.I.U. Tower, later known as the Lincoln-Leveque Tower. Our space was very crowded, because the building is a tapered tower. As it soars into the air, each floor is smaller. The lawyers' offices were arranged in a circle around the perimeter of the tower, and the secretarial space was in the center. The law library was not commodious, and many of the books were scattered throughout the various lawyers' offices. This was not a good arrangement, but no one seemed to be worried about it. It was understood that no conference with a client was so confidential that another lawyer could not barge in if he needed a book.

When I arrived and took my place on the masthead in sixth place, which also was six lawyers from the bottom, there was no office for me. Several of the five lawyers below me offered their offices, or at least a joint occupancy with them; but I opted for a small corner which was formed by the hallway that also circled the suite of offices. It was tiny, but temporary. Before I arrived, the firm had committed to a large suite of offices in a sleek new modern office building under construction by the John W. Galbreath Company, at 100 E Broad. We expected to move in the spring of 1965, and when we did, I was to have one of the nice offices in the new facilities, with all new furniture of my choice. Those promises worked out as honorably as did the partnership and compensation promises.

A casual reference to the first few matters I handled, from my little office in the hallway, will show the variety of my new practice:

- I mentioned the ancient estate I handled for Bob Barton. That was my beginning, and my end, in the practice of probate law. During the next 25 years I sometimes helped other lawyers with probate work which involved corporate or partnership law. But never again did I start and finish an estate. I have no idea how probate lawyers manage to get to the office every morning, and stay awake throughout the day.

- One of our partners was treated very poorly by a local trial judge, who granted a summary judgment in a case he was handling. The judgment was docketed by the judge without any notice or hearing, both of which were required by law. I went to the judge in behalf of my partner and tried to refer to his egregious error as a simple "oversight." He then turned on me, and said he would continue to run his court and docket without any advice from me. I took the matter to the court of appeals, and got the trial judge reversed. I made an enemy on the trial bench, but made a friend in our office. Both for life.
- Another of our partners was wrongfully sued by his client because he failed to know about an unrecorded easement in a real estate transaction. There was no way he could have known of the existence of the easement, and the lawsuit against him was vindictive rather than rational. I defended our partner and obtained a summary judgment, after both notice and a hearing. Chalk up another lifelong friend in the office.
- I represented a national warehouse developer based in New York, who wanted to acquire three warehouse sites in Columbus. I acquired the tracts, negotiated all the necessary permits with the City, arranged for railroad sidings to the sites, and drafted the building contracts with the general contractor.
- I obtained an injunction against a labor union which was picketing illegally.
- I helped Bob Barton try a personal injury case in the common pleas court. My job was to pick the jury, and do most of the research. He permitted me to present part of the final argument. Our client got a judgment against him, but the judgment was less than the amount our client had offered in settlement prior to trial. This is a good example of why it is so difficult for a trial lawyer to determine his won-lost record. If you read the account of our trial in the newspapers, you would assume we lost. If you knew that our client had offered more than the

judgment, you would know we won. In order to keep their sanity, most experienced trial lawyers do not keep a box score.

There were other matters for me in the first six weeks or so. And, during that time I continued to serve as "general counsel" to Industrial Nucleonics. IN kept my office and secretary in place, and nearly every morning I dropped by for an hour or so to check on the Tracerlab litigation, and to take care of other routine matters. The company leased many of the nucleonic devises to its customers, and one of my responsibilities was to prepare those leases. If the company sold the equipment, I approved the customer's purchase order. I prepared the employment contracts for new engineers and executives; prepared the grants of stock options; and continued to supervise the work of the other corporate lawyer and the two patent lawyers.

If you think about my first few months at the Bricker firm, you will notice that there was a great variety in my work. I was a probate lawyer, a trial and appellate lawyer, a real estate and commercial law lawyer, a labor lawyer, a research lawyer, and an "in-house" corporate lawyer—all at the same time.

That condition changed after a few months. When we moved to our new offices in the spring of 1965, we were in a position to expand, and within a short time we hired a half-dozen of the brightest young lawyers available from national law schools. The Honorable Russell Leach, a local municipal judge who became bored watching other lawyers at work in his court, resigned from his bench, and joined our firm. He was capable of doing the work of three lawyers, and he took over nearly all of the non-corporation work I had been handling. Because he knew his way around the local courts and community, he did this same work a lot faster and better than I.

Richard Pickett, a gifted lawyer who had worked closely with John Eckler for years, began to serve as the lead lawyer on the John W. Galbreath work. Eventually he took it over entirely, and near the end of his career, Dick took a leave of absence from our firm, and joined Galbreath as its full-time vice president. William Leighner was responsible for much of our tax advice, and also was our best probate lawyer. Bill Chadeayne slowly replaced Bill Evatt as the premiere bond lawyer in Ohio. Nearly everyone in the firm found a niche. Because of my varied background, I was able to assist other, younger lawyers in a variety of assignments. But for the most part I stayed in the corporation, securities and complex litigation areas of the law.

Most of us believed that a varied background was a good thing for a young lawyer, and we insisted that all the new law graduates who came with us not specialize for a couple of years. We required them to clerk for several months with each of the experienced lawyers who were working primarily in real estate, trial work, probate, corporation and labor law. Because of the governmental backgrounds of our founders, we did a lot of lobbying at the Ohio general assembly, and we required the new lawyers to try their hands for a while in that politically charged environment. Most of them hated it. After a few years, we encouraged the new men to settle down in the area of the law of their choice. During the rotation process most of the new lawyers considered the process a waste of time and money. Looking back now, most of them who had to go through the system agree that getting a taste of everything made them better lawyers in the long run.

You may notice that I refer to all of our lawyers as "men." They were *all* men; and so were all the judges; and all the department heads in government; all the in-house lawyers at the corporations; and all of our clients. We never had a woman lawyer apply for work at our office until the mid-1970s. Until the time of my retirement we never represented a corporation which employed a woman in a senior position. The situation is altogether different today. We have two women on the Supreme Court. The Speaker of the House is a woman. The superintendent of schools is a woman. So is the head of the chamber of commerce. The public transportation system is run by a woman. Nearly half the lawyers at Bricker & Eckler are women. Many businesses, especially smaller businesses, are headed by women. In the days when one of the largest public relations firms in central Ohio was represented by our office, the founder was my personal friend and I did his legal work. Today, his daughter heads the company, and she is represented by a woman lawyer. "Nothing personal," she explained to me, cheerfully.

Our practice of rotating new lawyers from department to department was abandoned in the early 1970s. The lawyers who came to us after 1972 or so, knew exactly what kind of law they wanted to practice, and if you tried to indoctrinate them in something else, they would threaten to accept employment with another firm. It was a young lawyers' market after 1970, and each top graduate from a good law school had at least two or three offers of employment from which to choose.

We noticed something else starting in the early 1970s. The lawyers we began to hire were remarkably intelligent. There were two reasons for this. The possibilities for employment in the colleges and universities leveled off after the vast expansion following World War II. Higher education had all the professors it needed, and there was very little incentive for anyone to prepare for teaching by acquiring a masters and doctorate. As a result, the top college students who in normal times would head for graduate school, headed for law school where the opportunities were unlimited.

The second reason was the social unrest of the 1960s, most of which was blamed upon the war in Vietnam. Many bright young college students in those turbulent times decided that they were going to re-arrange society and make it better. They decided that a career in law afforded many opportunities to save the world from itself; so they flocked to the law schools in unprecedented numbers. We had brand new law graduates without any clinical experience, coming to us and insisting that they would practice only civil rights law, or only environmental law, or only class action law. They shied away from any employment with a corporation, or with the department of a private law firm which represented corporations. When we first heard these attitudes being expressed with great earnestness, we thought the youngsters were kidding us.

This was a difficult phenomenon for the founding lawyers in our firm to understand. Bill Evatt died in 1970, and Bob Barton in 1972, so they missed much of the changing times. Senator Bricker fumed in private, but kept his cool in public. Although it was clear to me that the young people were short-sighted, if not amusing, I was able to remain sanguine, because I was a trustee of a small, Presbyterian college during most of the 1960s, and had lots of opportunities to understand the youngsters. Also our own children were in either college or high school by this time, and I learned a lot from them. Times change; law firms change; and there is very little anyone can do about it. John Eckler took this attitude too, and the fact that he was our leader helped keep most of our lawyers from touching off riots.

The social revolution ended in the 1980s as quickly as it began. Law students coming to us were suddenly less job-oriented and more career-oriented. They wanted to know exactly how profitable our firm was; exactly what their beginning salary would be; exactly when they would "make partner," as they put it; and exactly what their incomes would be in five years, and again in ten years. They cared less about what they were going to do, and more about how quickly they would become rich doing it.

I found this attitude to be more offensive than the attitude of the do-gooders in the 1970s. After all, I was now an old-timer myself, and I did not find it funny when the young graduates, both men and women, wanted to know my income. Only my wife, my partners and the IRS knew those numbers. Nor did I enjoy explaining our firm's retirement plan to a 25-year old lawyer.

I was genuinely pleased when conditions were such that I could avoid some of the diversity, and begin to concentrate entirely on corporate, securities and complex litigation law. I think that from my early days with the Durfey firm in Springfield, I had known that this is what I wanted, but only after 15 or more years of experience was I able to realize this goal.

One of our new associates took over the Industrial Nucleonics work in 1965 and 1966. He, instead of I, began to go there daily and take care of the routine work. Gradually John Eckler began to assume the responsibility for the Tracerlab litigation. I lost a lot of respect with the Chope brothers early in 1965, when I began to work with Jim St. Clair and other lawyers in Hale and Dorr in putting together a possible "settlement package" for presentation to the Tracerlab lawyers. Obviously we could not present it until it was approved by Bert and Roy Chope, and they were both very disappointed when they learned that I had been working on a settlement without discussing it with them. They looked upon it as a show of weakness in our case. I think the source of most of their disappointment sprang from the fact that they never understood how lawyers work.

The case went to trial in the summer of 1965, without either Eckler or me being invited to the trial table. Exactly what St. Clair, Eckler and I feared would happen, actually happened. Both Chopes turned out to be opinionated witnesses. They were evasive, contradictory and overly sensitive about being accused of stealing trade secrets. They were too close to the facts to be objective about them. As a result, on the 34th day of the trial, St. Clair, with the support of John Eckler, recommended to the Chopes that they settle to keep from losing badly, perhaps even losing the entire company. The Chopes had enough of lawyers and courtrooms by that time. They settled by paying about twice what St. Clair and I possibly could have negotiated for them earlier in the year. I say "possibly," because one never knows about these things. We surely could have engineered a settlement better than the one which ended the ordeal.

I had no time to be unforgiving. By the summer of 1965 I was committed to the busiest and most stressful period of my career. Here is a sampling of what I was up to:
- I represented a group of ten investors from southern Ohio which organized a holding company and conducted an intrastate offering of common stock. We used the proceeds from the stock sales, to found a life insurance company; to organize an open-end investment company, commonly known as a mutual fund; to acquire a National bank; and to found a real estate corporation. With an initial capital of under $50,000, the holding company's assets grew within three to five years to $120 million.
- Our firm represented Pure Oil Company, an Ohio corporation which had been in existence for many years. When Union Oil Company of California, later UNOCAL, entered into negotiations to acquire Pure Oil, I was asked to defend Pure Oil's rights. The merger was completed in July of 1966, and immediately 83,000 former Pure Oil shareholders filed a dissenting shareholders' lawsuit in Ohio, objecting to the merger. They demanded an appraisal of their shares, and to be paid for them in cash, rather than with Union Oil stock. Union Oil asked me to defend that litigation, which twice went to the Ohio Supreme Court between 1966 and 1970. It was, by far, the most significant litigation in which I ever participated. At the end of a long, legal battle, things worked out well for Union Oil. One nice footnote to this case was that I had to make many trips to Los Angeles. My parents were living in California at that time, so I got to visit them frequently; and Union Oil saved a lot of money on hotel bills I didn't incur.
- In addition to the founding of the life insurance company men-

tioned above, between 1966 and 1971 I represented four other groups of investors which founded life insurance companies.
- In 1967 I represented a group of investors which founded a State-chartered savings and loan association. This was the first such charter granted in Ohio in more than 25 years.
- In 1967 I filed a wrongful death action in behalf of the estate of a scientist at Industrial Nucleonics, who was killed when an airliner crashed on a flight between Columbus and Toledo. He left a widow and three small children. The litigation ended in an out-of-court settlement for the largest amount ever paid in this type of case. Since then much larger settlements have been paid. We settled because the insurance company representing the airline knew we were prepared to go to trial, and were anxious to do so.
- In 1966 I filed a large number of Form 10s with the SEC for corporations in central Ohio. In 1964 Congress passed several substantial amendments to the Securities and Exchange Act, which required that any corporation which employed 500 or more persons, and had annual sales in excess of a million dollars, had to register its shares on Form 10 and thereafter clear annual proxy material with the SEC. 1966 was the first year for these filings, and they were a bonanza for lawyers who liked to do securities work. The Form 10s were long and complicated and required many exhibits. The annual proxy material also presented the securities lawyer with steady work each year. The first Form 10 I did was for a long time client of our firm, Buckeye Steel Castings. When the word spread that I knew how to prepare and file these documents, I received assignments from numerous other local corporations not normally represented by Bricker & Eckler, and from lawyers who had no background in securities law.

There were many other exciting matters to handle, but I think you can get an idea from the few I mentioned, how the character of my practice turned toward corporate work as soon as we acquired more lawyers to help us. The secret to being able to take care of substantial assignments is the assembling of an adequate force of lawyers. A single lawyer, or even a few lawyers, can not attract the larger cases, or handle them if they are attracted. The complex case must be broken down into pieces, and each piece must be assigned to a team of lawyers for research. The partner in charge deals with the client and the court, and makes certain that each team working on the pieces is on schedule and properly focused.

An example of how this works is a gigantic law suit which came our way from Union Oil in the year 1971. By this time our firm had expanded to 20 to 25 lawyers, which made us the third largest in Columbus. Eventually we would become more than a 100 lawyers, but the gang we put together in the early 1970s was exceptional. In those days we recruited only at Harvard, Yale, Michigan, Northwestern, Chicago, and of course Ohio State because most of our founders studied there. We did not necessarily take only top students academically, although we got our share of those; but we sought good students who appeared to us to be willing, even likely, to out-hustle the other side.

The law suit sent to us by Union Oil was a class action brought by two Union Oil credit card holders in the Cleveland area. These two plaintiffs believed, or at least their lawyers did, that Union Oil was violating the Truth In Lending Act, only recently enacted by Congress. The Act was not easy to read or understand. In length, along with the regulations promulgated to administer it, it was about the size of a Sears catalogue—but there were no pictures. Much of it consisted of bureaucratic gobbledygook which sounded something like: Except as provided elsewhere in this Act and the regulations, and subject to the limitations in paragraph A above, and in accordance with paragraph Z hereinafter, to the extent that either may be applicable, on and after the effective date, or such other date as may be provided ... etc., yada yada yada. Some of the paragraphs in the regulations were several pages in length, with no place to breathe if you were reading them aloud. One of our lawyers, an honor student at Harvard, looked over the Act and said that it could scarcely be contained by the human mind.

It was vital that Union Oil not be found to have any liability, because if that were the case, the Act provided that each person in the class would be entitled to a flat, statutory payment of $100. According to the plaintiffs' complaint the class consisted of the two credit card holders who were named, "together with all other persons to whom credit cards were issued after ... (a certain date)."

If Union Oil lost, it would owe its 4,979,998 happy and contented credit card holders, and its two unhappy card holders in Cleveland, pretty close to a half-billion dollars, one-third of which would go to the plaintiffs' lawyers. The potential loss exceeded the net worth of the company, despite the fact that Union Oil was at the time the 18th largest domestic, integrated petroleum company in existence.

George Bond, Union Oil's intelligent and Stanford educated general counsel, had tears in his eyes and a prayer on his lips when he assigned the case to us. I had a little flutter in my heart myself, part of which was gratitude since I still had two kids to put through college.

Consumer advocates will tell you that the procedural device known as the class action is absolutely necessary in our society, because it keeps corporations honest. A single, unhappy consumer can not make much of an impression on the defendant, if he has a legitimate complaint and has been injured in some substantial way. But if he can be laced together with "all other persons similarly situated," he can catch the attention of the corporation in a hurry.

On the other hand, corporations and their lawyers, will tell you that consumers are not nearly as well protected and rewarded by class actions as the lawyers are who file them. My own feeling is that among potential dangers to society, class action lawsuits rank somewhere near mass famine and widespread unemployment, and perhaps a little ahead of contagious diseases.

Union Oil had done its best to comply with the Truth in Lending Act. After it became law, but before it became effective, Union Oil retained one of the largest law firms in New York City, to render an opinion on whether the company was in compliance. Copies of Union Oil's application for a credit card, and the credit card agreement, and even the credit card itself, along with all of the printed materials used in marketing the card, were submitted to the New York firm.

For a modest fee which was only slightly less than the national debt, the firm opined that Union Oil was in "substantial compliance" with Truth in Lending, whatever that means. It was like telling a man whose house was on fire that he was in substantial compliance with the fire codes. There was lots of language in the opinion which was designed to save the backside of the law firm.

I don't have to tell you that Union Oil won our case. The fact that Union Oil is still in business today, is proof enough of the victory. What I do want to tell you is how we organized in order to win.

The first thing I did was put together a team of our brightest minds, and its mission was to learn everything possible about the Truth in Lending Act. We explored the legislative history of the Act, and took note of what was said about the intent of the legislation while it was still in committee. One of those team members was sent to the law firm in New York, to learn what it had looked into before rendering its opinion. The partner in charge of rendering that opinion had been practicing banking law most of his life, and somewhat against his better judgment he told us everything he knew. Union Oil insisted that he do so.

A second team in our office looked into Rule 23 of the Federal Rules of Civil Procedure. This is the class action rule. We already knew quite a bit about it, and personally I had defended a couple of other smaller, less fatal, class action suits. We reviewed our own files, and studied all the literature on the subject in the law reviews and other commentaries.

A third team went through the complaint and made a list of every precise thing the plaintiffs' lawyers were alleging to be in violation of the Act. Each of these matters was analyzed in the light of the exact language in the Act and the regulations. The regulations were studied in the light of the Act, because we intended to attack any regulation which was not faithful to the spirit and words of the legislation.

Our last team put together a list of possible motions we might be able to file in good conscience, in order to knock out the suit right at the pleading stage.

Because I was the lawyer who would make the appearances in court, I went to Cleveland and interviewed every trial lawyer I knew, on the whims and caprices of the Honorable Thomas Lambros, who had the case. I was admitted to practice in the US courts in Cleveland, but I had never appeared before Judge Lambros. I went to Cleveland a second time and dropped by His Honor's chambers and introduced myself. I told him that I did not want to discuss any feature of the case on an *ex parte* basis, but I did want to shake his hand and let him know that we would be seeing a lot of each other in the coming days. As it turned out the case ambled on until 1975, and I spent weeks on end in Cleveland. I even became a fan of the Cleveland Native Americans baseball team.

I met frequently with the lawyer in charge of each team, but was careful not to meet with the entire team. It was the job of the team leader to deal with his own team, and I had enough to do otherwise. This was not the only case I was handling. About every ten days or so, I would meet with all four team leaders simultaneously, and we would get a broader view of where we were going.

Whenever anything significant took place in the courtroom, I would take all four team leaders with me to the court. We did not want Judge Lambros to get the idea that Union Oil was not taking this case seriously.

I prefer not to go further into this major litigation, and I would imagine that you are grateful for my attitude. I wanted to go this far to demonstrate how a law firm puts the wagons in a circle before the battle starts, and why it takes a lot of Native Americans (I nearly said "Indians") to make up a tribe. The day of the solo practitioner is gone, for a lawyer who wants to handle substantial cases.

There are two afterthoughts to the Union Oil credit card case I want to mention. In 1995, twenty years after the case ended, and almost ten years after I retired, Judge Lambros retired from the Federal bench. He could have joined any law firm, but he selected Bricker & Eckler. I didn't know of his coming with us, until after it happened. He told the managing partner of our firm that he still had a memory of me, and he even quoted one of my briefs I filed with him years ago, where (according to him) my opening lines were: "Lawyers who file class action cases stick together like birds in a dead tree after a rain."

The other afterthought has to do with how taxing and unending the practice of law can be. When the credit card case ended, I went immediately, without even a day of rest, into an equally intricate law suit filed in the Federal courts in Denver. That one took another few years out of my life with my family. I think lawyers' spouses and children suffer more than lawyers. And they don't have nearly as much fun.

Bricker & Eckler expanded at a time when the practice of law was undergoing tremendous technological stresses. In the mid-1970s, some of our younger lawyers began to campaign for us to enter the computer age. When I began to practice in 1951 we used manual typewriters, which we bought for under $100 each. Then came electric IBMs, and we were certain that their $600 price tags were going to bankrupt us. The first copy machine we acquired, in about 1952 or 1953, cost a small fortune and required a lot of maintenance. We used to spill the liquid which made it work, all over our carpets.

Then came typewriters with magnetic card memories in them, and they were close to $2500 each. A new and improved copy machine came along every year or so, and each time the price was higher. Fax machines and smart telephones followed as did cellular telephones and pagers. But the most polarizing equipment of them all was the computer.

Half of our firm believed that we couldn't exist for more than the next two minutes if we did not lay out the money for a mainframe Wang, which was so temperamental that it would require its own clean room, and could be approached only by persons wearing surgical masks and white gloves.

The other half was absolutely against such an acquisition. For one thing, many of us were scared to death of what Nellie Henry's homemade accounting system would do to the innards of the contraption.

Good cases could be made on both sides, and it got to the place where our lawyers were spending more time making those cases than they were devoting to clients' matters. The scales were tipped in favor of getting a computer by two factors. First, our leading competitor got one. Could we do less? Second, we all agreed that the computer would be used *only* for research, bookkeeping and the like. Under no circumstances would it ever be used to attempt to evaluate the worth of any lawyer.

After about a year, our understanding was modified by a second agreement among us, that the worth of lawyers would indeed be evaluated by our computer, but the numbers would be available only to the executive committee of our firm. No way would everyone become privy to such sensitive information, which would be based upon such things as seniority, number of hours worked, billings, new clients attracted, and the like.

Within two hours every lawyer in the office, and most of the secretaries, knew how "valuable" everyone was or was not.

This presented an administrative nightmare for persons like John Eckler, who were trying to run our firm by keeping everyone happy. The distrust among us, cost us much more than the several hundred thousand dollars we spent for the gadget. I never had any personal complaint over the way the computer sized me up, because it treated me with respect; but we sure had some mad lawyers, who thought more of their performances than did the Wang.

One comedian among us started the rumor that one night after hours, Nellie Henry approached the computer and typed in, "Is there a God?" Instead of coming back with the well known answer, "There is *now*," the computer came back with, "Well there *is*, Nellie, but don't worry about it ... *He* would never think of challenging your authority." Life in the computer age can be brutal.

As the years rolled on I built up a great respect for Senator Bricker. He grew mellow with age. I often had lunch with him, and it was like taking a seminar in practical government. In the late seventies, when he was approaching 85, he avoided driving his car at night. He was in great demand at Republican rallies all over Ohio, and because I enjoyed being with him, I often drove him to these gatherings. Once we went to Logan, in Hocking County, my home town. All of my high school buddies were there, and they were impressed by the fact that I was associated with a former governor and senator. Many of them thought I was his chauffeur, and were envious of that.

Senator Bricker straightened things out in my behalf. I was very grateful for the nice things he said about me, but he overdid it a little. For example, he got carried away with this bit of his own oratory:

"When I was running for attorney general, many years ago, I campaigned on the steps of your courthouse. A little red-headed boy came up to me, and I could see that he was a very serious young man, and I said to him, Son, what do you want to be when you grow up? and he said, Sir, I want to be a lawyer, and he did grow up and he did become a lawyer, and as a matter of fact he is my partner, and I never had a better partner, and he is the lawyer who drove me here tonight ..." I didn't know whether to laugh or cry, but all my buddies saved the day by giving me a standing ovation. Senator Bricker could have sold molten lava to the people of Pompeii.

In 1983 this dear old man walked out of our offices for the last time. For years he had told us, cheerfully, every time he left for the day, "If you take in any big fees, just put the money in the bank." It was his final exit line. It was a sad but proud moment for me, a few months later, when he told John Eckler that he didn't think he could make it back to our offices, and he wanted me to have the use of his office. I occupied it for years in fact, but in spirit it always was his.

We had some tragedy along the way. In April of 1966, Bobby Barton, the son of Robert Barton, our founder, was killed in an airplane crash. He was a childhood friend of Jack Nicklaus, and he and his wife and another couple were on the way to Augusta for the Masters. They were going to be the guests of the Nicklaus' in the house Jack rented for the week. They encountered ice and fog. Bob was an experienced ex-Air Force pilot, but the combination of weather and overloading of the small twin-engine Beechcraft, which he leased, got the better of him. The plane went down just short of the runway at Johnson City, Tennessee. All four were killed, and seven children were orphaned. Jack Nicklaus wanted to withdraw from the 1966 Masters, but his wife Barbara recommended against it, and told him that his young friend would have wanted him to play.

Nicklaus won that Masters, his second in a row. He insisted that the trophy be put on display in our office.

Robert Barton, the father, never recovered fully. Until his own death in 1972, he spent most of his days staring silently out of the windows of his office. He never tried another law suit. His spirit died with his son and daughter-in-law.

In 1976 John Selby, the partner who appeared immediately above me on the masthead, died in a diving accident. He and his wife were experienced spelunker instructors and scuba divers, but he failed to manage his air tank properly and it was a fatal mistake. One of the young men we recruited shortly after I came to the firm died of a heart attack at his desk. Another young lawyer who came to our firm after I retired also died, I believe of cancer. I never knew her.

For the most part, though, we had happy times. In 1982, Senator John Glenn, the former (and recent) astronaut invited me to accompany him on a business trip to the Persian Gulf. For years prior to then, I represented Senator Glenn, and his family, in personal matters, but never in his public responsibilities. In the 1960s we served together as trustees of a small, Presbyterian college which is his alma mater. Senator Glenn would sometimes ask me to fly with him in his airplane, when the weather was a bit ragged for one pilot. Flying with him was like flying with Lindbergh. If we dropped into an airport for fuel, a half dozen line boys tried to fill his tanks at one time. Of course they all wanted autographs. If John were flying from Columbus to Washington, it was not unusual for the traffic controllers to give him something "useful" like the winds aloft over Council Bluffs, Iowa, so they could brag about having handled John Glenn. He took it all in stride. He is the finest pilot I have ever observed at close range. His airmanship is perfect.

The Head of State of United Arab Emirates invited Glenn to Aba Dahbi to "discuss some personal business." Another US

Senator had just been indicted for participating in personal business which was in conflict with his public duty, and Glenn thought I should go along to keep everything pure. Traveling with a national icon was lots of fun. Over the years I have had as much trouble as any traveler, getting Margaret and myself through customs. On this trip, at both London and in the Gulf, we whistled through what can be an endless process, with the help of an armed guard.

The highlight of the trip for me was filling in for the senator with a speech before the chamber of commerce at Dubai. Aba Dhabi is the capital, but Dubai is the commerce center of United Arab Emirates. We were on the way to the speech when Senator Glenn received a telephone call in his limo. The message was that the Head of State wanted to entertain John at his oasis. A helicopter would take him there immediately. Glenn asked for permission to bring me along, and that was refused.

As a salve to me, John asked me to make his speech for him. I readily agreed, thinking it would be fun. I asked him for a copy of the talk, so I could make sure I could pronounce all the names and places. He said he had no text. He had intended to wing it.

To make matters worse, I had 20 minutes to get ready. The crowd of perhaps 500 persons were all dressed identically in mid-East, black and white, flowing garments. They looked like a room full of distinguished penguins. They were profoundly disappointed that the famous astronaut had not shown up. Many of them never understood who on earth I might be. I spoke through an interpreter, and all of my light-hearted pitter-patter must have been lost in the translation. When they were not yawning, they sat like mannequins, while I described the life and times of the people of the Great State of Ohio, a subject which interested them not at all.

Late in the speech I made a reference to the fact that more and more business was being conducted through joint ventures.

When the interpreter said "joint ventures" the room came alive like a choir loft on Sunday morning. These were proud and honorable rug merchants by birth and heritage. They and their progenitors had engaged in world bartering for 50 generations. They could care less about whether Ohio was an agricultural state, or that it was bordered on the north by Lake Erie. They wanted to hear more about whether you could make any money with a joint venture. It turned out that at least half of them were graduates of the Harvard School of Business, and spoke English as well as I did. After my talk mercifully ended, they gathered around the dais for a solid hour, and pumped me for information about those joint ventures. Even the interpreter was awake by this time.

It was so sad to see John Eckler's health deteriorate. As early as 1970 he began to show the strains of his responsibilities. The nature of his practice was stressful. He may have been the busiest lawyer in Columbus. He developed an ulcer, which in some ways was a badge of honor in our line of work; but it was painful. He began to keep bottles of white pills on his desk, which he called "my chemicals." His only son, a Naval officer and a hero of the Vietnam war, died suddenly in July of 1970, and the deaths of Bill Evatt and Bob Barton, near that time, hit him hard.

Many of us who could see his failing health encouraged him to take more trips to get away from the strain of management and practice. He did go to Africa a time or two, in his capacity as a trustee of World Neighbors, but since he and Mary went with a client and his wife, he was not entirely away from the office. The women might go sightseeing. The men discussed stock options, and buy-out agreements.

The Branch Rickey family owned an island in Canada, and we encouraged John and Mary to spend more time there. We tried to keep him informed on our activities. My colleague, Bill Chadeayne, could not suppress the urge to send letters to John with important "news" like: "The fire in the Bricker & Eckler vault last week was not nearly as devastating as reported in the newspapers."

In 1978 John Eckler reached his 65th birthday and was supposed to retire as chairman of our firm, and from our practice. But he just didn't want to do that, and none of us ever brought up the matter. The firm was his life, and had been since the end of World War II. He was born to lead: as president of the student body at Ohio Wesleyan; as captain of his ship in the Pacific; as the administrative assistant to Senator Bricker; and as the head of our firm since 1949. He held important offices in the local and national bar associations; and he seemed to be a past president of every service club and worthwhile organization in Columbus. The only person who ever won more civic awards than Eckler, was Senator Bricker. Both of them wound up being burned out.

The responsibilities of running our firm transferred so slowly to Richard Pickett, that you couldn't see it happen. Dick was (and is) one of my closest friends in the office, and we owned several airplanes together. He left our firm shortly after the transfer of authority to him was complete. He didn't particularly want to leave, nor did we want to lose him; but the John W. Galbreath Company, whom he served for many years, wanted him to come full time to their organization as vice president. The Galbreath company was undergoing a change of the guard too, as John Galbreath, the boyhood friend of Senator Bricker, was succeeded by his son, Daniel Galbreath.

Time does indeed march on. Senator Bricker died in his sleep in 1986. John Eckler spent his last few years battling Alzheimer's Disease. I drove him home one night and he introduced me to Mary as "this nice young man who brought me home." It finally got so bad that he did not recognize Mary. He died in 1994 the same way he lived, with dignity. One of the sad moments of my life was when I presented his eulogy at the ceremonies celebrating his life. I tried to do it in the confident way I knew he would want.

The laughter, and the wisdom, of John Bricker and John Eckler will echo in the halls of Bricker & Eckler forever.

It was now time for me to leave the firm too. We were 105 lawyers bound together by the heritage of the Brickers, and Evatts, and Bartons, and Ecklers who had taught us always to put the interests of our clients first. Our practice was healthy. I was exhausted. I never had any special training in management, and it was clear that a younger generation of lawyers with a greater admiration for planning and budgets and (I hesitate to use the term) monthly reports, needed to take over.

Who is to say what is good or what is bad in this complicated world. I think the younger lawyers, who have come along in recent years, committed professional suicide some time ago. They want to be organized. They want to measure this year against last, and to predict what the next year will bring. Bill Evatt would say they have become certified public accountants. For all I know, that is the way to go. After all, their computers can not just stand silent. There must be something for them to do.

For me, though, a lawyer of another school and a man of another generation, I wanted no part of a Bricker & Eckler which was not headed by either a Bricker or an Eckler. I missed my long time secretaries, Jo Barrett and Mary Ellen Wildermuth, who understood my way of doing things. Both of them left our firm, and I decided to do the same thing.

I did not want to sit and vegetate.

So, what the Heck, I decided to become a golf writer

As the years rolled on I built up a great respect for Senator Bricker. He grew mellow with age. I often had lunch with him, and it was like taking a seminar in practical government. In 1983, this dear old man walked out of our offices for the last time. For years he had told us cheerfully, every time he left for the day, "If you take in any big fees, just put the money in the bank." It was his final exit line.

The Honorable John W. Bricker, former Attorney General of Ohio, Governor of Ohio and United States Senator

John Sagan was my fraternity brother and a close friend. John earned his masters and doctorate in economics before joining the Ford Motor Company. Within a short time he became vice president and treasurer of Ford, and found time to chair the Federal Reserve Board in Chicago. For more than 20 years we served together as Ohio Wesleyan trustees. He died two days before Christmas in 1999. Earlier in 1999, John and his wife, Margaret, the daughter of a former Methodist Bishop, gave a million dollars to Ohio Wesleyan.

John Sagan, Margaret Pickett Sagan, myself and Marg, May 1998

Mother and Dad Hanna, with Marg, July 1973

When Marg's parents needed some extra help in their later years, we could fly to the Moline, Illinois airport, near the family farm, Seldom Rest, in 90 minutes. The auto trip to the farm was at least 11 hours, each way. It is hard to overstate the convenience of having a private plane.

Matt died in 1986, and my mother in 1993. They are buried in the same grave. You can see the Pacific from their resting place. They were more than just persons who grew up in Ohio, and had more than their share of struggle. They married, moved to California for the happy life, and wound up with a view of the ocean which only their spirits can see. For our family they were our vitality ...

My mother, Ada Grace Chesser, and my step-father, Matt

Their headstone, Oceanside, California

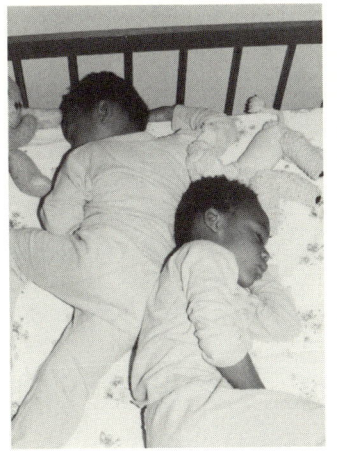

The little babies came to us often in the middle of the night. About midnight one night, a father came for his kids. He said he didn't want any trouble, he just wanted his children. His children looked like little angels in their PJs. The father touched them both gently. I began to explain the law of kidnapping to him. It was a relief to see the man relax. It was clear that he was a caring father.

Two of our 60-some foster children

There has never been a day in our lives when Jim and his sisters have not made us proud. Jane, the doctor; Laura, the teacher; and Jim, the research expert, are the closest of friends. It makes us happy to see them looking out for one another. They are in near daily contact by telephone or E-mail.

Our three children, Laura, Jane and Jim, in 1957

and again, more recently

Our Grandsons, Ian (on top), Andy (to the left) and Greg Huntington

Growing older has not lessened my wants. I want to watch our five grandchildren go through the same stages of maturity as our kids did. I want to see them become good citizens and persons, just like our kids did.

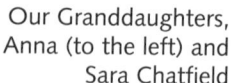

Our Granddaughters, Anna (to the left) and Sara Chatfield

A NEW CAREER FOR ME

My becoming a golf writer, which I started to do even before I left the law, contradicts the bromide that you can't put an old dog through a retraining program. Retraining for a new career is happening frequently these days, all over industry, as persons who once worked at making things, are retraining to communicate with computers which now make things. You can teach us old dogs, but it isn't easy.

It was natural for me to want to be a golf writer. I had represented the Nicklaus companies, and had served for many years as a lawyer and manager for several prominent professional golfers and golf promoters. I read everything printed about golf and golfers, and enjoyed all of it. I had held leadership positions in several golf associations, and had conducted a considerable number of golf tournaments. I was the honorary co-chairman of the 1987 Ryder Cup matches. I even played a little, but always with more fun than success.

So I approached the possibility of writing for golf magazines with great enthusiasm. I was encouraged by one of our finest golf journalists in the United States, Mr. Ken Bowden. Ken is a former top-editor of the most popular golf magazine on the American market. For the past 20 years or so has written nearly every word Jack Nicklaus has uttered in public. Several of Ken's books have become best sellers and are classics in the world of golf literature. Everything Ken Bowden writes holds your attention like a hand full of aces.

He told me that it wouldn't be easy. He said that I should try to write something some golfer might like to read. He told me how to get started, and then sounded like a TV commercial for sneakers, as he urged me to Just Do It. I began to send my stories to every publisher I ever heard of.

The rejections I received were works of art. Some of the editors knew me as a lawyer, and more than one of them advised me not to give up my day job. None of them ever said, "this stinks." They said things like: " … thank you for thinking of us … your story is intriguing but does not fit in with the themes for our magazines for the next few months." Now and then a publisher or editor would turn me down, but suggest another magazine they thought I should contact. I did that a few times, until I realized the first magazine was just trying to put the second magazine out of business.

I got nowhere for 18 months. Letters to the Editors would not publish anything I wrote. The TV Guide wouldn't publish a schedule of programs if I wrote it.

I made some fundamental mistakes, until I got the hang of things. If I went to a tournament which was very exciting, I might sit down and write a cracker-jack article about all the drama and hair-raising intensity. I would send it off with a conviction that only an editor who was half dead would fail to be gripped by my literature. Within days, a rejection would come back reminding me the tournament I was writing about was over, done, and no longer news.

What I learned was that most magazines plan their editions for the Masters, which is played in April, around the first of each year. Maybe a little later if you are an established writer. A neophyte writer should submit his stuff the preceding November or December. Anything written by a novice on the US Open, played in June, should be in the hands of the editors prior to March. Armed with that important, practical information I began to submit my copy months in advance, and with a new-found confidence. It made very little difference. My stories usually were rejected before the tournament I was writing about, was played. I am telling you, I was getting no where.

I also learned that most amateur writers write badly, especially lawyers, and especially me. We assume our readers have no intelligence or ability to use their imaginations. We try to spell out everything. All of our lives, if we are lawyers, we have tried to avoid ambiguity and unintended meanings. We want to make the whole shebang clear, even if we have to start each sentence with "whereas." We use a lot of parenthesis, and dashes and exclamation marks, maybe even two or three of them back-to-back if we want the reader to get the point. There is no crispness, or proper use of pronouns. The adverbs stand in the way of the verbs, and we insert adjectives as every third word. If we intend to tell you something funny, we tell you ahead of time it is going to be funny.

Maybe not all new writers make such common mistakes, but I did. I still do, but I am better than I was. I read things I wrote 15 years ago, and cringe. I had no idea I was so bad. I was crushed when, a time or two, an editor blue-penciled my work and sent it back without a single encouraging word. I used to do that to our new law clerks and summer interns, when they wrote their first contracts and leases. But that was ... well, different.

One thing I noticed was how inconsistent editors can be. If I sent the same story to more than one editor, which I did frequently, I might get it back with a brassy remark that I should learn to put in more commas, so the reader would know where to breathe. Another editor would mark the same copy, " ... too many commas."

Fortunately I didn't have to write for a living. I could laugh at the rejections, even when some of them made me mad. I have no idea how I would have reacted if I were dead broke with a family to feed. I might have bought an AK-47. Just for sport and recreational shooting of course. No one would want to harm a fussy little editor.

Finally, when I was about to turn to bowling or fly-fishing, an editor of a regional magazine, which is distributed only in Ohio, printed one of my stories. He must have been, at heart, a Las Vegas blackjack dealer. I could have kissed the guy, and I never met him. My tale concerned a fictional character I dreamed up, who discovered the "secret" of the golf swing. It had something to do with how you hold your eyebrows. He began to win every tournament he entered. He soon was on the PGA Tour, warming up next to Palmer and Nicklaus. The story had a couple of odd twists, but I will not tell you more, in case you run across an old copy of *The Ohio Golfer Magazine* in your dentist's office.

My story was so outlandish that it picked up some interest. Several readers wrote letters to the editor about it. One reader took my insane plot seriously, and offered the sober thought that he didn't think it could ever happen. Duh. Instantly, I was famous within a mile of two of my house. Now, when I sent copy to an editor, I could refer to myself as a published writer.

Jeff Groezinger, the editor of *Ohio Golfer* who took such a chance with my first story, asked me to do a monthly column. *Golf Digest*, a national magazine, read one of my columns and asked me to submit a story. I did. It was published. *Golf Illustrated* saw my story in *Golf Digest* and asked me to submit something. As they say, whomever they are, the rest is history. I have had somewhere around 650 pieces published.

My *Ohio Golfer* column, which the magazine called "Beyond the White Stakes," ran in every edition for 10 years. For the benefit of non-golfers, the out-of-bounds stakes at a golf course are painted white. I wore out four editors of the magazine, but all of them were willing to run my columns. I wrote on every subject you could think of. As I look back through the issues, I see that some of my efforts were good, and some very bad. I am tempted to dazzle you with some of the good ones, but it would be unfair to do that without including the dogs. Anyway, good writing is like beauty; it lies in the eyes of the reader, and rarely is there unanimity on what is good or bad. Especially among editors.

In the fall of 1993 I hit the jackpot. I wrote a story on the 1993 Ryder Cup matches, which I covered at The Belfry near Birmingham, England. I was annoyed by the indifferent play of the American team, even though the US won 15 to 13, and I remember saying in my story that " ... even my gums are aching."

The editors of *Today's Golfer*, which is published in Peterborough, England, and distributed in ten countries, read my story and decided that an American golf writer with aching gums should be the American Correspondent and Columnist for their magazine. I submitted several samples, and the following spring, my column entitled "Letter From America" made its debut. I have been in every issue of the magazine since then. When I was tagged-out by leukemia early in 1999, the editors kindly cut back my schedule. Since I have been ill, I have written only about the four major tournaments, and the 1999 Ryder Cup matches. That is a big enough load for me just now. When I am well, I go to about 20 to 25 PGA Tour tournaments each year, and attend several more in Europe.

Golf writers differ significantly from lawyers. The first time I walked into a media tent, I thought I was in a shelter for the homeless. Except for a few older writers, the journalists were wearing blue jeans and sneakers. They needed haircuts. They were actually friendly. They were helping one another. A writer who had no idea who I was, asked me how to spell a word. Another asked me if "Singing in the Rain," starred Frank Sinatra or Gene Kelly. I couldn't figure that one out, until a friend reminded me that V.J. Singh, the current Master's champion, was leading the tournament, and because it was raining, the writer probably was going to use the line, "Singhing in the Rain." I wished I had thought of it.

My initial reaction to the golf writers was they lacked hard and harsh experience. None of them had spent an evening in a drafty courthouse with a nervous client waiting for a jury to bring in a verdict. None of them had to listen to the opposing counsel, an A-plus student from the Harvard Law School, give a masterful summation to a jury; knowing that in a few minutes they would have to stand up and rebut every point. All these writers did was spin clever phrases, or unfair opinions, and sit back and listen to people either laugh or cry.

You won't find a bunch of lawyers sitting around in fatigues, and asking one another for help. Very early in my Municipal Court practice in Springfield, a veteran lawyer on the other side of the case volunteered to file my subpoenas for my witnesses, because he had to go to the courthouse anyway to file his own subpoenas. Nice fellow. He sent me the receipts from the Clerk, indicating that all my requests were filed. When I got to court, ready for the trial, I had no witnesses. None of them had been served. I went roaring into the Clerk's office to complain, and learned that before my subpoenas were delivered to the sheriff for service, the other lawyer had withdrawn them. He had put them on the record; he could take them off. Nice fellow.

Golf writers would never do that. They wouldn't even think of doing that. Their minds work in a different way. Strategy plays a very minor part in meeting a deadline. Syntax and punctuation are paramount. Trying to remember who came in second in a tournament three years ago, and where the US Open is going to be played next year, occupy the minds of writers.

Writers and lawyers both deal in plots, but writers create them, and lawyers exploit them. Writers spend hours looking for the right word. Lawyers never use one word anyway, so it doesn't matter if it is the right one. Years ago, I filed a "brief" that was seven volumes in length, and took up three feet of shelf space. Editors now ask me to express myself in 750 words or less.

When I attended tournaments as a lawyer and player-manager for the contestants, everyone treated me fairly. If I asked where the ninth green was, someone would point to it. Now I am there as a member of the media. I am now in heaven. The same security guy who throws lawyers out of the locker room, holds the door open for the media types. Lunch is free. So are the drinks. No one points me to the ninth green; I am now escorted there, sometimes in a golf cart. What a difference.

There is another important difference in the two vocations. Lawyers are thriving, and increasing in numbers and importance in our culture. They are career-oriented and aggressive. They are in demand, and highly paid. A young law graduate from a good law school can write his own ticket. He can join a big firm or a little one; or go into business; or go into politics; or work for the government; or teach. A golf writer is a member of a dying breed.

We will always need good golf writers, but not many. A talented golf correspondent for the New York *Times* a few years ago, today is the vice president of public relations for a corporation. Another has given up writing for famous magazines, and now writes for a website you never heard of. Can you imagine spending an afternoon composing a literary effort which can be obliterated in an instant, by clicking a button marked "delete?" Fewer and fewer people are reading words printed on paper these days.

Fifteen years ago my editors would accept a feature story of 2000 words, maybe even 2500. Today they would rather have a photograph with a clever caption under it. My first columns ran 1200 to 1400 words. They are half that, now.

Sometimes I write something which is better than average. My editors will sense that, and splurge a little by spending some money to have my copy illustrated. Several times I have lucked out by having my stories illustrated by the famed New York artist,

Jack Davis, the man who created Mad Magazine, and introduced its foremost character, the freckled-faced little guy who smiles at you and says, "What? Me, worry?"

Nothing boils my water quicker than having one of my friends say something like, "I saw your article in Such and Such Golf Magazine. Those were the funniest cartoons I ever saw." The only thing that will make me madder is the friend who says, "I saw your article …" and then stops right there. He does not say he liked it, or that he didn't. He doesn't agree or disagree, or mention anything about its content. He just says he saw it.

I am tempted in those cases to say, "Welll???" But I don't.

After you have written for awhile, you tend to view everything as a potential story. I play golf, and on another fairway I spot a handicapped young man swinging a club with one arm. I have to interview him. I walk past the caddie yard, and a young kid in the back of the crowd is asking for work with his eyes. He gets it from me. I have to know how he learned to beg, using mental telepathy. If I play a crowded course in the middle of the summer, I wonder what it would look like under two feet of snow and I am the only person on it. So I show up in February, just to get a story.

I like to write about golf, because I like golfers. Everyone likes famous golfers, but I am talking about the hackers you never heard of who play day in and day out, for nothing but the trophy. Show me a person who tells his boss he is working and then goes golfing, and I will show you a lucky person who will soon be out of work so he can play golf full time. The chances are also that he will be virtuous, and patient, and good-natured, and honest in almost everything he says except what he tells his boss. And if his boss is a golfer, he will understand.

I hope I get to be a golf writer for many years to come.

There was a time when I wished I could fly forever. Those days finally came to an end. This might be a good place to tell you about owning and operating a small, private airplane.

FLYING FOR FUN

FLYING FOR FUN IS AS DIFFERENT FROM BEING A GOLFER, as being a golfer is different from being a lawyer. And all for different reasons.

A lawyer can spend days plotting out his strategy. The flyer must make his decisions immediately. The golfer can take a chance, and if he screws up, he gets a bogey. The flyer who screws up, makes the headlines.

Flying for fun also differs from flying for the Navy. There were exceptions, but for the most part Navy flying was not fun flying. The Navy would have us in the air on days when the fog was so thick that you could hardly find the hanger door. The war was on. We were trained to kill, and to keep from being killed. Not much fun connected with that, unless you are psychopathic.

For years after I left the Navy, I could not afford to own even a small plane. I might never have gotten into private flying, were it not for Richard Pickett, one of my partners and best friends at Bricker & Eckler.

Dick was an enthusiastic United States Air Force ex-aviation cadet. He got caught up in the same sort of "purge" that ended the flying careers of my two roommates at Iowa Preflight School. They were sent to Great Lakes and never heard from again, despite the fact that they met every requirement of the syllabus at Iowa City. Dick's enthusiasm for flying never left him.

In the late 1960s, as we both were prospering a little, Dick Pickett began to talk to me earnestly about the possibility of the two of us buying a small airplane. At that time, Dick and his brother owned a tiny little Cessna Skyhawk, which was about the size of the sofa in your living room. Dick took me up a couple of times, and let me play with the radios. He even let me shoot a shaky little landing or two. He knew that would do it.

We decided to buy a real airplane. The deal was sealed when Dick's brother, Dr. Robert Pickett, said he would like to join our partnership. Bob had considerably less flying time, but he had more money in his checking account than Dick and I had together in total assets. And he was honest.

With whom you own an airplane is very important. There has to be a lot of honesty within the adventure. If one pilot makes a hard landing, he has to tell the others. He has to understand that the mechanics must look over the aircraft for possible structural damage. If a pilot sees even a little smoke coming out of the cowling, he has to report it. If he thinks an instrument is giving a questionable reading, he has to speak up. He has to know in his heart that his partners are being as careful as he is.

We gave a lot of thought as to what kind of a plane to buy. Personally, I wanted to buy a sleek little low-wing monoplane which would look like a fighter plane. I wanted an airplane you would like to stand in front of and get your picture taken. I also wanted something stressed for acrobatics. Dr. Bob, the one of us with money, wanted an aircraft which would get us there fast, something like a Beechcraft Bonanza, the hottest selling plane in America among medical doctors. There is a widespread belief among pilots, that more doctors are killed every year in Bonanzas, than any other plane. Of course it isn't true. It is just envy.

Fortunately, we had Dick Pickett in our group. He kept holding out for a slightly larger version of the small Cessna Skyhawk which he and Bob then owned. A Cessna is not all that sleek. It is a high-wing monoplane, and when you see one you think more "kite" than you do "fighter." Its advantage is that because you are sitting under that high wing, you can see the ground below you. This is important during landings, which is when many accidents occur. Not only can you see the runway, as you land, but also you can see the traffic below you in the traffic pattern. Because of the design of its wing, the payload of the Cessna is much better than some of the sleeker models.

When it comes to airplanes, the design of the wing is everything. Orville and Wilbur Wright would tell you that. In those early days, the importance of the shape of the wing was not thoroughly understood. The power plant, and the steering apparatus got much of the engineering attention among the pioneers. There were few wind tunnels in those days.

When moving air hits the leading edge of an aircraft wing, part of the air slips under the wing and part of it slips over the bulge in the top of the wing. The same two parts rejoin and become one again, at the trailing edge of the wing. Because the part which passes over the top of the wing travels a greater distance to get to the point where it rejoins its counterpart passing under the wing, it must travel at a greater speed. The greater speed results in a lower air pressure, and this phenomenon, first discovered in the 18th Century by an Italian physicist by the name of Venturi, creates a "lift" on top of the wing.

I hope I don't have to go through all of that again. Just take my word for it. Don't argue with me. The Navy said so. It must be true.

With the help of a national publication known as Trade-A-Plane, we picked out a Model-182 Cessna, which was for sale in Alabama. The C-182 was close to being the smallest four-seater Cessna manufactured at that time. We ruled out a two-seater. Dick Pickett knew that with me as a co-owner, it was important that our airplane hold a foursome, including four sets of golf clubs. Because he was our leader, and the best pilot among us, Dick flew to Birmingham and brought home the prettiest little Cessna the company ever made.

Our little bird was ten years old, but it was well equipped for instrument flying and had been well maintained. It cost us less than $25,000, which we split three ways. If you wanted to buy the exact airplane today, from its present owner, it would cost you at least $125,000. A new Skylane, which is what Cessna calls its C-182, comes out of the factory these days at around $227,800. Believe me, 1970 was *the* time to buy an airplane.

Never in the history of general aviation has an airplane had the tender care we gave our C-182. When we bought it, its logs indicated that all of its periodic engine and other checks were in apple-pie order. But we had them all done over again, by mechanics at Don Scott Field, Ohio State University's airport. We trusted the men at Don Scott, most of whom we knew. More importantly, they knew us, and knew that we might be injured if they overlooked anything. They knew also that we would have a fit if they were careless. We washed and waxed the plane, and noticed that it gave us five additional nautical miles per hour, with the same engine and prop settings. Even on days when we were not flying, we would go out to Don Scott and just pat our airplane on its cute little tail, and talk to it in the hanger.

Dick and his brother each had a private pilot license, and both were instrument rated. When I left active Naval duty in 1945, I was issued a commercial pilot license, which is a bit more significant than a private license, and a lot less significant than an air transport, or airline captain's license. My commercial ticket was still effective in 1970, and I was legal to fly, subject to an updated medical certificate and a "currency" flight or two with an instructor. To go with my license, I had the tremendous experience of having learned instrument flying under Navy guidance and discipline. Being comfortable and competent on instruments, is an important aspect of private flying. In my last few months in service, I took some extra training, and received the Navy's highest grade of instrument flying.

That was all good. But the problem was that between 1945, when I was at the top of my game, and 1970, when I was relearning to fly our little Cessna, the technology of instrument flying was entirely different. Also, the Cessna had about half as many bells and whistles as the torpedo bomber, and was a much less stable flying platform. The TBF weighed 19,000 pounds without a torpedo aboard. The C-182 weighed less than our family car.

In 1945 we flew cross-country from electronic beacon to beacon, as did Charles Lindbergh in his prime. When we arrived at our destination, we shot our instrument landings with the help of "cones of silence" which were formed by A/N "beams." The letter "A" in the Morse Code is dot/dash, or DIT space DAH. The letter "N" is the opposite, dash/dot, or DAH space DIT. The beams we homed on, were known as A/N beams because on the "A" side of the beam you heard a dit space dah in your headset. If you turned ever so slightly toward the "N" side of the beam, which was called "bracketing the beam," you heard a solid tone, which was the beam. The dit space dah merged with the dah space dit, and the spaces would fill in and form that solid tone.

Of course it was primitive. Ten years before I learned to fly, aerial navigation was even more primitive. The pilots had no beams at all. They just flew from beacon light to beacon light, many of which were built on high hills or mountain tops, so you could see them at a greater distance. For the benefit of the first air mail pilots, in the 1920s, bon fires were built and served as "beacons."

The A/N beams disappeared between 1945 and 1970, and so did the bon fires and beacons on the hills. As I relearned instrument flying, I was introduced to the VOR. That stands for Very-high frequency, Omni-directional, Radar. These are the cone-shaped little towers you see out in the open fields, as you drive through the countryside. Many are painted in red and white stripes, others all white. The VORs are built and maintained by the Federal Aviation Administration (FAA), the same agency which licenses pilots, and at one time, prior to "deregulation," rigorously regulated the airlines.

Each VOR transmits on a different frequency, and by tuning the navigation-side of the aircraft's radio to the proper frequency, the pilot can identify which VOR he is using for navigation. The cockpit instrument also tells the pilot his position in relation to the VOR. A distance measuring device, known as the DME, tells the pilot how far he is from the VOR.

In 1970, if a pilot wanted to fly from Chicago to New York, as an example, he zigged and zagged from VOR to VOR, changing frequencies for each VOR along the way. It was that simple. When he arrived in the New York vicinity, he shot his instrument landing by flying down an electronic "glideslope," with the help of an instrument which told him if he were above or below the glidescope, or to one side of it. This arrangement, known as the Instrument Landing System, or ILS, was a big improvement over the old A/N beams. It beat Lindbergh's beacons, too, by a bunch.

These days, the entire process of navigating is greatly simplified for the pilot. When General Jimmy Doolittle first flew in the 1930s without any visual reference to the horizon, he had only needle, ball and airspeed instrumentation. Those, along with an altimeter, were the key instruments in the first J-3 Piper Cub I flew in 1943. In the military trainers and fleet airplanes of the 1940s we added artificial horizons, the A/N beams and radio altimeters. We also had "Identification—Friend or Foe" (IFF) capability, which later developed into the first post-war transponders. Radios became much more reliable. The old "coffee grinders" in our TBFs gave way to electronic tuning devices, which were quicker and more precise. The cutting-edge, weather-radar equipment which guided me around the Caribbean in 1945, can be seen now only in museums.

I had much to re-learn, and much to learn over and over again, as I began to fly again in 1970. The changes in technology never cease. In a smartly equipped light plane today, which would include the nearly new Piper which John F. Kennedy, Jr. owned and flew until July of 1999, the cross-country navigation is accomplished by global positioning. All of the customary information a pilot needs to fly on instruments—air speed, altitude, direction, artificial horizon, autopilot data, etc.—is collected in one place on an instrument which resembles a TV screen. It is not necessary, anymore, that the pilot constantly "scan" his panel from gadget to gadget, although many still do it out of habit. As back ups, the modern airplane may have a second global positioning instrument, and a full stack of professional-quality, very reliable, navigation and communication radios, along with one or two flight directors, a sophisticated instrument which simplifies the flying in holding patterns and on the glideslope. Of course it will have modern Radar, or a Stormscope, or both.

The days when the airplane flew a zigzag course from VOR to VOR are long gone. The VORs are lined up electronically from the take off to the destination, and are referred to as waypoints. The pilot flys a straight leg. No more zig-zag.

On the other hand, instrument flying is instrument flying, so I didn't have to relearn everything. Aircraft are now steered through the air, and flown straight-and-level, as they were in my day. I picked up the new methods within a few hours, and continued to keep up with them as they changed constantly. I remembered instinctively how to trust my instruments, even though those instruments continually changed through the years. Trusting the numbers is the big thing about instrument flying. You can not trust your feelings. You may or may not be in a turn, without knowing it. If your plane is losing altitude, the airspeed will go up. If you are climbing, the airspeed will go down. If you are turning, the turn indicator and the compass will tell you. Sounds simple, doesn't it?

Well it is—if you are careful not to panic, and if you practice as much as possible. Instrument flying is not like swimming or riding a bicycle. You can't stay away from it for long periods of time, and then expect to do it as well as you ever did. It is for this reason that the FAA requires pilots to stay "current," by constantly flying a minimum amount of time in the cloud or under a hood

A pilot has to be discriminating, and a slave to details. My favorite aviation story is about an airline captain who aborted a takeoff, which caused extensive damage to a big jet. The airline hauled him before a board of inquiry and asked him what happened. He said it was the co-pilot's fault. They asked him to explain, and he said that during the takeoff the co-pilot did not say what he was supposed to say. The captain reminded them that when the plane approached the takeoff point, the co-pilot was supposed to say "rotate," so the captain could lift the plane off the runway. "Well what *did* he say?" they asked. "He said *I think we can make it!*" replied the captain.

Thinking we can make it, is not enough. In aviation everything is checked so it can be re-checked. The safe pilot removes the gas cap and looks into the tank to check the fuel level, and its color. The old, safe pilot dips his finger into the fuel, to make certain it is wet. The best way to become an old pilot is to become a pilot who never gets over his lifelong habit of checking and double-checking. Safe flying is what makes flying fun.

I might have carried the safety habit a little farther than I needed to. After I had been flying light planes for a few years, I decided that it would be wise to have a good instructor give me a checkflight now and then. Sometimes I would even fly with an FAA licensed checkpilot, and let him endorse my logbook. Then,

I noticed that because I was acquainted with many of the instructors and checkpilots at Don Scott Field, they were tending to overlook my short comings. They were being nice to me. Instead of demanding that I shoot more night landings, for example, and chewing me out if I didn't, they would merely note that I was a bit shaky, and should give some thought to getting more practice at night.

I talked it over with Dick and Bob Pickett, and decided to go somewhere where we were unknown, and find a hard-nosed check pilot. Dick and I flew to Opa-Locka, in Florida, the former Naval air station where I learned to fly the latest model TBM in 1945. The flight instructors there did not know me from a bag full of shag balls. I found the toughness I was looking for, and I think my family was more comfortable flying with me because I took this attitude. Dick Pickett did not really need this kind of extra attention. He was a natural pilot, and would have made an excellent airline captain. Of course our community would have been deprived of one of its best lawyers, had Dick chosen that career.

Owning an airplane is like owning a boat. The minute you get one, you start looking around for a bigger, faster one. Within two years, we became restless with our little Cessna Skylane. We moved up to a Cessna-210, the first of two we would acquire. We wanted more TAS, true air speed. Pilots brag about their TAS. Non-flyers always ask, "How fast will it go?" This is a somewhat meaningless question, because the answer depends upon wind speed and direction, and air temperature. Pilots want to know the TAS.

The C-210, or Centurion, is Cessna's answer to the Beechcraft Bonanza. If the Bonanza had a reputation for knocking off doctors, the Centurion was hard on lawyers. There is no rational reason why either airplane should harm anyone who is being careful. The Cessna-210 is an elegant airplane. It's landing gear retracts during the flight. It has a 300-horsepower engine, and a TAS of almost 200 miles per hour at cruise settings. Because its electrical system is bigger and heavier, it can support more and stronger radios which give much better reception. Its service ceiling is higher, so the pilot can get above more of the weather. Our second Centurion was turbo-charged, and we routinely flew it above 20,000 feet. The C-210 has a payload of around 1800 pounds, which is the best in its class. It seats six persons on leather seats, and handles four sets of golf clubs without any strain. The Centurion is a Lincoln instead of a Ford.

Cessna does not manufacture the Centurion these days. It makes a similar airplane with a fixed-gear configuration, which it calls the Stationaire. The cost of a new Stationaire is $310,000. We bought each of our C-210s for about $60,000, which we split three ways, and both were in nearly perfect condition. Them was the days.

Dr. Pickett did not like either of our Centurions, because they were pretty complicated for the sport and recreational flying he preferred. He asked Dick and me if we would buy him out of the partnership. We agreed to do it, but only after he agreed that whenever he and his family wanted to go anywhere, all they had to do was tell Dick or me, and we would fly them anywhere, anytime. As soon as Bob left our arrangement, we brought in a new third partner, Tom Maish, the president and owner of a local company. He was a thoroughly dedicated pilot with lots of hours, and with unlimited trustworthiness. He was comfortable with our latest turbo-charged Cessna 210, which, naturally, was bigger and faster than our first one. When the time came that Dick Pickett and I could no longer fly with the same proficiency and ability—our zest never waned—Tom bought out both of us.

Most thoughtful pilots know when it is time to hang it up. If the pilot does not know, the FAA will tell him. Although I didn't have to, I elected to renew my medical certificate once a year. It got harder and harder as the years rolled on. When my family doctor discovered that I had an elevated blood pressure, my fate as a pilot was sealed. The FAA required that I get a stress test every year. The results of that test, along with my annual FAA medical examination, were sent to the medical section of the FAA in Oklahoma City. Each year the FAA doctors would sit on my case for about four months. Meantime I was grounded, and could not keep up my flying proficiency. If I had tried to fly during that interval, which I never did, we would have had no insurance on our airplane. It came to the place where I was paying for 12 months of flying, and flying only eight months. Dick had about the same experience, although he did last a little longer than I did.

It was tough to quit. After all, I came along in flying not long after the pioneers. More than that, I had learned to depend upon the plane. My law practice included frequent trips to most of the larger cities in the Midwest, and I used to look down on the crowded Interstates and feel sorry for the folks who were bound to the ground. It was handy to go to Augusta each April, in less than two hours; to Pinehurst in less than that; and to Florida in three or four hours, depending upon the winds. Dick and I took our plane as far west as Denver. Several times we flew out to the Bahamas, which was nothing for an old Navy pilot. It was far enough from land for Dick, however, who referred to the trip as "maximum shoreline separation."

Often on a Sunday afternoon, Dick Pickett and I would just go out and fly. We spelled one another under the hood, to keep up our skills in instrument flying. In my Navy days, I literally flew "under the hood." It was a canvas apparatus which was stored behind the pilot's head, and which was pulled up to the front of the canopy and hooked, like the top on a convertible. When I re-learned instrument flying, we used a plastic helmet with long blinders on it. Today, the pilots wear what appears to be a pair of eye-glasses, which block out all periphery vision. Whatever the device, when "under the hood" the only thing the pilot can see is the array of flight instruments in front of him.

Dick Pickett and I would sometimes purposely fly in bad weather—never in dangerous weather—so we would not fear being in the cloud when we got in it unexpectedly. Other times we would simply fly to somewhere we had never been before, just to see what the world looked like. We might start as late as mid-afternoon, on a Sunday, and wander as far away as Wisconsin, or Missouri. We didn't go anywhere in particular; we just flew for the fun of it. When our kids enrolled in various colleges, we often would fly them to and from, at spring break and other times. When Marg's parents needed some extra help in their later years, we could fly to the Moline, Illinois airport, near the family farm, Seldom Rest, in 90 minutes. The auto trip to the farm was at least 11 hours, each way. It is hard to overstate the convenience of having a private plane.

I also flew a lot with a professional pilot, who is my close friend and golfing buddy. John Tremaine is a retired colonel in the Air Force. He has considerably more than 20,000 hard hours in every kind of airplane you could imagine. He ended his flying career as the chief pilot for a large, Columbus bank. In addition to supervising the work of the other pilots, he took his regular turn at the controls of the bank's King Air and one of its huge, multi-million dollar business jets. I learned much about flying from John. He was a professional, and the pros do things a little differently. He improved my radio procedure so much. He didn't try to give me lessons, but I just sat next to him hour after hour, and watched his smooth way of doing things. Despite the fact that his regular, weekly flying schedule might take him all over the United States, and perhaps even to Europe, he always looked forward to taking me up in my little Centurion whenever he could. Flyers are like that.

With my law practice ended, and my flying days over, the only thing I have left, aside from the love of my family—which always has been at the top of the list—is golf writing.

And one other thing. I have the haunting images of the evening my daddy jumped in the river.

It is time I told you about those feelings which have been with me all of my life.

AUGUST 1, 1927

My father, James William Hoskins, enjoyed a short life. He was born in 1895, at a time when there were still people alive who remembered Daniel Boone and Simon Kenton. Those two pioneer woodsmen had much to do with the fact that the Hoskins family located in southeastern Ohio.

In the days when Boone and Kenton roamed the frontier land, part of which was the Ohio Country, a vast forest extended all the way from Virginia to Wisconsin. The terrain was rugged, the foliage thick, and in places impenetrable. Boone began to explore the forest around 1770 or so, largely because he couldn't keep out of it. He had that same restless spirit which brought the first Europeans to the east coast of the United States 150 years earlier. Simon Kenton, on the other hand, fled into the woods, a decade or two after Boone, to keep ahead of the law. He thought he had killed a young man who was about to marry Ellen Cummins, the love of Kenton's life. In truth, he had only injured him. Had he known that, he might have stayed put in Virginia.

At different times in their wanderings, both men passed through Fort DuQuesne (with a capital "Q"), sometimes known as Fort Pitt, and now Pittsburgh. Like hundreds of other explorers and soldiers, they floated down the Ohio River on rafts, and explored what was known as the Middle Ground, which stretched from Fort Pitt westward to the great river known then as the Messipi. It was said of the Middle Ground that only "the foolish would enter it."

Boone headquartered in Can-tuc-kee, and centered many of his explorations in the eastern part of Ohio. Kenton settled for a few years on the Kanawha River, near the present site of Charleston, West Virginia, and for years explored the western part of Ohio.

Following the Revolutionary War, the Federal government wanted to do something to placate a group of Americans known as the "Refugees." They were not dedicated "Royalists." They were Colonists who were not in total sympathy with the rebellion against England and King George. Many of them were born in England, and most of them had relatives and friends living there. They would have preferred that the disputes over taxation without representation, and the other underlying causes of the Revolution, be resolved short of a war. To avoid personal, often family, conflicts, they fled to Canada and became known as "Refugees."

After the war, consideration was given by the Federal government to some inducement to bring home the Refugees and their offspring. In 1798, a tract of real estate in the center of the Ohio Country was set aside, and called the Refugee Tract. It was less than a mile wide, from north to south. It began at a point in central Ohio near the present-day Capitol Building in downtown Columbus, which did not exist then, and proceeded eastward some 45 miles to a point near Buckeye Lake, which also did not exist then. The Refugees who were willing to settle this land and live on it, could do so without any question, and without recrimination.

Had it not been for the earlier explorations by Boone and Kenton, the land in central Ohio would not have been opened, so that the Refugee Tract could be created. Had it not been for the

Refugee Tract, the culture of Ohio would have developed much differently than it did.

The long and narrow Refugee Tract, stretching across the midsection of Ohio, served both as a belt and as a barrier. The refugee families, who settled it, came in from the north, because most of them lived in Canada. Many of them did not make it all the way south to the Refugee Tract, which was their goal. The trip was long and difficult, and many of the families gave up the effort, and settled in northern Ohio. To this day, more than 200 years later, many families in the northern part of Ohio have French names and French characteristics. A recent Ohio governor, from Cleveland, was named "Celeste."

The southern part of Ohio, which generally is all of the land south of the southern border of the Refugee Tract, was settled by Americans from Virginia and other southern colonies, many of whom were the sons and daughters of large-land owners. There was not a drop of French-Canadian blood in any of them. They were accustomed to plantation living, so they settled on larger tracts of land in the south of Ohio. When you visit our southern Ohio cities today, places like Lancaster, Circleville, Athens and Chillicothe, you notice that even the architecture is different from northern Ohio. The southern homes have columns, and large front porches. The northern homes have steeply-pitched roofs, so the Canadian snows will slide off. Our current governor, who comes from Cincinnati, is named "Taft," a familiar name in Virginia.

The cultural differences caused by the Refugee Tract, which itself was made possible by the adventures of Boone and Kenton, are a fact of life in modern Ohio politics and commerce. In our current General Assembly, which convenes at the western terminus of the Refugee Tract, there are daily clashes between the French inspired tradesmen from Cleveland, and the agriculturally inspired Virginians from Cincinnati. Our southern governor, Taft, has little in common with our former northern governor,

Celeste. It is possible that the great growth in the Columbus area—it now is the largest city in Ohio—is due to the amalgamation of the two cultures.

In the light of these developments, it was no historical accident that the Hoskins family, from Virginia, settled in southern Ohio, southeastern Ohio to be precise. It was more of a foregone conclusion, dictated by historical circumstances. Exactly when the first of the clan appeared in Ohio, and where their migration originated in Virginia, is lost in time. I have read the general genealogies on our family, but they are vague and uncertain. The dedicated genealogical research of Mary Conaway, one of my cousins, has chased the family back to an Ira Hoskins, who was born in Pennsylvania around 1800, and located in the vicinity of New Straitsville, according to all of the census reports from 1830 through 1860. Ira was the father of Samuel Harvey Hoskins, who was born in Ohio in the 1830s. My grandfather, William R. Hoskins, was Samuel's son. That's about all we know, and some of that is rather indefinite.

My grandparents kept a family Bible with many pages of names and dates of births recorded faithfully, but with virtually no indication as to where or when any of them were born, or whom their parents might have been. From the futility of my mid-seventies, I now look back sadly upon the questions I could have asked, but didn't, when I was a youngster.

We also know that my grandparents, William R. and Ida Bainter Hoskins, moved early in the 20th Century from New Straitsville to a small farm in a little community in Athens County, known as Connett. At the time of that move, the Hoskins family was large, seven sons and a daughter. Connett was not, and still is not, a city or even a village. It is just a place. Everyone who needs to, knows where it is, so there aren't any signs warning you that you are about to miss it. There is not much to miss. There is no commercial activity in Connett, just a Methodist church and a large cemetery where most of my paternal ancestors are buried, except my father.

My father is buried some ten miles to the west, on Asbury Ridge, the home of my maternal ancestors, and the place where my mother was born.

The decision to bury him in the Clark Family cemetery plat was influenced at the time of my father's death, by my Grandpa Clark, a man who often looked ahead. He foresaw the day when my mother would join her husband, among all the other Clarks. What Grandpa Clark did not realize was that Mother would remarry, move out west, and sleep eternally in the soft California soil overlooking the Pacific.

My mother and father did not know one another as children. When my dad returned from service in France after World War I, he needed work. He learned that the Josh Clark family, up on Asbury Ridge, was in the process of building a new house. Josh and Ida Clark spent the war years in Barberton, Ohio, which is a little city near Akron. Grandpa wanted to do something for the war effort, and when he learned that the rubber companies in the Akron area were in need of workers, he uprooted his family from Asbury Ridge and traveled all the way to Barberton, in a wagon which contained all the Clark family belongings. The rubber factory where Grandpa Clark worked made tires for military ambulances, and my father, whom none of the Clarks had ever met at that time, was at that moment an ambulance driver in France, in the thick of the war.

The contractor who was building the new Clark home on Asbury Ridge was glad to hire the returning veteran, Jim Hoskins. The Clark family remained in Barberton while the new house was being built, but they came down a time or two to see how the new house was progressing. That is when my mother and father met.

She was fifteen, and had not yet started to high school in Logan, the nearest high school. He was 23, and had just a few years to live. But he didn't know it.

All of her life, even as a youth, my mother was a tiny person. At full maturity, she was just a little more than five feet tall. Because she had two older brothers and a younger one, she had to speak up to survive. When she graduated from high school in 1921, an achievement in those days, she declared her intent to marry Jim Hoskins, of Connett, and there was very little her family could do about it. She was determined, even resolute, in almost everything she did. We have noticed that enviable trait, which must be a generation-skipping trait, in all of our children, especially our daughter Jane, the medical doctor.

The Clarks had nothing against the Hoskins boy, a man actually. He was a veteran, and from a God-fearing family. He worked wherever he could find it, and helped a lot on the Hoskins family farm at Connett. Everyone spoke well of him. He was in the process of learning the barbering trade.

Ada Grace Clark and James William Hoskins were married in 1921. Their first home was at Connett, just across the road and up a small hill, some thousand yards or so from the Hoskins family farm house. It was in that little house that I was born in August of 1924. There are several little houses clustered in the immediate vicinity of the one in which I was born, but I no longer know which was ours. I really do not think it makes very much difference. My chances of becoming a President, or the winner of the US Open, and warranting a flag in front of my birthplace, seem rather slim at this point.

When I was about two, my parents moved to Philo, Ohio, which is a small community directly across the Muskingum River from Duncan Falls, Ohio. Philo and Duncan Falls are about seven miles or so downstream from Zanesville. My folks selected Philo, because my mother's two older brothers, Ray and Herman Clark, lived there at that time with their families. My father rented a small barber shop on Main Street in Philo, which he operated for the final ten months of his life.

On the evening of August 1, 1927, just five days before my third birthday, my father kept his shop open until a little after six p.m. As she always did, my mother had dinner waiting for him at our home, which was within easy walking distance of his shop.

My mother remembered that for a month or so she had been having a problem with my refusing to drink my milk. Sometimes I would drink it for my dad, but not for her. On the last evening of his life, I would not even drink it for him. We were having chocolate cake, and my dad hit upon the idea of dropping a piece of the cake in my glass of milk, stirring it, and feeding it to me with a spoon. It worked, and it was one of my mother's last memories of my father expressing his love for me.

After dinner, the three of us went over to the waterhole in the Muskingum River, to cool off and watch the swimmers. To get there, we walked to the general vicinity of my Uncle Ray's house. Across the road from his house, there was a path leading down toward the river. It was steep at first, and then leveled off across a valley to the river's edge. The foliage along the path was so high that my dad had to carry me on his shoulders, which we both liked. When we arrived at the waterhole we noticed that there was an unusually large group of teenagers swimming that evening. My mother spread a blanket on the river bank. We had no sense of impending doom. That's how it is with accidents. They sneak up on you. If we could invent some form of warning horn, like those on airplanes which send out a warning when you try to land with your wheels up, we might be able to avoid so much distress.

It probably wouldn't work. I remember the story they told us at flight school. The cadet was flaring in for a landing with his wheels up, and the tower was screaming at him, "Don't land … don't land … your wheels are up!" After the crash the tower asked the cadet why he didn't hear the tower yelling at him. "I heard you, but I couldn't tell what you were saying … that darned

Wheels Up Warning Horn was making too much noise."

We sat together as a family for the last time, watching the kids play in the water. They decided to race across the river, and took off with considerable splashing and howling. One young lady, Doris Logston, got a late start, and found herself at the back of the pack. The other swimmers were kicking water in her face, and she was becoming disoriented. My mother said later that she did not notice this emergency as it was developing, because she was pouring ice water from a jug.

Dad noticed. Doris was beginning to flail in the center of the river, and he sensed that he might have to give her some help. "Jim, be careful," were my mother's last words to him as he jumped in the river.

He didn't dive, he jumped, according to my mother. I saw him go in too, but my reporting was less consistent than hers. For some time after the accident, I "demonstrated" how my father jumped, to whomever would take the time to listen to me, or watch me. It probably was a way for me to vent my emotions, or I might have been simply showing off, by drawing attention to myself. If I were in a nice, soft haymow, I might dive, as I shouted, "This is the way my daddy jumped in the river." If I were parachuting from atop a low wall onto the hard lawn, I might go feet-first while holding my nose and shouting my attention-getting line, which I had found to be appealing to those who thought I was pretty cute.

When the other swimmers reached the opposite shore, and pulled themselves up on a rock, they learned that there was a drama unfolding behind them. They figured out quickly that it was their friend, Doris, who was involved in some way, and there was another person in the water who was swimming strongly toward her. Mother and I cheered too, when we saw that my father had reached her and appeared to be towing her back toward our bank.

After telling me to stay back, Mother took our picnic blanket down near the edge of the water. She remembers that several men joined her, and together they hauled the water soaked and thoroughly scared Doris Logston up on the bank. My mother claimed that at that instant, she was within a few feet of my father while he was alive in the water, and as far as she could determine he was not injured in anyway.

For the next minute or two, all the attention was on Doris. They spread her out on the blanket, and helped her cough up the river water. The kids returned from the other side of the river, and gathered around her, helping to cheer her back to normal breathing

Someone said, "Where's Jim?" My mother's heart froze at that question, and she said later that it was then that she knew that he was not going to be found, and that in fact there wasn't even any use to spend any time looking for him. But of course they did anyway. The teenagers explored the river and the area around the bank where he had brought Doris ashore. The water had been reasonably clear, but it soon became riled from all the activity. Many people in Philo owned rowboats, and several were put into the water. Someone ran up to my Uncle Ray's house, and up to our house, to see if my dad had gone to one of those places to change clothes. Mother stayed at the waterhole, and even refused to leave when twilight turned into one of the darkest nights in the history of my family. For hours she shouted across the river, "Jim … Jim."

Everyone in Philo and Duncan Falls who could, turned out at the river bank early the next morning. A river rescue crew from the sheriff's office was there too, and by noon they realized they would have to widen the search for my father's body. Later that day, he was found about a mile downstream from the waterhole, still fully clothed

These tragic events, on the evening of August 1, made almost immediate alterations in our tranquil lifestyle. Grandma and Grandpa Clark came to Philo as fast as they could get there, and as soon as it was decided that the funeral and burial would be at Asbury Church, they returned home to assist with the preparations, and took me with them. The gentleman who owned the barber shop which my father rented, said that if my mother could clear out my father's property within a day or two, he would refund the August rent. Her two brothers, Ray and Herman, had the place cleared out in a matter of hours. People from as far away as Zanesville brought food to our house, which was largely a ceremonial act, because there was no one there to eat it. Some of the food was taken to the Hoskins farm at Connett, where my father's body lay at rest in my grandparents' living room for several days before the funeral.

The night after the drowning, Mother was appalled to notice a letter neatly addressed in my dad's handwriting to an insurance company. She opened it and found what she expected to find, the August premium for my father's life insurance, which she knew was due on the last day of July. While she had the letter open, she wrote a note to the company advising them of his death, and thanking them in advance for the proceeds of the policy. She hoped they wouldn't notice that the policy was expired at the time of the death.

People for miles around Connett, Nelsonville and New Straitsvlle, the little town where the Hoskins family lived when my father was born, called at the Hoskins farm to pay their respects. The funeral was conducted at the Asbury Methodist Church. The Masonic Lodge, of which my father and many other male members of the Hoskins and Clark families were members, conducted a ceremony. The local newspaper reported that traffic was backed up for great distances on Asbury Ridge.

The death, standing alone, would have been enough to arouse a considerable amount of sympathy, but when you added the plight of my mother and me, there was overwhelming commiseration and warmth of feeling.

Exactly how my mother coped with the situation is beyond me. We talked about it years later when we both were adults, and her own impression was that she just lived from day to day. Having grown up in the home of a dedicated lay preacher where there were daily family prayer meetings, mother obviously had a spiritual underpinning. She was not articulate about her beliefs, and in fact kept them pretty much to herself. She was not overjoyed at my own religious exposure as a youth on Asbury Ridge. She understood, even agreed with, my brief rebellion against my grandparents, which grew out of that experience. I had the feeling that she might have gone through the same experience. We never discussed any of that. We rarely discussed religion, even in a general way.

I don't think it was religion that sustained Mother, as much as it was a minute by minute, hour by hour, day in and day out determination not to fail. When the Monarch Accident Insurance Company, of Springfield, Massachusetts advised her that they had no obligation to pay the proceeds of my father's policy, she would not accept that decision. In arguing with them she did not beg, or cry out about her need. Rather, she insisted that the "decent" thing for the company to do was to pay the claim. She pointed out that many times my father had sent his premium to the company in advance of the due date. Shouldn't she get some credit for that? She stated that my father's death had created much interest in Zanesville and Philo, and also down in southeastern Ohio where he was buried. She left it for the company to figure out that paying the claim might be the sensible thing to do. She did not rant or rave, or threaten to boycott Monarch, or anyone else.

It must have been hard for my mother not to use drastic tactics. She had less than fifty dollars in cash, but of course she did have her father and mother, and her brothers, none of whom was going to let us starve. She also had the Hoskins family behind her, and many of them would have "taken us in" without any hesitation.

The insurance policy was what was known as an "industrial" policy. It had nothing to do with any particular "industry," and I have no idea how the name developed in the insurance business. In such policies, which were very popular in the 1920s, the indemnifications were small, and the premiums were not paid annually or even semi-annually. They were paid at very short intervals, like monthly or even weekly. Often the agents of the company would call on the policyholder to collect the premium. My dad had kept his policy in effect since he and mother moved to Philo. The insurance companies, Monarch included, did not make much money on each industrial policy. By the same actuarial reasoning, they could not lose much on just one policy. They had to have volume to succeed, and a lack of volume would sink them.

Mother seemed to sense this. After thinking it over, Monarch decided to try out a compromise on her. After carefully explaining, again, that they had no obligation to do so, they offered to pay the proceeds of the policy if, in return, my mother would write them a letter of thanks for their generosity. The company would write the "thank you" letter for her, and she would have to agree that her letter could be used in Monarch's advertising.

This was a classic win-win solution. In our scrap book, we still have a copy of Monarch's neat little blue brochure, which explains how important it is that policyholders pay their premiums on time. The letter the company asked my mother to sign, doesn't sound much like her. In it, she thanks nearly every executive in the company, by name and title, and refers to my dad as "Mr.

Hoskins." In the text of the brochure, Monarch states, "Fortunately, Mr. Hoskins developed the habit of paying premiums promptly ..." I think it also was fortunate, for us, that "Mr. Hoskins" left behind a smart widow who was very patient, and who knew how to make a tantalizing argument, and stick with it.

We had one more good thing happen to us shortly after Monarch paid off. My Uncle Ern, my father's youngest brother, heard about the mission of the Carnegie Hero Fund, of Pittsburgh. This organization was founded by Andrew Carnegie in 1904, and its purpose was to encourage heroism, and to make life a little easier for genuine heroes and their families. The Fund had a staff of investigators which looked into all cases of heroism which were called to their attention. They asked for much information from Ern, which he gathered and sent to them. The Carnegie investigators conducted many interviews, and had several discussions with my mother about her needs. There are three classifications of Carnegie medals: gold, silver and bronze. My father's large, bronze medal, is ensconced in a genuine leather and velvet case. On one side of the three inch medal is a bas relief of Mr. Carnegie. On the other side, it reads: "Awarded to James W. Hoskins, Who Died Attempting to Save the Life of Doris O. Logston From Drowning, Philo, Ohio, August 1, 1927."

A small pension came with the medal, and that money along with the insurance proceeds, helped out my mother immeasurably. The "Carnegie Man" came around once a year to make sure we were spending their money wisely. On one of those occasions when I was in grade school and reading well, my mother remembered that I questioned the man at some length as to why the medal said my dad was "attempting" to save Doris Logston's life. She said that I told him, with conviction, that my dad *did* save her life, and the medal ought to say so.

As to Doris Logston and her family, we don't know what happened to any of them. They had not lived long in Philo prior to the drowning, and in the years since then all of them have moved away. My mother was a little irritated that no member of the Logston family came to the funeral, or called upon her to express sympathy. In her later years, she dealt with this oversight much better; and she concluded finally that in all probability the Logston family was just too confused by the whole thing to know what to do. As a youth, it didn't bother me any. It still doesn't.

I have tried to tell this story as honestly as I can. Everything I have reported is based upon accounts of the tragedy which I heard from my family over the span on my life. I have mentioned earlier that I have no personal memory of any of it. Very recently a relative who lives in San Diego called to my attention a very old, very yellowed newspaper account of my father's death which reports that my mother was in Connett when "word was received" that my father had drowned. I then remembered that I had seen that clipping, perhaps 50 years ago or more, and I remembered my mother's reaction to it: "They got it all wrong!" I am absolutely certain that I have given the true story here, just the way it happened.

A year after my father's death the event was to a great extent erased from most memories. Those of us closely involved, of course, have never forgotten about it. I quit showing everyone how my daddy jumped in the river. My mother's older brothers got back to their own lives in Philo. With the exception of my Grandma Hoskins, the remainder of the Hoskins family moved on routinely. My mother was fully occupied in Columbus spending a large chunk of the Monarch money on her education. Grandma and Grandpa Clark had a fulltime visitor—me. The August 1, 1928 newspapers took no note of the first anniversary of the tragic drowning.

But not everyone got off easy. My Grandma Hoskins, I have noted earlier, "went out of her mind," and stayed that way until she died in 1941. Those close to her said that " ... Jim's death was too much for her." She had worried desperately about him when he was in France in World War I. Having his life snuffed out at age 31, was too much.

The other person most affected was my mother. She had more at stake than anyone. There was no one with whom she could share the decisions that she now had to make alone. The decision to enroll in the Buckeye Business College, in Columbus, was an example of a tough call for her. It was a two-year course, and employment upon graduation was almost guaranteed, if you were willing to remain in the Columbus area. The tuition for the two years was about $250. Her living expenses in Columbus, and the trips to Asbury Ridge to visit me would eat up another $300. That would be more than half of all the money she had in the world. Porter and Hazel Hoskins, my dad's oldest brother and his wife, offered her room and board at their home in Columbus, but she didn't feel right about accepting. In 1924, when I was about six weeks old, Mother had to have an emergency operation at Grant Hospital, in Columbus, and Port and Hazel had kept me during her recovery. She believed that was enough for them to do.

Mother's goal was to get what she regarded as the best education she could afford. Then she wanted honest employment, which along with her Carnegie pension would provide food, clothing and shelter. She wanted the two of us to be together, in our own home.

She looked upon all of that as life after death.

Clayton C Hoskins

LIFE AFTER DEATH

OUR LIFE AFTER THE DEATH OF MY FATHER might have gone quickly for Mother. For me, life was very slow. She was in Columbus, attending business school, and I didn't see nearly enough of her. Mother would try to come to the Clark farm on Asbury Ridge when she could, but it was a tough trip. My parents did not own a car before his death, and of course his death made that possibility all the more remote. Despite the inconvenience, Mother came to see us about every other weekend. Sometimes she would catch a ride with a person coming to southeastern Ohio. Grandpa Clark, who did own a car, would drive to Logan, or Nelsonville, to pick her up.

Her visits were golden. She would nearly always bring me a gift, usually something to wear. I have no idea whether Mother paid anything to her parents for my room and board on the farm, but my guess is that she did not. I can not imagine Grandpa and Grandma accepting anything.

The three years between the death, and the time for me to start to school, seemed like an eternity. The time from one Christmas to the next was forever. In the summer of 1930, however, it was time to give some serious thought to school, an adventure which would consume the next 21 years of my life, if you consider my Navy career to be primarily schooling, which it was.

Mother rented a two-room, mostly furnished apartment on Poplar Street in Nelsonville, from a well-known business lady in town, Mrs. Highlah Herald. Mrs. Herald was a milliner. She made and sold women's hats. Her little house on Poplar Street had a bay window which extended out into the sidewalk, and it was there that she displayed her hats. In the 1920s and 30s all women wore hats, and you couldn't buy them just anywhere. Mrs. Herald filled a real need, and had a brisk business.

Our two rooms fronted on the house, but we were asked not to use the front door. We came in by walking along the east side of the house, to the back porch. We also left from the rear. If we received any mail, we had to go around the house to get it. For us ingress and egress were through the kitchen, which had no running water. Beyond the kitchen, to the front, was our second room, which served as our living room and our bedroom. Mother and I slept together in a double bed. There was a heating stove, which burned both coal and wood, in our front room, and it was adequate to warm the kitchen as well. There was no bath, and the toilet was located on the back porch. We shared it with Mrs. Herald.

This grand layout cost my mother two dollars a week, payable each Friday evening. Mother was employed at a time when many people were not. She was a legal secretary for a Nelsonville lawyer, Mr. Preston Thompson, who paid her six dollars a week, which she received each Friday afternoon.

Numbers like this are shocking, in this day and age. But we had enough. A full restaurant meal, which I can not remember ever having, was about 25 cents. When I got big enough to make the trip, Mother sent me to a nearby family grocery for food. There were no supermarkets or chains. She would give me a glass milk bottle with two dimes rattling in the bottom of it, and with that I could buy a quart of milk, a loaf of bread and a few slices of luncheon meat. Often we would bring produce from the Clark farm, and sometimes Mrs. Mary Chesser would give us a loaf of her homemade bread and a little package of the butter which she had just churned. We kept this in an "ice box," which was just that. Twenty-five pounds of ice were delivered to our house, twice a week.

Mrs. Herald was a bit unfriendly. She was not mean, or ill-natured. She just treated us like "renters," and kept her distance when she could. She had rules other than the one which kept us from using our front door. We had an inside door between our front room and her millinery shop. She asked that we not lock the door on our side, so that she could come into our part of the house when she wanted to. In her mind this was a right she had as a landlady. Her side of the door was locked, however, and she told us time and again that we were not to enter her shop through our door. We had to go out our back door, go around the house to the front, and enter her shop from the front porch. Sometimes when Mrs. Herald had to be away for a while during evening business hours, she would ask my mother to watch for customers. I don't think she paid Mother for this service, but she did give her a hat one time.

Mrs. Herald had figured out that if she gave me very many privileges around the property, I would be a troublemaker. No doubt she was right about that. I probably would have jumped into a box full of her hats, to show her how my dad jumped in the river. I was full of energy, and excited most of the time over the reality of living again with my mother.

I was enrolled in the Central Elementary School, which was located on the north side of the public square in Nelsonville. I could walk to and from school from our apartment. The last time I was in Nelsonville, years ago, the school was gone. It had been replaced with a supermarket.

School was very easy for me. I started first grade able to read most kids' books (*A Child's Garden of Verses*, for example) because my Grandma Clark spent hours with me telling me about the words and letting me read to her. Mother did the same thing when she came to visit. Any kid who can read a little when he starts to school has a big advantage, because he can concentrate on some of the harder stuff, like cutting and pasting.

The highlight of our day was when the free milk was delivered. I have no memory of who sponsored or financed this program of free milk, but I hope he got re-elected year after year. The milk came in half-pint glass bottles, and the teacher proceeded up and down the aisles with a flat carton of 20 or so bottles to a carton. We picked out the one we wanted (they were all alike), and used the same straw day after day. I kept my straw in my pencil box.

The milk was cold, and was as welcome as a milkshake would be today. We drank it very slowly, to make it last. Milk was pasteurized then, but it was not homogenized. We would dip our straws into the cream on top, and stir it up, if we wanted to. Sometimes the cream was a treat, and we just drank it without mixing it. The teacher then passed by again with the empty carton, into which we inserted our empty bottles. It was not true in my case, but for many of the little kids in my class, this milk was their only breakfast.

This good life in Nelsonville lasted until my fifth grade, when Mother had an opportunity to become the deputy to the newly elected Hocking County prosecuting attorney. Mr. Lanning, a Republican, had practiced law in Logan, the county seat, for years, but his secretary did not wish to join him in his new office in the courthouse, and thus a job opportunity opened up. Many legal secretaries applied, because appointments like this one came along infrequently. All jobs were scarce. Mother was selected. Being a single-mother, a term we never heard of then, might have helped her some. But it was her business college education in Columbus which gave her the biggest edge.

I was not that happy about leaving Nelsonville. I was doing very well in school, and had lots of friends. I had even learned to like Mrs. Herald. As the years passed, our landlady came to the conclusion that we were pretty nice people, for renters. Somehow or other she learned that my mother was the daughter of Josh Clark, of Asbury Ridge, and his fame as a powerful, lay preacher had spread as far as Nelsonville. If we were in that family, we couldn't be all bad.

We moved whether I liked it or not. Actually I did like it, almost immediately. Mother's new salary, of $600 a year, doubled her income as a legal secretary in Nelsonville. That meant a bigger house for us to rent, and we were the only people in it. Within a year, we enjoyed the luxury of our own car. The new job meant that Mother's responsibilities were much greater. When she worked for Mr. Thompson, about all she had to do was not disclose any secrets of the office. Working in a prosecutor's office was different. She now was being paid by the taxpayers, and the business she was helping conduct was public business. She cautioned me time and again, not to mention to anyone anything I might know or learn concerning her work. This must have been good training for the time when I would have my own law practice.

It was interesting to see how the elected officials, whatever their political affiliations, supported one another, for the common good. The county sheriff, a Democrat, looked after my mother as if she were his younger sister. He learned that Grandma Clark's doctor had "prescribed" a little snort of whiskey now and then for her heart, and that presented a practical problem because no member of the Clark family would be caught dead buying the evil stuff. The sheriff solved the problem. One of his responsibilities was to cooperate with the Federal agents in breaking up the stills, which were common in most of the remote parts of the county. He rebottled the contraband after the case was over, and slipped a pint now and then to my mother. She would pour a drop or two of the rot-gut into the bottle cap, and ignite it with a match. If it burned pure and left no residue, she would give it to my grateful grandmother, who would sip it, hoping that God Himself was not looking. Any sheriff that thoughtful today would be indicted, and some TV reporter would win a Pulitzer for "exposing" both him and my mother.

Mr. Lanning was a kind man. I have mentioned how he let me caddie for him after my mother fired me for snickering. He did other kind things for us, as did his wife, Mrs. Gladys Lanning. In the 1980s, nearly 50 years later, when I was practicing with Bricker & Eckler in Columbus, Mrs. Lanning telephoned me in a frail and shaky voice, and asked me to come down to Logan and help her prepare her will.

Our house on Front Street was all ours. No hat shops. Mother bought some furniture, and received some hand-me-downs from her folks. My bedroom was on the second floor, with a great view out toward the street. We bought a used piano, which was terrific for my mother because she had been playing since her childhood. Unfortunately, she thought I should do the same thing, and arranged for me to take lessons from a local piano teacher, Mrs. Elizabeth Dollison.

You had to feel sorry for poor Mrs. Dollison. She had a lot of success with virtually all of her students. With me, nothing happened. I did not show the slightest trace of talent. I did not want any talent. I had no thought of developing any talent. I refused to practice. My lessons were every Monday evening, at six o'clock. At five-thirty each Monday I became deathly ill. It happened every week, automatically. The malady might differ a little from week to week, but you could count on the fact that every Monday I was lingering on the edge of death. I was ready for the last rites. My disease, whatever it was, was terminal.

Mother was every bit as stubborn as I, and a lot smarter. She rustled me out of my stupor, week after week, and sent me off to

Mrs. Dollison's studio, which was in her home. She must have groaned when I knocked on the door. When she asked me how I was, I always gave a grim, health report. "I am half dead, is what I am," I would tell her, "And exactly why my mother has insisted that I come over here when I am in this condition, I do not know … I sure hope you don't catch whatever I have."

The fact is I had much more than my fair share of musical talent, and my mother knew it. Almost every week, I would "master" the week's lesson at a time when Mother wasn't home. Having learned to play the tune, I would then refuse to do so. Sometimes I would play the week's lesson in a rhythm never contemplated by the composer. I learned to do a few simple boogie-woogie movements in the left hand, and it was amazing how many of the simple melodies in my lesson book could be adapted to that beat. Mrs. Dollison left the room to take a telephone call one Monday, and while she was gone I played my lesson to the boogie beat. She came in and heard me, and asked me if I could play a couple of other tunes in my book for her. I gave her a concert. She seemed to enjoy it and sat down on my left and began to beat out a really complicated two-handed boogie-woogie, while I picked out the melody at my end of the piano. We could have gone on tour. I had no idea she had ever heard of Jelly Roll Morton, or Fatha Hines. It turned out she was a regular type person.

My musical talent, limited as it was, came to me honestly. My Uncle Ern, my father's youngest brother, was a tenor of great renown in Hocking and Athens Counties. His voice was as pure as Nelson Eddy's voice, and he along with Jeannete MacDonald were on the radio every Sunday evening. Ern's favorite accompanist was my mother, and together they played at weddings and funerals all over the area. When I got to be about ten, and had heard my Uncle Ern sing all my life, I began to try to sound like him. The problem was that I wasn't old enough to be a tenor. I was a soprano. A boy-soprano, like Wayne Newton. Mother and I worked up a couple of numbers, and began to accept invitations to play and sing before the local service clubs, and at local churches. Everyone has his fifteen minutes of fame, and Mother and I had at least a year of it, until my voice changed. I used to sing Scotts-Irish ballads, such as "Danny Boy" and "Did Your Mother Come From Ireland?" When my preteen voice gave away to the ravages of old age, I began to sound like a fog horn. We had to find another outlet.

That would be the trumpet. I took to it honestly too, because my Grandpa Clark was the loudest cornetist in the vicinity of Asbury Ridge. I never heard him at his best, because in midlife he lost all of his teeth. But I was told that in his prime he was awesome. In those days, cornetists were rated by how far you could hear them. Grandpa was a certified three-miler, even more if you were down wind.

I took to the trumpet almost immediately. When I began, I took group lessons at the junior high, playing an old instrument which was owned by the school system. Our next door neighbor was the Hammond family, which owned and operated the only music store in town, where I began to take private lessons. Mr. Hammond recommended that we consider buying a King cornet, with a sterling silver bell. Grandpa Clark offered to give us his old instrument to use as part of the total payment, which was a little less than $400. That was either 1939 or 1940, and at that time a new four-door Ford retailed for about $400, same as the cornet. Today the Ford is about $20,000, give or take a little. The cornet is no doubt worth less than that, but it is worth plenty. Recently I brought mine down from our attic and gave it to our grandson, Greg Huntington, who is showing a lot of talent on his old trumpet.

My new cornet made me popular in Logan. No one had one like it. Everyone wanted to blow it, or at least finger it. We had a community dance band in town, made up of former high school players who wanted to stay together and hopefully make a little money playing gigs at Ohio University and other nearby colleges. The lead trumpeter was a young man by the name of Harry Shaw. He might be the best trumpeter ever produced at our high school, and he liked to borrow my King cornet. He brought it back once full of tobacco smoke, and I wouldn't let him have it after that.

I managed to win several prizes in regional and statewide solo contests. One of those was at Ohio State, and another at Oberlin College, both exciting trips for me. I played about all of the cornet solos of Herbert L. Clarke. My favorite was "Willow Echoes," which I played at my high school graduation. In my junior year I helped organize a brass sextet from among the members of our high school band. We played serious music, and also a little Dixie and Ump-pa-pa. We won a First in a national band contest in Kellogg Hall in Battle Creek, playing a medley of Steven Foster standards. The trip to Michigan was exciting in another way: Battle Creek was the farthest away from home I had ever been. The clouds of World War II were then gathering on the horizon, and that record would soon be broken.

Baseball was my other passion. I played the game from the time I was very small. For hour after hour, out on my grandparents' farm, I would gather gravel off the road and throw it at the mailbox. In a short time the road was bare, and the mailbox was virtually ruined. When we moved to Logan I got into the church league, which was the precursor to the Little League program. At 12, I played regularly on the Catholic church's team, and because the average age for the players was around 15, I was "written up" in the local newspaper. A couple of years later the Methodist and Presbyterian teams both wanted me, and I went with the Methodists because they had the best team. That lead into high school baseball, and in the summers with the American Legion team.

By the time I was 16 there was no doubt, in my mind, that I could play in the Major Leagues. It was just a matter of time. I received a letter recently from my boyhood friend, John Buchanan, in which he remembered that in the 1941 American Legion state finals played in Springfield, Ohio, I handled 14 straight chances at shortstop without an error.

I had forgotten that, but I remembered something else from that state tournament. There was a little, fat fellow in a straw hat hanging around our dugout. I had no idea whom he might be, but felt it was okey for him to be there, because our manager, Mr. Clint Webb, who also was editor of our local newspaper, was not asking him to leave. After my first time at bat, the gentleman came up to me and asked me if I would consider using a lighter bat my next time up. I said I would, but I didn't. He asked me a second time, and I still didn't. When he asked a third time, in the seventh (and last) inning, I blew my gaskets. Mr. Webb told me after the game that this gentleman was a scout for the Philadelphia Phillies, and he had come to the game specifically to watch our pitcher, Mark Wylie, and me. Mark Wylie did play professional baseball after the War, and he is the father of Mark Wylie, who until a couple of years ago was the pitching coach for the Cleveland Indians. My 14 errorless chances at shortstop did not impress the big-time scout, but my temper did. We lost the championship, and I never was scouted again. I should have at least *tried* a lighter bat.

In my junior year, at a time when the war in Europe already was under way, Mother received an opportunity to accept a job with the Federal government. It would have meant a move to Cleveland. She understood why that would be most disruptive for me, so she did not insist that we move. On the other hand, the pay was so good at $1260 a year (twice her income from the prosecutor's office), that she could not turn it down. Wanting to do something for the developing war effort, was part of it too.

Fortunately, there was a solution. Before the Chesser family moved into the farm home immediately north of the Clark farm on Asbury Ridge, possibly around 1910 or so, the place was occupied by the Nathan Clark family. It was the Nathan Clark family, you may recall, with whom my mother lived during the weekdays when she commuted to Logan for high school in 1918. The Nathan Clark family had several daughters, one of whom was Margaret, a life long friend of my mother. Margaret married Bob Mackey, and in 1941 they lived on Furnace Street in Logan. Mother approached Margaret Mackey and asked if I could move in with them for at least the remainder of the 1941 school year. Bob and Margaret had no children, and they liked the idea of trying out parenting, even with a teenager.

Bob was a tool dresser for a local oil drilling company. He was big and loud and gruff, and a pushover if there ever was one. In an honest and sober way, he would try to give me "fatherly" advice on how to deal with women, and break down laughing in the middle of it. Margaret Mackey was a homemaker deluxe, and for the four or five months I was with them, I had the time of my life.

It was lonesome for my mother in a small apartment in Cleveland. I went up to visit her a time or two, and liked it even less than she did. In the summer of 1941, Mother learned that she could transfer to an even better job at Wright Field, near Dayton. She collected me from Bob and Margaret Mackey, and we left the hills of southeastern Ohio forever.

Our life together after the death of my father continued in Dayton. It was back to small apartments for us. Ours was located near the downtown area, and I commuted to Kiser High in north Dayton by city bus. I am sure it was a fine high school, but it was not what I was used to. My old friends were not there. I missed being in the brass sextet, which was doing well without me. There wasn't as much spirit at the new school, and there was no small-town community cheering for us. I played on the basketball and baseball team, and did well on both. In addition to playing first chair cornet in the band, I was the student conductor. Our director of music thought I should make a career in music, and arranged for me to receive a modest college scholarship. You guessed it: at Ohio Wesleyan.

Within a year I was at Ohio Wesleyan sure enough. But it was as an aviation cadet. Battalion bugler, in fact. You know that story.

Mother married Matthew P. Chesser just before I graduated, and ended her loneliness. It also got her out of one-room apartments forever. Ultimately, it took her to her grave in California. You know that story too.

So there isn't much more to tell. I am left now with memories, and they are good ones. And I am left with Wonder. Glorious, endless Wonder. No more flying, no more law practice, and who knows, maybe not much more life. My doctor told me that in all probability I will never again play golf like I once did. I shot back at him, "Well, for *that* we can all be grateful!"

But the remark made me think. Growing older has not lessened my wants. I want to fly again, and have a client again, and tee it up again with the best of them. I want to be with Marg forever, and to take care of her for as long as she needs me. I want to watch our five grandchildren go through the same stages of maturity as our kids did. I want to see them become good citizens and persons, just like our kids did. I would like to watch our kids grow up all over again. It would be fun to take family trips with them again. I want to "take in" foster kids, again, just as we did in the 1960s.

We got started in the foster care program, at the insistence of Jane, our oldest. She was leaving for college, and pointed out that we now had an extra bed in the house. Her argument was that we had the room, and there were lots of little kids who needed help. The fact that in some ways the foster children could be a pain in the neck never occurred to her; or if it did she gave that depressing fact little notice, because she was going to be far away in a Swarthmore College dormitory.

After endless questions from a caseworker who came to visit us, we were "certified," and permitted to accept youngsters into our home for temporary care. It opened up a new world for all of us.

The little babies came to us often in the middle of the night. Sometimes a caseworker would bring them, and other times a deputy sheriff or a police car would bring them to us. Sometimes the kids were removed from their homes to safeguard them; other times they simply had no homes. Once, two little kids who were hardly old enough to walk were abandoned in front of a downtown men's clothing store, as their family was passing through town.

Marg and Laura, our daughter, usually gave them baths and some hot food, while I dashed to a nearby Kmart to buy them inexpensive pajamas and other things they needed. They were always scared to death when they arrived, but in a day or two they called us Mommy and Daddy and gave us good-night kisses. In all, about 60 toddlers lived in our house for short periods of times.

There was one terrifying experience. The names and addresses of foster parents are closely guarded secrets, but somehow or other our caseworker slipped up. About midnight one night a taxi pulled into our property, and the biggest, widest, tallest African-American man I ever saw stood in our doorway and declared that he had come for his kids. How we remained calm, I am not sure.

I asked him in and offered him a chair. He was so distressed. He said he didn't want "any trouble," he just wanted his children. He added that if we did not cooperate, he would simply take the children, whether we liked it or not.

As a practicing lawyer, I knew that this distraught father was about to get himself into a mess. In all probability his life already was a mess. Not knowing what else to say, I asked him if he were a lawyer. He said he wasn't.

"Well, I am," I told him, "and I would like to give you a little free legal advice ... but before I do, let's go back to our bedroom and take a look at your children."

His children looked like little angels in their Kmart PJs. They were clean, and sweet like most sleeping children are. He touched them both gently, before we went back to the living room. He was a new man after he saw that the kids were safe. I began to explain the law of kidnapping to him, and how a long term in the pen would not make his life any brighter. It was a relief to see him relax. It was clear that he was a caring father, and his main concern, like most of us, was the safety of his kids.

The minute our guest left in the taxi, we called the caseworker. Caseworkers are nice people. They are underpaid, and overworked. However, like anyone else who screws up, big time, they have to know about it so they won't do it again. According to Marg, our caseworker learned about this mistake in words from me which she would not soon forget. To let her know it was nothing personal, I made a lawyer-like deal with her: I would not tell her supervisor that we had been visited by a father, if she would in turn not "rat" on the father and get him in a lot more trouble than he could handle. We also resigned as foster parents for awhile. We were ready for a break, anyway. Laura summed it up for all of us, shortly after she changed a diaper one night: "The kids are cute … but they sure are a whole bunch of bother."

Despite the bother, I want to be a foster parent again. These are only some of my wants. Some of my wants will come to pass, and others won't. What makes life exciting is that you never know which will be which, and what will be what. If I died today, a fair-minded person would be hard pressed to argue that I missed much in life.

In addition to my wants, I will be obsessed for all of my days by the many Wonders which engulf me.

I should tell you what they are, before I go.

MY WORLD OF WONDERS

I WONDER IF ANY OF MY FATHER's DNA remains around the old waterhole at Philo? For more than 70 years, the Muskingum River has been surging past the site where they found his body. Has he been all flushed away? Floods once were a problem on the Muskingum, but those have been fixed effectively now, with a series of flood control dams. I wonder if the waterhole itself exists? Probably not. The Ohio Power Company built the "world's largest" power plant close to the place where he died. It must not have been the "world's most efficient" power plant. It became obsolete, and the mammoth structure was torn down years ago. I'll bet there is no waterhole. No DNA.

I wonder what happened to the demented lady who kept me under gun point in my office? Did she shoot her beloved? If she shot at me, would she have hit me? Her psychiatrist thought not. He didn't have as much at risk as I did.

I wonder what ever happened to Ensign Valentine's family. I didn't tell you about him, until now. He was an instructor at the primary flight school at Ottumwa Naval Air Station in Iowa. He was killed showing a cadet how to do short field landings. We all liked him. He had a young wife. I wonder if she did as well with widowhood as my mother did? I wonder about my instructor, too. His name was Ben ... Something-or-other, but of course I knew him only as "Sir." He was not killed to my knowledge. But he loved to fly so much. It must have killed him when the war ended.

I wonder about our oldest daughter's guidance counselor in high school. Our daughter was the valedictorian of the class of 1968. In the year before she graduated she received dozens of unsolicited invitations to apply for admission to some of the most prestigious colleges in the US. She finally selected Swarthmore, which may be the toughest school in the country to get into. It took her months to fill out forms and meet all the requirements, but it was the fulfillment of a life's dream for her. A few days before her graduation, her guidance counselor called her in and said, "Honey, have you given any thought to going to college? ... you *really* should." She recommended a couple of nearby state universities which she thought would be suitable for Janie.

I wonder if Margaret and I will again hike to the bottom of the Grand Canyon? We did it when we were 63. Going down was easy, except that when Marg hit the bottom, her legs gave way and refused to work on the level ground. They wanted to keep going down. Coming back out of the Canyon, the next day, was a psychological victory. We had to keep telling ourselves that we could do it.

I wonder if our daughter Laura would still shiver like a wet dog if we took her down to the Presbyterian Camp in the hills of Fairfield County? She wanted to go swimming the minute we got there. She was so excited over being at the camp, that she just stood on the edge of the pool, grinning from ear to ear and shaking like a jack-hammer.

I wonder if our son Jim will ever again fly to Reykjavic, and solo hike the complete perimeter of Iceland? He was a teenager when he did it. It took him six weeks, living in a tent. Or will he ever again visit the little village of Thunguy, in Senegal, where for 27 months he lived among the people in a mud hut, and taught them how to grow enough food to last a year, and not merely 10 months. Marg and I went to visit him in his village after he had been there 18 months. He spoke their language. He suffered with them. They loved him just as we do.

There is so much to wonder about. Why do so many people call persons "individuals?" I wonder what the New York *Times* will use for advertising income when every living American owns an expensive wrist watch? Why do so many of those good looking people on TV, who make their livings with words, pronounce the adverb "often" as off-Ten? Why do they call some things *very unique*? They should have had Professor Diem as their debate coach. What if the dean at Northwestern had thrown me out of law school, instead of warning me, when he found out I was cutting so many classes. What if the border guard in Czechoslovakia, which then was behind the Iron Curtain, had tossed Marg and me in a local jail somewhere? You read about things like that. He had been drinking, and for some reason was very angry with us. He kept our passports for more than two hours. How did Jane and Laura ever attract David Huntington and Jim Chatfield, our two fantabulous sons-in-laws? You see what I am doing to you? I am softening you up, leading toward the biggest "I Wonder" of all:

I wonder what would have happened to me if my father had not jumped in the river? That question is why I wrote this memoir. As a free moral agent, James William Hoskins did not have to jump into the river and die. Doris Logston was not a person for whom he had any societal responsibility. There were other men around. He could have justified himself later by saying, "I would have gone after her, but ..." If the banks of the river that evening were a democracy, my mother and I would have voted that he not put his life on the line.

There is the possibility that my young father had no choice in the matter. We Presbyterians call that "predestination." You have to at least consider that possibility. I wonder if there is a God who (or which) controls this kind of split-second decision? Consider this: God wanted young Doris to stick around for awhile, so he put my dad in the right place at the right time.

If that kind of a personal, potent Force is loose in the universe, and it may be, it would have been less dramatic, and more humane, if The Great Decision Maker had not let Doris go near the Muskingum on August 1, 1927. That would have been easier on my grandmother, who went out of her mind. Perhaps being dramatic and not being humane are two of those "mysterious ways" in which God moves, His mission to perform.

It appears to come down to this: If my father had not made an attempt to save the young lady, that would be proof that he was free to make his own decisions, even the decision not to be a hero. That is not all bad, because man yearns to be free. But if his going to his death was a Divine Decision, then the whole tragedy was a religious experience, and he really was not a hero. He was more like a martyr. Mother and I should have given the money back to Andrew Carnegie.

Generally speaking, our society does not bother to make these kinds of fine philosophical distinctions. The Carnegie Hero Fund did not look into Divine Intervention. The fact that my father did not hesitate even a second made him a hero, officially. We have a bronze medal in a leather case to prove it. Perhaps the Carnegie folks consider a martyr to be a hero.

I do know this: If my father had opted to chicken out, I might have plodded my way through life as a kid with only one father. I would not have come under the influence of Matt Chesser. Most young men escape from Philo as soon as they are old enough. Would I have stayed, or got out of town? Where would I have gone?

If I stuck around Philo, I probably would not have married Doris Logston. She was eleven years older than I. Anyway, if my dad hadn't saved her, she might have drowned herself that night.

I wonder if that has ever occurred to her, wherever she is?

Would I have become a Navy officer and pilot? Or, would I have been drawn into WWII as a foot soldier, and killed in the Battle of the Bulge? That happened to half a dozen of my high school classmates.

Did my father's deadly plunge contribute to my becoming a lawyer? When I lost a case, was that his fault? When I completed a complicated adoption and handed the sweet little male baby to his new mother on Christmas Eve, was my father entitled to the incredible timing? Did his death lead me to meet Margaret Hanna? To father three magnificent children? To have a life so crammed full of joy that it is a crime that it was given to only one person?

I would feel much better if I didn't make up your mind for you on any of this. I'll tell you what I think, and then you make up your own mind.

I have told you earlier that I think there is a God, and that I believe reincarnation is a sure gone conclusion. If there is no life after death, a lot of things are going to go unanswered.

I think life is such a huge mystery for all of us, that it may take death itself to solve it.

The purpose of death may be to unlock life.

Should that be true, aren't we silly to dread death so much?

My first question after death is going to be: What Was THAT All About?